My People

Abba Eban's History of the Jews

ADAPTED BY DAVID BAMBERGER

My People

Abba Eban's History of the Jews

VOLUME I

BEHRMAN HOUSE, INC., PUBLISHERS
NEW YORK, NEW YORK

DESIGNER: *Betty Binns*
ARTIST: *Arvis Stewart*
PROJECT EDITOR: *Geoffrey Horn*

© Copyright 1978 by Abba Eban and David Bamberger

Published by Behrman House, Inc.
1261 Broadway
New York, N.Y. 10001
MANUFACTURED IN THE UNITED STATES OF AMERICA

"Ethical Will" by Judah ibn Tibbon. Reprinted by permission
of Ktav Publishing House from *Masterpieces of Hebrew
Literature*, edited by Curt Leviant.
"Ode to Zion" by Judah ha-Levi. Reprinted by permission
of the Jewish Publication Society from *Selected Poems of
Jehudah Halevi*, edited by Heinrich Brody.

Library of Congress Cataloging in Publication Data

Bamberger, David.
  My people.

  Includes index.
  SUMMARY: A history of the Jewish people focusing
primarily on the period before the American Revolution.
  1. Jews—History—Juvenile literature. [1. Jews—
History] I. Eban, Abba Solomon, 1915–   My people.
II. Title.
DS118.B344   909'.04'924   77-10667
ISBN 0-87441-263-3

2   3   4   5   6   7   84   83   82   81   80   79

To Carola

ACKNOWLEDGMENTS

The task of adapting Abba Eban's monumental history of the Jewish
people was a great challenge which could not have been met without
invaluable assistance from others. Bernard J. Bamberger and Henry
Bamberger spent many hours reading and annotating the manuscript.
The advice and criticism of Morrison D. Bial helped shape the book
in its early stages. Neal Kozodoy of *Commentary* proved a rich source
of ideas for the special topics.

For the photo research, the Israel Museum in Jerusalem and the
Jewish Museum in New York City were particularly helpful. Myron
E. Schoen of the UAHC-CCAR Commission on Synagogue Admin-
istration deserves special thanks for his generosity—and boundless
patience. Among the many tourist offices and consulates which lent
their services, CEDOK (a Czechoslovak travel service) and the Australian Government Tourist Office in New York City were most
generous.

The sources of the quotations in text are as follows: page 63, "The
Sanctuary in Flames," from Josephus, *The Jewish War*, translated by
G. A. Williamson (Penguin, 1959); page 106, "Genius at Work," from
the Maimonides entry in *Encyclopedia Judaica;* page 133, "A Letter
from Jerusalem," from *The Holy City: Jews on Jerusalem*, compiled
and edited by Avraham Holtz (Norton/B'nai B'rith, 1971); pages
144–45, from *Masterpieces of Hebrew Literature*, edited by Curt
Leviant (Ktav, 1969); page 187, "Waiting for the Messiah," from the
Memoirs of Glückel of Hameln, translated and edited by Marvin
Lowenthal (Harper, 1932).

In March 1978, as this book was in its final stages of preparation,
Palestinian terrorists invaded Israel and in a few hours killed 35
civilians. One of their victims was Gail Rubin, whose photograph of
the Sinai Mountains appears on page 3. We are proud to be able to
preserve, in some small way, her legacy of beauty and devotion to
the State of Israel.

G.M.H.

Contents

To the reader

You hold in your hands one of the most amazing of all stories. It is
the story of my people – our people – the story of the Jews.

In 1968, I published this story in a book of over 500 pages. Since it is
far too large to use as a textbook, we have prepared this new edition
especially for you. The story is very long – 4000 years long. We will
therefore tell it in two volumes. The second will concentrate on the
last 200 years. This one deals primarily with the period in which
Judaism was formed and grew to maturity, up to the time of the
American Revolution. The last chapters, however, summarize the
story of the Jews in the modern world. In that way, this first book will
give you a picture of the vast sweep of our history. When you
have finished studying it, you will understand more about your
community, your grandparents, your parents, and, most especially,
about yourself.

Of course, Jews have always affected the non-Jewish world and
been influenced by it. We have therefore begun each section of the
book with a general history of the period we are about to discuss. In
these chapters you will find many names which are familiar to
you – Julius Caesar, Muhammad, Napoleon. You will see how their
lives affected the history of Judaism.

When all the influences have been accounted for, however, we shall
still not have explained the special and distinctive features of Jewish
history. These must be sought within the innermost recesses of the
Jewish religious spirit and the Jewish national genius. By telling the
story of our people as they themselves lived it over thousands of
years, with all the sympathy and understanding at our command, we
may hope to come somewhat closer to that solemn and thrilling
mystery which lies at the never-dying heart of the people of Israel.

ABBA EBAN

PART ONE

The Ancient World

The Biblical Period

Our story begins thousands of years ago, but for those of us who live in Israel the Biblical Period seems like only yesterday. The land of Egypt is today the key to peace in the Middle East, just as it was even before there was a Jewish people. The cities named in the Bible are often modern cities in which we still live. Most important, the Biblical promise that the Hebrews would inherit the land of Canaan was the force which inspired the creation of the nation which is our home.

The Bible is part of our lives in other ways as well, ways that are harder to define. Throughout Jewish history, up to the present time, we Jews have never forgotten the personalities and situations of our Biblical past. Generation after generation, we look for a new Joseph to plead our cause, a new Moses to lead us forth from tyranny, a new Solomon or Aaron to dazzle the world with his wisdom and brilliance. Our entire way of understanding the meaning of our past comes from the Bible. Our vision of where we have been, and of where we are going,

The World of the Bible

How can we imagine the world of the Bible?
Many places mentioned in the Bible still stand: the
mountains of the Sinai peninsula can be photographed
looking much as they did 3200 years ago. For other
scenes—like that of the Israelites carrying the
Tabernacle through the wilderness after the Exodus
from Egypt—an artist must try to capture in paint the
scene which the Bible creates with words.

has been determined for us in large part by the history of our Biblical
ancestors and by the experiences they underwent thousands of years
ago – the experience of enslavement followed by redemption, of
degradation followed by uplift and salvation, of exile followed by
return. Our faith that Jewish history is working toward a positive and
glorious end derives from the promise made to Abraham, Isaac, and
Jacob, a promise that has sustained us over the centuries and that
continues to sustain us today.

So turn your attention now to a history which is very old and yet very
modern – the history of the Biblical world.

ABBA EBAN

The ancient Hebrews were the first people to abandon idols like these (above and right, both of Assyria) and worship the One God of all humankind. But their worship of God was very different from ours. Everything you see in this scene—the Temple of Jerusalem, the High Priest, the sacrificial fire, the animals to be sacrificed— has disappeared from our religion since the Romans burned Jerusalem.

Above, an enameled lion from Babylon, which the Hebrews
may have seen after they were exiled from Jerusalem; below,
a wall painting from ancient Egypt showing how bricks were
made, much as our ancestors must have made them before the Exodus.

1

INTRODUCTION TO PART ONE

The Ancient World

Tonight the sun will set behind the Great Pyramid in Egypt, as it has for more than 4500 years. Slowly the shadow of the giant monument will stretch across the desert. Somewhere in the sandy waste, a family of nomads will settle down for the night, just as their ancestors have done for longer than anyone can remember. Finally, the land that was once the kingdom of the Pharaohs will be covered by darkness.

A thousand miles to the east, in the land once known as Mesopotamia, the waters of the Tigris and Euphrates rivers will flow into the sea, as they have since long before the first human was born. Farmers will sleep near their crops, much as some of the earliest farmers did when, weary of hunting for game, they came to the banks of these very rivers and decided to grow their own food.

In the night, the air will seem to echo with the names of the empires that once ruled these ancient lands. Some of these names are familiar, others are all but forgotten: Babylonia, Egypt, Sumeria, Chaldea, Assyria. . . .

And tomorrow the nomad will continue his endless journey, and the farmer will return to his crops.

The birth of civilization

In these lands—Egypt and Mesopotamia—civilization had its beginnings. Here people first learned to live in settled communities under the rule of organized governments. Here they developed writing, mathematics, astronomy, medicine, painting, sculpture, warfare, and many other arts and sciences. Architects designed huge palaces, tombs, and temples, some of which are the largest ever built.

Hundreds, even thousands, of gods were worshiped, for it was believed that every part of nature held a divine being. Sacrifices were offered to these gods in hopes of a rich harvest. Sometimes kings and queens were regarded as gods; when one died, the servants might take poison so that they could continue to provide for the ruler's needs in the world to come. Gradually, however, this type of human sacrifice became rare, and new forms of nature worship developed.

Abraham—a man with an idea

In the midst of the great nations, a small tribe grew. Its first leader was a prosperous shepherd who was born in Mesopotamia. His native city was a rich one, but the shepherd was not satisfied there. He therefore moved his family west to Canaan—the land that is now Israel but which was then the home of backward tribes and warring city-states. He visited Egypt for a short time; perhaps he saw the pyramids, which at that time were over 500 years old. But the splendors of Egypt did not attract him, and he returned to the harsher life of Canaan.

What made this man reject the comforts of the great empires? Only an idea—a belief that the nations of the world were wrong to worship many gods; a belief that for him and his family there should be forever only One God; a belief that God had promised to make the land of the Canaanites into a homeland for his children and his descendants.

Only an idea. But strangely, while the names of some of the world's great empires are known only by scholars, this man-with-an-idea is remembered and revered throughout the world.

He was Abraham. With him our story—the story of the Jews—begins.

"But," you may be asking, "how do we know there really was such a person as Abraham? The Bible talks about him, but it also talks about the world being created in six days and says David fought with a giant. I've had enough of stories. I want to know what's true!"

Fair enough—though it must be said that it is not always simple to identify the truth. Most of us would agree, for example, that there never were giants on earth, but this still leaves the possibility that David defeated some very tall, strong warrior in single combat. On the other hand, it is also possible that this battle is only a legend, a beautiful story designed to teach that the righteous can sometimes overcome seemingly hopeless odds.

For that reason, this book will not be concerned with David and Goliath, or with many other stories whose background is uncertain. Our purpose here is the understanding of history. For that reason, every statement made in this book is, to the best of our knowledge, accurate fact. In the few cases that we retell legends and folktales, it will be because the fact that people believed them is itself important to our history.

Why then have we begun by talking about Abraham? Isn't he the subject of stories and legends? He is, to be sure; but scholars believe that the basic outline of his life, as we have given it, is indeed historical, and that Abraham did live about 4000 years ago.

Archaeology and the Bible

We know that many tribes moved between Mesopotamia and Egypt around the year 2000 B.C.E.,* so the travels of Abra-

* B.C.E. = Before the Common Era. See "Beginning at the Beginning," p. 11.

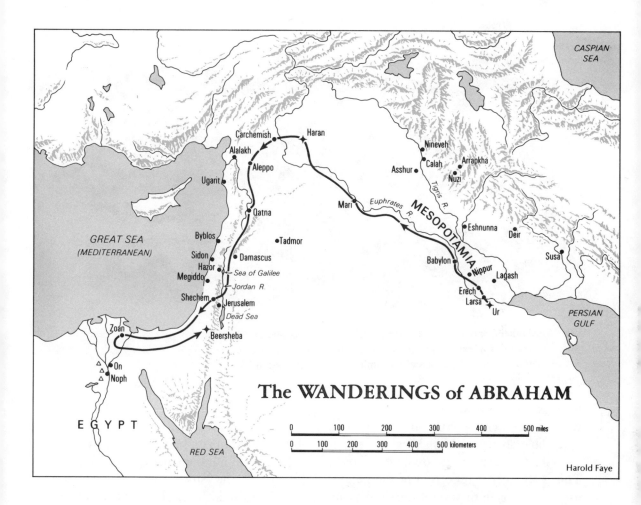

The WANDERINGS of ABRAHAM

Harold Faye

You can retrace the path of Abraham by following the lines and arrows on the map, which is based on Genesis 11–13 and on discoveries made by archaeologists during the last 150 years. Abraham's long journey began at Ur, in Babylonia (lower right). The Bible says that after Abraham's father, Terah, left Ur with his family, they all settled in Ḥaran, where Terah later died. Genesis next says that when Abraham was seventy-five years old, God commanded him to leave Ḥaran for Canaan, the Promised Land. You can see from the map that Abraham—along with his wife Sarah, his nephew Lot, and their servants—reached the Canaanite city of Shechem but then left for Egypt. (This was to avoid a famine, the Bible tells us.) Finally, Abraham returned to Canaan with Sarah, while Lot settled further east, in the plains of the River Jordan.

Abraham, Sarah, and Lot enter the land of Canaan. Since we have no pictures of Abraham, the artist has used the work of archaeologists to guess at what Abraham and his family might have dressed like.

ham, as described in the Bible, fit in well with our general picture of the period. The Bible stories tell of Abraham riding a donkey, never of his owning a horse. This is also a true reflection of the period, for it was not until several hundred years later that horses were tamed.

Perhaps most important, the Bible tells us of specific towns which Abraham visited. These places no longer exist, and for a time people thought that they had never existed. Then archaeologists discovered the buried ruins of these very towns. What is more, studies proved that some of them had been destroyed shortly after the year 2000 B.C.E. They were only small villages and their names would soon have been forgotten, except by those who happened to learn about them in stories passed down from generation to generation. This chain must, of course, have begun *before* the destruction of the towns—

which means our record of Abraham's travels must date back to the very period in which Abraham seems to have lived.

"I am still not convinced," you may say. "Even if the stories of Abraham are very, very old, that still doesn't prove that a man named Abraham ever existed. We have no birth certificates, no photograph, no mention of him except in the Bible."

Again you are right. Still, one fact is absolutely certain—the story of the Jews has a beginning. It begins at the moment when a man came to believe that there was but One God, a God who had promised his family a home in what is now the land of Israel. The Bible tells us that the man was called Abraham, but even if it could be proved that this was not his name, it would make little difference. The man did exist, and he changed the life of humanity.

The life of Abraham, then, marks the

Beginning at the
Beginning

"How old are you?" You have answered this question hundreds of times, but have you ever thought about it? What does it mean? It really asks, "How many years have passed since *the day you were born?"*

How old is the Jewish people? Was Judaism born with the Exodus? With the birth of Abraham? Either of these would have been possible choices. It was decided, however, that since our God is the God of all mankind, it would not be right for us to count years from a specifically Jewish event. Instead, it was decided that our calendar should begin with the real beginning for *everyone*—the first day of creation.

To find that date, it seemed enough just to go through the Bible and add up the years "from the beginning." The number that was reached is, of course, much smaller than the real age of the universe. In the year 1977–78 the Hebrew date was only 5738.

When Christianity developed, Christian leaders wanted a calendar of their own. They felt that the real beginning of history was the birth of Jesus, and they dated everything as happening either before or after that event. It was later discovered that Jesus was probably born four years earlier than they had thought, but by that time the Christian calendar had become standard throughout the world.

Standard—but for us as Jews it presents a problem since it is based on the doctrines of another religion. Even the letters B.C. and A.D. are statements of belief. B.C. stands for "Before Christ"—and remember that "Christ" is not a name but a title meaning "Messiah." A.D. stands for "Anno Domini—In the year of the Lord." Yet for us Jesus is neither the Messiah nor the Lord.

When dealing with the non-Jewish world, we have no real way to avoid using the common calendar. When writing for Jews, however, many like to replace B.C. and A.D. with the initials B.C.E. and C.E. These stand for "Before the Common Era" and "Common Era." In this way, we can use ordinary dates, while reminding ourselves that they are based on beliefs which we must respect but do not share.

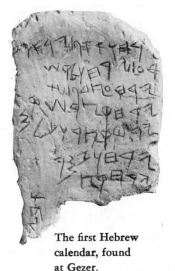

The first Hebrew calendar, found at Gezer.

Historians think this mask shows the face of an early Mesopotamian ruler. Most ancients believed their kings were gods, and worshiped images of them.

opening of the first great period of Jewish history, which lasted almost 2000 years, until the victories of Judah Maccabee in 165 B.C.E. It is the period which the Bible describes, and in which the books of the Bible were written, and so we call it the BIBLICAL PERIOD.

Ancient empires

During most of this period, our people were ruled by great kingdoms. Three *old* nations grew until they were strong enough to try to rule the known world. Each built a large but short-lived empire. Then three *new* nations entered the Near East and succeeded in ruling the area for a long time. In time, however, these also declined and disappeared.

The three *old* nations were the kingdoms of Egypt and (in Mesopotamia) Assyria and Babylonia. At first, they worked to develop their own lands. But each, in turn, became strong enough to try to gain new territory. Each conquered a huge area, yet none was able to rule very well. The Egyptian armies could control little more than the valley of the Nile. The Babylonian empire lasted less than fifty years, the Assyrian empire was at its height for only thirteen. These last two nations are, nevertheless, very important in Jewish history. It was in fighting the Assyrian and Babylonian armies that the kingdom ruled by David and the Temple built by Solomon were destroyed.

The last of the old empires, Babylonia, fell just before 500 B.C.E. Now younger nations from other areas of the world were able to conquer the entire Near East.

The first of these *new* nations was Persia. The Persian armies conquered an enormous area, from Europe to the foot of the Himalayan mountains. What is more, the Persian rulers were able to control this area by practicing religious toleration. Whenever possible, citizens of the empire were allowed to practice their own beliefs and customs. The Jews, for example, were permitted to rebuild the Temple in Jerusalem. For 200 years the Persian kingdom prospered under such tolerant rulers. Then new kings came to the throne—kings who were cruel and tyrannical.

Their cruelty made them unpopular, thus weakening the state at the time another new nation was growing. This was Greece, the first great power to come from Europe. Its armies were led by one of the most brilliant of all generals—Alexander the Great—who had destroyed Persia and conquered the known world by the time he was thirty-three. Then, at the height of his power, he took sick and died. His empire was divided among three generals, so the Greeks never actually ruled the world as a single nation. Nevertheless, Greek culture dominated the life of Europe and the Near East for centuries, leaving a heritage that has deeply influenced the modern world.

At first the Greeks too were tolerant. They also changed. Antiochus IV attempted to force Greek paganism on the Jewish people—and it was this act that brought about the revolt of the Maccabees, the expulsion of the Greek army from Israel, and the first Ḥanukkah.

This triumph marks the end of the Biblical Period, but we should mention the third new nation, which was to be the most successful of all in governing the Western world. Its rule over Israel was so long and so important that we have devoted Part Two of this book to it. That nation was Rome.

The wonder of Jewish history

Even in this brief outline, you may have noticed a pattern in history: a nation begins to grow, defeats other nations in war, builds an empire, weakens, is destroyed by another power, and disappears from the pages of history.

At first, Jewish history follows the same pattern: tribes settle in Canaan, establish an empire under David and Solomon, and then see their land destroyed by the conquering armies of the Assyrians and Babylonians.

But the people of Israel did not disappear. How did the Jews survive and prosper when larger and stronger nations disintegrated and vanished from the face of the earth?

This is the wonder of Jewish history. And this is the question we will begin to answer in the next three chapters.

SUMMARY *This book will concern itself with the facts, not the legends, of Jewish history. This history begins when a man, whom the Bible calls Abraham, came to believe in One God who had promised his family a homeland in Canaan.*

In the ancient Near East, the site of early Jewish history, three states became strong enough to carve out empires. These were Egypt, Assyria, and Babylonia. None, however, was able to control a large area for very long. Then three new nations—Persia, Greece, and Rome—managed to dominate the known world for hundreds of years. But the only people able to survive the entire Biblical Period and defy the pattern of history up to our own time was the people of Israel.

2

"Like the Other Nations"

Workmen swarmed like ants on the face of the sheer stone cliff, measuring, drilling. . . . Gradually forms emerged from the stark hillside—forms so huge that the stonemasons could sit and rest on the gigantic hands which they carved. At last, their work was completed—four colossal statues of their Pharaoh, each 67 feet high, gazing out over the River Nile.

When the Pharaoh inspected this remarkable monument, even he must have been awed. Here was the supreme tribute to his wealth, to his position as the world's most powerful ruler. But it was more than that. It was a visible statement that the Pharaoh was far more than an ordinary man. In Egyptian religion he was divine, the child of the all-powerful sun.

The statues still stand today. Yet, impressive as they are, they are only one of the vast projects of the Pharaoh Raamses II. He had a passion for building, and since his reign lasted nearly seventy years, he had plenty of opportunity to see temples, monuments, and even entire cities built at his command.

Yet not even the wealth of Egypt could support these projects without strain. There were not enough native Egyptians available to do all the work. For this reason, Raamses made slaves of foreign peoples who had until then been living peacefully in Egypt.

Thus the Bible almost certainly means Raamses II when it speaks of the king who set taskmasters over the Israelites "to oppress them with forced labor; and they built garrison cities for Pharaoh: Pithom and Raamses" (Exodus 1:11).

וַיִּבֶן עָרֵי מִסִּים לְמַעַן עַנֹּתוֹ בְּסִבְלֹתָם
וַיִּבֶן עָרֵי מִסְכְּנוֹת לְפַרְעֹה
אֶת־פִּתֹם וְאֶת־רַעַמְסֵס

The Exodus

The next episode in Jewish history is a very familiar one. It is the story of the

Exodus—the escape of the Israelites from Egyptian slavery. For thousands of years that story has been told at every Passover seder: how Moses led the people of Israel across the "Red Sea" (what scholars now call the Sea of Reeds) and brought them through the desert to receive the Torah at Mount Sinai. It is a wonderful tale, well worth retelling; but we have promised to deal only with accepted facts, and there is disagreement over how much of the Biblical story is historical. Some believe that miracles occurred just as the Bible describes them. Others try to find "scientific" explanations. Still others think much of the story is legend. There is debate over how many Hebrews were in Egypt, their route of escape, and where Mount Sinai was.

But there is general agreement on the central fact: the Exodus *did* take place, and through it the people of Israel were reborn.

One God, one Law

The Hebrews saw their escape from the Egyptian armies as dramatic proof of the power of God and a visible sign of His love. Finding God "on their side," they might well have felt free to do anything they wanted. Instead, they decided it was their duty to do whatever *God* wanted. They saw themselves as having entered into a special agreement, or "covenant," with Him, in which He would care for them—but only as long as they obeyed His Law. This agreement became the central fact of their lives. The symbol of it, the sacred stones bearing the Ten Commandments, became their most prized possession.

Perhaps even more remarkable than this new relationship between God and His people was the nature of the Law which the Hebrews pledged themselves to obey. In other nations of that time, each class of

Raamses II, Pharaoh of Egypt, had these statues built at Abu Simbel to show the world that he was more than a man —he was (he thought) divine. Today the giant statues can still be seen, though not where the Pharaoh built them. In the 1960's they were cut apart, transported, and then put back together on another site, to make way for waters rising upstream of the Aswan High Dam.

society had its own laws. A slave would be punished much more severely than a nobleman for the same crime, while the king might be regarded as divine and completely above the law. In Judaism, no social class enjoyed special laws. All people were regarded as equal before the Supreme Lawgiver, the God "who brought you out of the land of Egypt, out of the House of Bondage."

אֲשֶׁר הוֹצֵאתִיךָ מֵאֶרֶץ מִצְרַיִם
מִבֵּית עֲבָדִים

Thus, a new kind of society was born among the former slaves. They now saw themselves as one people with a common memory and a common purpose, with one God and one sacred Law. What they lacked, however, was a land of their own. And so, after living for many years in the deserts of Sinai, they headed north to the land of Canaan.

The conquest of Canaan

The Exodus occurred about 1225 B.C.E., the entry into Canaan shortly after 1200 B.C.E. In the next 200 years—by about 1000 B.C.E.—the Hebrews took control of the land that, according to their tradition, had been promised to Abraham many centuries before.

Of course, conquering a country was not a simple matter. The Hebrews were not united—though they called themselves a single family, they were divided into twelve separate tribes. Each traced its history back to a different son of Jacob, the grandson of Abraham. Each had its own leadership, and each settled in a different part of Canaan. They could rarely take territory by force, because the native Canaanites who controlled the inland area

and the Philistines who controlled the coast had far stronger weapons. (They had recently learned to use iron, while the invading Hebrews had weapons made of softer, "old-fashioned" bronze.)

The Hebrews preferred to settle peacefully when they could, but peace too presented problems. Their new neighbors taught them many things about the land and how to farm it. Much of this information was no doubt useful, but some was pure superstition. The Hebrews would be told what god to worship to make the soil fertile, what god to pray to for rain, and so on.

Such practices had no place in their religion, but settlers could easily justify using them: "Everybody does it." "It's a nice practice." "It won't do any harm." "I don't mean anything religious by it." (Today, some Jews say the same things about having Christmas trees in their homes.) So Judaism faced a constant battle, not only against warring enemies who sought to destroy the Hebrew people, but also against attractive influences that could have weakened or even destroyed the Hebrew religion.

In the face of these challenges, valiant leaders appeared. The Bible calls them SHOFTIM, שׁוֹפְטִים. This one word is often translated "judges"—sometimes the shoftim did rule in legal matters—but basically they were tribal chiefs and heroes. The most famous among them is Samson, whose legendary strength was said to be due to his long hair. More accurate, from a historical point of view, is the Biblical account of the great leader Deborah, the woman who inspired the Hebrew forces to rout an army of the Canaanites.

But the most important of the shoftim was the last: Samuel.

Samuel chooses a king

Samuel lived about 1050 B.C.E. By that time, the Hebrew tribes had been living in Canaan for 150 years, each with its own laws. Sometimes those laws came into conflict. To settle these disputes, Samuel traveled throughout the country, deciding cases and establishing legal standards. In effect, he became a one-man Supreme Court; but unlike modern judges, Samuel had no police or soldiers to enforce his decisions. He must have been remarkably fair and wise for the Hebrews to have accepted his judgment.

Samuel was more than a judge, however —he was also a prophet. Today we often speak of a prophet as someone who predicts the future, but the word really means "a person who speaks for God." Samuel was one of a remarkable series of men who said God had given them a message to bring to the world. The full importance of the prophets for our story will be seen in the next chapter. For the present, it is enough to realize that our ancestors were quite convinced that God had given them laws through Moses, and was making them clear through Samuel.

In time, the Hebrews came to feel that

A Chosen People "For you are a holy people to the Lord your God, and the Lord has chosen you to be his own treasure out of all the peoples that are upon the face of the earth." (Deuteronomy 14:2)

כִּי עַם קָדוֹשׁ אַתָּה לַיהוָה אֱלֹהֶיךָ וּבְךָ בָּחַר יְהוָה לִהְיוֹת לוֹ
לְעַם סְגֻלָּה מִכֹּל הָעַמִּים אֲשֶׁר עַל־פְּנֵי הָאֲדָמָה.

These words from the Torah tell us that the Jews are a "chosen people." But what does it mean to be "chosen"? It means that in giving us His Laws and Commandments, God singled out the Jews for tasks that no other nation has been commanded to perform. With those commands came God's pledge of special protection—as long as we continued to serve Him and obey His Law. And when we accepted God's Law, we became not only a chosen people but a "choosing" people too.

Historically, the ancient Hebrews were the first to base their life as a nation on the idea of One God, the God of all nations and all peoples. In a very real sense, the ancient Hebrews were also "chosen" to bring that message to the world. How well they succeeded you can discover for yourself in the chapters that follow.

they were a nation. They controlled land; they had a developing body of law. Yet they had no central government, no unifying political institution except the prophet Samuel himself, and he was growing old. The people felt it was time to be "like the other nations." They asked Samuel to select a king for them.

At first he refused. Was not God the only King of the Hebrews? The kings of the other nations oppressed their people. Would a Hebrew king be any different? In the end, however, Samuel had to give in to the will of the people. They needed a leader, and there was no one to follow him as prophet and judge.

Saul

And so, Samuel chose Saul to be the first king of Israel. The new ruler was anointed with oil, a ritual which to this day is a sign of becoming a king. Aside from that, he had none of the finery we usually connect with kings. He had no standing army, no court, no tax revenues —he had only Samuel's blessing and the agreement of the tribes to let him be their leader. In effect, he ruled by popular consent. Yet despite this shaky foundation, Saul remained in control for twenty years, during which he made the monarchy a firmly established institution.

Nevertheless, Saul was a very unhappy man, tormented by fits of depression as well as wild and uncontrollable trances and rages. According to the Bible, a musician was brought to play the harp for Saul in the hope that music would soothe the troubled ruler.

That musician was David.

David

The life of David has fascinated humanity for 3000 years. The story of the shepherd who rose to be the greatest king of Israel is appealing and exciting. Folktale and legend have gathered around this heroic figure. The Biblical account of David's life is, on the whole, fair-minded and accurate. It shows him as a man with weaknesses as well as strengths, a leader who had flaws but also unusual charm and extraordinary ability.

First brought to the court as a musician, David soon became a spectacularly successful soldier. This gained him widespread popularity but, at the same time, the ferocious jealousy of the king. David, fearing for his life, fled to the hills, where he gathered a loyal band of followers. After Saul was killed battling the Philistines, David became ruler of his native tribe, Judah. This set off seven years of war with the tribes of the north, but at the end of the long struggle, he was declared king of the entire Hebrew people.

His next acts combined military skill of the highest order and shrewd politics. David defeated the Philistines and captured Jerusalem, יְרוּשָׁלַיִם —a settlement so strategically placed on a ridge of mountains that no Hebrew tribe had previously been able to conquer it. There, in a place which had never been the subject of tribal warfare, David set up his capital. In addition, he planned to build a Temple there as the center of Jewish worship. Thus Jerusalem, עִיר דָּוִד , or the "city of David," began the long history which would in time make it the holy city of three world religions.

David continued to triumph in battle, conquering for the Hebrews an empire far

Saul sent for David in the hope that the young musician would cure his depression and fits of rage. This worked for a while, but Saul later became jealous of David and even tried to kill him.

larger than the modern State of Israel. But more important for the history of Judaism, David was a man of deep feelings and spirit. In fact, the Bible tells far more about his personal life—his joys and tragedies—than it does about his military exploits. Tradition states that he wrote the wonderful book of Psalms, and although it is not certain how many of the poems in it are actually his, it is King David who gave poetry and music a key role in Jewish life and worship.

Even more important, however, is what David did *not* do. He did *not* become a dictator. He did *not* claim to be divine or have statues built to glorify his image. He did *not* silence or execute the prophet Nathan who criticized him. He seems to have realized, as did those who wrote about him, that in Israel it was God's laws that remained supreme. Before God, all

people—even the greatest of kings—were regarded as equal.

Solomon

The beginning of David's reign was a central event in Jewish history. (The approximate date is easy to remember—1000 B.C.E.) When he died, some forty years later, he left a strong and rich nation to his son, Solomon. Solomon was able to concentrate on peacetime projects. The Bible describes him as the wealthiest ruler of his time, and archaeological discoveries have largely backed up this claim.

Solomon's most famous accomplishment was the building of the Temple of Jerusalem. Since the time of Moses, the Hebrews had always had a central shrine—a tent or building containing the ark with

In the Biblical
Period

Young people in the Biblical Period never had to worry about
homework assignments, for no regular schools existed. A
child began helping at home from an early age, and in that
way learned an occupation—raising crops, tending herds, or,
occasionally, operating a small business. From the family
each child also learned about his or her religion, the history
and customs that had been passed down through the ages.

Before the Babylonian exile, the people spoke Hebrew,
which was then written in an old Canaanite alphabet. After the
exile, the language of the land of Israel was Aramaic,
another Semitic tongue. (It is the language of the KADDISH,
קַדִּישׁ .) The letters of Aramaic were adopted for Hebrew and
are basically the same as the ones we use today. But during
the Biblical Period, most people could neither read nor write.

The standard diet of the age would seem somewhat
boring to most of us. Its basic ingredients were grain,
fruit, and goat or sheep milk. Meat was eaten only on special
occasions, such as religious festivals, and usually it was mutton
or lamb. Cows and bulls were scarce, so any kind of beef,
particularly veal, was a luxury.

Salt was readily available from mines or from evaporated

seawater, and it was used heavily in cooking. Pepper and most other spices, on the other hand, had to be imported and were extremely expensive. Sugar was unknown until the Middle Ages, but wild bee honey was used to sweeten food. There was also a substitute honey made from dates and grapes.

Yet if the meals themselves were rather dull, they were at least accompanied with fine wines. Then, as now, the land of Israel was known for outstanding vineyards.

During the Biblical Period and for centuries later, the land was home to the bear, leopard, cheetah, wild ox, hippopotamus, and lion, some of which were a threat to farms and flocks. (The Bible says that, as a young shepherd, David had to defend his father's lambs from lions and bears.) Domestic animals such as the dog and ass were common, as were horses and camels after Abraham's time.

One animal you would not have seen was the cat. Cats had been known in the Near East for centuries—they had long been worshiped in Egypt—but they did not become popular in the land of Israel. Mice did have to be kept under control, so another animal was kept in the house—a pet mongoose!

Making bread the ancient way: from right to left, women grind the grain to make flour, mix the dough, roll it out, shape it into large cakes, and then bake the loaves in a clay oven. Sometimes the fire was built outside the oven, sometimes within.

Archaeologists at Megiddo unearthed this horned altar, used for burning incense in Solomon's day.

the tablets of the Ten Commandments. Now they had a beautiful building as the visible center of their religion.

Yet, just as in Egypt, the Hebrews were being commanded, against their will, to construct impressive monuments. Although the people were not slaves, they were sometimes drafted to provide labor for the king. In addition, they were heavily taxed to pay for his projects. When Solo-

mon died and his son and successor refused to reduce these burdens, the enraged citizens rebelled, and the country exploded in civil war.

Judah and Israel

When the fighting ended, the kingdom of the Hebrews had been permanently split. The Southern half of this "divided kingdom" was the tribe—now called the kingdom—of JUDAH. This was the tribe of David and Solomon, and its people, plus the small tribe of Benjamin, remained faithful to the royal family and to the Temple of Jerusalem.

The Northern tribes, on the other hand, united into what was called the kingdom of ISRAEL. They chose their own kings and established their own religious centers at Beth-el and Dan. There, tragically, the God of Israel was worshiped in the form of an idol, a golden bull.

Now, 500 years after the Hebrews had escaped from Egypt, they had truly become "like the other nations." Divided into warring groups, with half the nation practicing official idolatry, they seemed likely to follow the familiar historical pattern: to disintegrate and then disappear.

That this did not happen is largely because of a handful of amazing men. We will consider them in the next chapter.

SUMMARY *After the Exodus from Egypt, Jewish history follows a pattern almost the same as that of all other nations. The Hebrews gradually took over territory, built a strong empire which lasted relatively few years, and saw their empire begin to decay. Only unusual circumstances could have prevented the Hebrew people from continuing to decline and, like other nations, becoming extinct.*

3
Revolutionaries in the Streets

When is an idea born?

So much around us seems obvious: the earth is round, the sun is the center of the solar system, mankind evolved from other animals. These are things that everyone "knows" today. Yet within the last few hundred years, these were startlingly new discoveries.

There are other kinds of ideas—ideas which cannot be proved by scientists but which have nevertheless been so forceful that they too have become widely accepted throughout the world. The principle that nations should work for world peace instead of world conquest was once a totally new idea. The idea that the rich should care about the poor—this too was once a new idea.

What everyone "knew"

These ideas would never have occurred to you if you had lived in 750 B.C.E. Then everyone "knew" that the earth was flat, that the sun revolved around the earth, and that there had been no basic changes in the earth or in living things since the world was first created.

You would have been sure that there would always be war. After all, the most powerful nation in the world, Assyria, had dedicated its religion to world conquest. And you might wonder if the *one* God of the Hebrews could stand up against the *many* fierce Assyrian gods if your nations were ever to meet in battle.

As for religion, it would have little effect on your life. If you prayed at all, you would so do in private, since you would know that organized worship was the job of the priests. Your religious duty would merely be to help your family bring animals and grain to be sacrificed—you would know that God had commanded these offerings. You would come in contact with many poor people (and might be aware that the slums were growing in your

When Amos preached in the Northern Kingdom, most people thought he
was a fool; only a few accepted the prophet's revolutionary ideas.

city), but it would not occur to you that
their problems were your concern.

Amos—prophet of righteousness

Walking through the streets you might
hear many people who claimed to have
spoken with God, or who, for a price,
would promise to tell your future on His
behalf. But if you were in the city of
Beth-el, you might hear a man who was
different from the others. In brilliant and
fiery poetry he would proclaim that all
your basic beliefs were wrong. He would
tell you that the God of Israel is a God of
Justice, who cannot stand to see the poor
oppressed or ignored. He would cry out

that the rituals of the priests were meaningless because they did not show the
true meaning of religion. "Thus says the
Lord," he would call out again and again:

I hate, I despise your feasts,
And I will take no delight in your solemn
*   assemblies.*
Take away from Me the noise of your
*   songs,*
And let Me not hear the melody of your
*   stringed instruments.*

וְיִגַּל כַּמַּיִם מִשְׁפָּט
וּצְדָקָה כְּנַחַל אֵיתָן.

But let justice well up as waters,
And righteousness as a mighty stream.
(Amos 5:21–24)

Most surprisingly, he would insist that the God of Israel was the God of the Assyrians, though the Assyrians did not realize it. The God of Israel was the God of all peoples, and He could and would use the Assyrians as a tool to punish the Hebrews for their lack of righteousness.

Would you have walked on, laughing to yourself about this fool? Or would you have stayed to listen, to believe, to memorize his every word? If you had done so, you would have helped pass on one of the most important books in the history of ideas: the book of the prophet Amos.

Of the life of Amos we know little. He was a shepherd of the land of Judah who felt God had told him to prophesy in the Northern Kingdom. There the royal palace had seen continual bloodshed and murder, as one family after another battled for control of the throne. Priests sacrificed before idols and assisted in the worship of foreign gods. Amos, speaking in the name of God, condemned all this—and was hated for doing so—but his ideas could not be ignored. They were to become a new and vital part of the religious heritage of our people: the idea that God cares more for the protection of the poor than for the prosperity of the wealthy; the idea that God is more concerned with justice than with ritual; and, above all, the idea that the One God of the Hebrews is the One God of all humanity.

Yet few in the Northern Kingdom accepted his words or believed him when he predicted that the nation would be destroyed. Nonetheless, as he foretold, the Assyrians attacked and, in 721 B.C.E., devastated the kingdom of Israel. Its inhabitants were transported to Mesopotamia, where they mixed with the native population, disappearing from history and becoming "the ten lost tribes of Israel." But, because of Amos and his followers, this was not viewed by the surviving Southern Kingdom as a sign of God's weakness. Rather, it was seen as proof of His power, and His determination to see our people obey His laws of righteousness.

Isaiah and Micah—prophets of peace

The teachings of Amos were echoed in Judah by the prophet Isaiah and his younger contemporary, Micah:

> *"What do you mean crushing My*
>   *people,*
> *And grinding the face of the poor?"*
> *Says the Lord, the God of Hosts.*
>   *(Isaiah 3:15)*

They called upon the people to turn to the ethical life:

הַגִּיד לְךָ אָדָם מַה טּוֹב
וּמָה יְהֹוָה דּוֹרֵשׁ מִמְּךָ
כִּי אִם עֲשׂוֹת מִשְׁפָּט וְאַהֲבַת חֶסֶד
וְהַצְנֵעַ לֶכֶת עִם אֱלֹהֶיךָ:

> *It has been told you, O man, what is*
>   *good,*
> *And what the Lord requires of you:*
> *Only to do justly, and to love mercy,*
>   *and to walk humbly with your God.*
>   *(Micah 6:8)*

Like Amos, they spoke of Assyria as the instrument of God's anger. Yet, while believing that God would use the fierce Assyrian warriors for His purposes, they could see beyond the wars and battles of their own time to a day of peace such as the world had never known:

And it shall come to pass in the end of
days,
That the mountain of the Lord's house
shall be established as the top of the
mountains,
And shall be exalted above the hills;
And all nations shall flow to it.
And many peoples shall go and say:
"Come, let us go up to the mountain of
the Lord,
To the house of the God of Jacob;
And we will walk in His paths." . . .
And He shall judge between the
nations, . . .

וְכִתְּתוּ חַרְבוֹתָם לְאִתִּים
וַחֲנִיתוֹתֵיהֶם לְמַזְמֵרוֹת
לֹא יִשָּׂא גוֹי אֶל גוֹי חֶרֶב
וְלֹא יִלְמְדוּ עוֹד מִלְחָמָה.

And they shall beat their swords into
plowshares,
And their spears into pruninghooks;
Nation shall not lift up sword against
nation,
Neither shall they learn war any more.
(Isaiah 2:2–4)

Thus, in the face of the successful Assyrian war machine, the ideal of world
peace was born. When, more than 2600
years later, the nations of the world decided to search for a peaceful solution to
their problems, these words of Isaiah were
carved into the wall facing the United Nations headquarters.

Jeremiah—the burdens of prophecy

What was it like to be a prophet? You
might think it would be a great joy to be
chosen to reveal God's word. In a sense,

Being a prophet was a dangerous life for
Jeremiah, who was thrown into prison because
of what he said.

perhaps it was; but it meant facing ridicule
and opposition, hatred and danger. We
know this particularly from the life of another prophet, Jeremiah, for in his case we
have not only his public statements but also
those he made in private sorrow.

In public he spoke against the sins of the
people as fiercely as had earlier prophets.
By his time Assyria had collapsed—as
Isaiah had predicted—but there was a new
great power, Babylonia. In ringing words,
Jeremiah declared that this nation would
destroy the kingdom of Judah. Since the
people had felt free to disobey God's commands, God would grant the Hebrews a
new freedom—freedom from His special
protection:

Thus says the Lord: You have not listened
to Me, to proclaim liberty, every man to

his brother, and every man to his neighbor; behold, I proclaim for you a liberty, says the Lord, to the sword, to pestilence, and to famine. And I will make the cities of Judah a desolation without inhabitant.

(Jeremiah 34:17)

For such words he was thrown into prison. There he poured out his heart to God. "Why do the wicked prosper?" he asked. He felt it would have been better if he had never lived:

Cursed be the day
Wherein I was born; . . .
Cursed be the man who brought tidings
To my father, saying:
"A male-child is born."

(Jeremiah 20:14–15)

But even in the depths of his misery, Jeremiah never doubted that he was speaking the truth. At all times he was certain that he had been sent to speak by the Lord of Hosts. And, in some of the most moving lines ever written, he admitted that, though he did not want to be a prophet, he could not avoid his mission:

I am a laughingstock all day long,
Everyone mocks me.
As often as I speak out, I cry out,
I am reproached and derided
For speaking the word of the Lord.
And if I say: "I will not make mention
*   of Him,*
Nor speak any more in His name,"
Then there is in my heart as it were a
*   burning fire*
Shut up in my bones,
And I weary myself to hold it in,
But cannot.

(Jeremiah 20:7–9)

Exile in Babylon

His prophecies of destruction came true. In the year 586 B.C.E. the armies of Babylonia, led by Nebuchadnezzar, captured and demolished Jerusalem. The independent life of the Hebrew nation was ended, the Temple of Solomon was left a ruin. Yet Jeremiah's effort to reform the people of Judah had not been in vain. In later years, they could understand that God had punished them for breaking His laws and thus breaking their covenant with Him. Furthermore, they could see that Jeremiah had proved, by word and example, that individuals can reach personal heights of righteousness and cannot escape the duty of trying to do so.

Nebuchadnezzar sent the inhabitants of Judah into exile in Babylonia. Tired, homeless, unhappy, they trudged east through the fertile crescent, reversing the trip that Abraham had made more than a thousand years earlier.

Now the prophets had a new task. Before the Exile, it had been their duty to bring a terrifying threat of destruction. Now it was their mission to reassure, to encourage, to inspire. The prophet Ezekiêl, in a series of wild and wonderful visions, spoke to the people of a glorious future, when Israel would be rebuilt and a new Temple would stand in Jerusalem:

Thus says the Lord God: Behold, I will open your graves, and cause you to come up out of your graves, O My people; and I will bring you into the land of Israel. . . . And I will put My spirit in you, and you shall live, and I will place you in your own land; and you will know that I the Lord have spoken and performed it.

(Ezekiel 37:12–14)

Exile and Diaspora

Nebuchadnezzar, king of Babylon.

The Babylonian armies, having conquered Jerusalem, sent most of the Hebrew people into exile (Hebrew: GALUT, גָּלוּת) in Babylonia. When they were permitted to do so, many Jews returned to rebuild Jerusalem and the Holy Temple; but particularly after the destruction of the Second Temple, communities outside the Holy Land were the major centers of Jewish life.

In time, Jews reached nearly every country in the world. This spreading of our people about the globe is generally known by the Greek word DIASPORA, which means "scattering." Living "in the Diaspora," Jews often came to think of themselves as Spaniards or Germans or Americans. But in their prayers and poems, they never forgot the land of Israel. They continued to dream of—and work for —the day when the galut, the exile, would be brought to an end.

It must have been even harder for the Hebrews of his time to believe in his message of hope than it had been for those who heard Amos and Jeremiah to believe their prophecy of doom. Yet Ezekiel's visions too were fulfilled. Not long after his death the empire of Babylonia started to crumble, and the armies of Persia began their conquest of the Near East.

"Second Isaiah"—prophet of hope

These events were observed by a man who was one of the most important and beloved of the prophets, but whose name we do not know. More than 2000 years ago his words were written onto a scroll that had been partially filled with the writings of Isaiah. For some reason, this more recent prophet's name was not included. We will never know who he was or the events of his personal life, and we call him simply the "Second Isaiah."

And yet, his writings have an importance unequaled in the prophetic books. To the exiles he brought renewed hope for a prompt return to Israel:

נַחֲמוּ נַחֲמוּ עַמִּי
יֹאמַר אֱלֹהֵיכֶם.

Comfort, O comfort My people,
Says your God.

The prophet continued:

Bid Jerusalem take heart,
And proclaim unto her,
That her time of service is
*   accomplished. . . .*

(Isaiah 40:1–2)

As the Second Isaiah predicted, the Persians rapidly overcame the Babylonians; and the Persian king, in one of his first official acts, permitted the Hebrews to return to Israel.

But the prophet did not merely provide accurate predictions of current events. He gave meaning to all that the Hebrews had endured and suffered. He explained that God—like any good father—had punished His children only to help them improve. Now they would be free of their guilt, stronger, and able to understand their duty as His people:

> I the Lord, in My grace, have summoned you,
> And I have grasped you by the hand.
> I created you, and appointed you
> A covenant people, a light of nations—
> Opening eyes deprived of light,
> Rescuing prisoners from confinement,
> From the dungeon those who sit in darkness.
>
> (Isaiah 42:6–7)

With these words, the Second Isaiah brought the prophetic phase of Judaism to a triumphant climax. Two hundred years before, Amos had declared that all nations should obey God's laws of righteousness, yet he did not say how they were to learn them. Jeremiah had been convinced that the Hebrew people would be saved from total destruction, but he did not say for what purpose they were to be saved. The first Isaiah and Micah had described an era of peace, but without specifying the part the Jewish people would play in bringing about that Golden Age.

The Second Isaiah brought the solution to these problems. The people of Israel had been saved so that they could teach God's laws of righteousness to the entire world. The Golden Age would be brought about because dedicated people would bring God's truth to humanity. Especially during the darker periods of Jewish history, this exalted message has been a continuing source of strength to our people.

Men shouting in the streets—men with revolutionary ideas claiming they had spoken to God. Men of vastly different personalities, from the fierce Amos to the kindly Second Isaiah, from the visionary Ezekiel to the heartbroken Jeremiah, yet each willing to risk ridicule, hatred, even death, to deliver the word of God. Each one forged a link in the chain of Judaism that gave it the strength to remain alive and vital when the Jewish homeland was destroyed. And in doing so, they made Israel a light to the nations—the bearer of ideas which changed the thinking of humankind.

SUMMARY *The unique event which kept the Jews from disappearing into the pages of history, as did other ancient peoples, was the appearance of the Hebrew prophets. These men gave meaning to the destruction of the kingdoms of Israel and Judah, explaining these events as part of God's plan for purifying and strengthening His people. At the same time, the prophets brought new ideas—ideals of peace and justice—which it became our duty to bring to the rest of the world.*

4

A Nation Reborn

Babylon, 539 B.C.E. For the first time in history the cry is heard: "Return to Zion! Rebuild the land of Israel!"

The reaction to this call was mixed. Few were still alive who had any personal memories of the land that had been destroyed nearly fifty years before. A new generation had been born in Babylon, the greatest city of the ancient world. There the Jews had maintained their religious identity, while reaching a standard of living they had never known in Israel.

So the vast majority chose to remain, developing an active and important Jewish community. In periods when there were very few Jews living in Palestine, Babylonian Jewry survived and often flourished. (More than 125,000 Jews still lived in this area in 1948, although cruelly oppressed by the Arab government in the modern state of Iraq. Nearly all of them escaped, with most heading for Israel during "Operation Ezra and Nehemiah" in 1950–51.)

We can easily understand the feelings of those who chose to remain in the country where they were born and raised. We ourselves may be enthusiastic supporters of the State of Israel, but most of us do not want to leave our homes to settle in the Jewish state. Others, however, are ready to give up everything just to live there. In Persian times, many Jews—perhaps as many as 50,000 of the several hundred thousand living in Mesopotamia—felt this same overwhelming devotion to the homeland of our people. And so it was a large and joyous throng who made the dangerous 800-mile journey to Jerusalem.

Rebuilding the Temple

What they found was depressing. The city of Jerusalem lay in ruins. Hostile foreigners had entered the deserted land and settled throughout Judah. The few Hebrews permitted to remain during the exile had intermarried with other peoples and were understandably hostile to the new arrivals from Babylonia who claimed the right to rule them.

Still, Jews in our own day, returning to an Israel more barren and more hostile than the Israel of the Persian empire, wept with joy at seeing the land of their forefathers. The reactions of the Babylonian exiles must have been similar. Eagerly they began the task of rebuilding, and within a year the foundations for a new Temple had been completed.

Then the work came to a sudden halt. We are not sure why—perhaps the major factor was the difficulty of raising food on the hilly land outside the ruined Jerusalem. Whatever the reason, it was eighteen years before the people, inspired by the prophets

Haggai and Zechariah, went back to work on the building. In all, it took twenty-three years to finish the Second Temple, more than twice as long as had been needed for the Temple of Solomon, and yet the new structure was far less impressive than the old.

The overall situation continued to worsen. The children of the returned exiles intermarried with the local non-Jews. Jerusalem remained uninhabited and defenseless. The priests of the Temple were unable to lead the people—in fact, they became corrupt. Within sixty years of the completion of the Second Temple and just eighty years after the end of the Babylonian exile, the community in Israel seemed about to fall apart.

The Jews who made the difficult journey from Babylon to Jerusalem found the Temple in ruins, but they soon began to build a new one.

Ezra and Nehemiah

It was two Jews from the exile, Ezra and Nehemiah, who revived Israel and made it again a center for Jewish life. Both men had risen to positions of importance in the Persian capital—Nehemiah was a friend and adviser of the king himself. Yet when they heard of the terrible situation in Israel, they left the splendor and comfort of court life for the ruins of Judah.

With Nehemiah as governor, conditions in Jerusalem changed rapidly. Before his arrival, attempts at rebuilding the city's defenses had failed because enemies had attacked and destroyed them before they were finished. Nehemiah divided his forces into two parts. While one group of men worked, the other stood guard, fully armed. In this way, the walls were soon completed, and once again Jews were able to live in the city of David.

Spiritual rebuilding was just as important. Major rituals were again observed—the Feast of Booths, Sukkot, was celebrated for the first time in memory.

Most important of all, ethical laws were given new life. Nehemiah discovered that poor Jews were being held in slavery by rich ones. He set them free, showing firmly that society in Judah would be built on the ethical principles established by God.

A major educational program was begun. Scholars were imported from the synagogues of Babylonia to teach Torah to the people of Israel. According to the Bible, Ezra read the Law of Moses in public assemblies. Then the entire community subscribed to an oath:

> . . . to walk in God's law, which was given by Moses the servant of God, and to observe and do all the commandments of the Lord our God, and His ordinances and His statutes.
>
> (Nehemiah 10:30)

The strength of Judaism

Judaism had entered a new era. By the time of Ezra, according to tradition, the Age of Prophets had ended; but under the Persian kings, another period of accomplishment had begun.

Yet, strangely enough, we know almost nothing about the 207 years (from 539 to 332 B.C.E.) during which the Persians ruled our people. One of the few things we really know about this time is that Judaism came out of it strong and secure, ready to pass every test it would face for the next twenty-three centuries.

First of all, the children of Abraham had become one people. Centuries ago they had been Hebrews, divided into tribes or rival kingdoms. Now they were JEWS, a name derived from Judah but now removed from any specific tribal or national identity. (The name of our religion—Judaism—also comes from Judah.) Whether they lived in Israel or Babylonia, Asia Minor or Egypt, wherever they might be driven in later centuries, the Jews would remain one people.

Furthermore, they would remain the people of the One God. For a thousand years, idolatry had been a constant problem in Jewish life. Hebrews had set up golden calves as symbols of God and had been drawn to all forms of pagan worship. During the Persian period, however, idol worship played no further part in Jewish life.

While they were separating themselves from pagan worship, the Jews made it possible for pagans to join the life of Israel. Before this, there had been no set way for a non-Jew to adopt the Hebrew religion. In the time of Ezra and Nehemiah, when intermarriage with foreigners was so widespread that it endangered the very survival of Judaism, the only way the two leaders could restore the unity of the Jewish people was to force all Hebrews to divorce their non-Jewish wives. In later years, however, the institution of conversion was developed. Through study, commitment, and ritual, any person could choose to give up his former religion and join his future to that of the Jewish people.

Religious life was strong. The center of Jewish ritual was, of course, the Second Temple, but since the destruction of the First Temple the Jews had also begun to worship in synagogues. It is hard to think of this as something revolutionary, but in fact it was just that. It created a democratic spirit among Jews by allowing groups of ordinary people to pray directly to God without the assistance of the priestly class and without animal sacrifice, which the Hebrews and all ancient peoples had performed. Today, nearly 2500 years later, the synagogue continues to serve as a house of prayer, meeting, and study. In addition, the synagogue has changed the religious life of the whole Western world by serving as the model from which Christianity and Islam developed their own houses of worship, the church and the mosque.

The strength which Judaism developed under the tolerant and enlightened rule of the early Persians helped the Jews survive when the later Persian kings became more and more dictatorial. The defeat of the Persians by Alexander the Great was a welcome relief to the Jews. Alexander was particularly kind to his Hebrew subjects, and they responded with loyal support. Many fought in his armies, and a large Jewish community settled in the new city which he founded in Egypt—Alexandria.

These Alexandrian Jews adopted Greek as their language, and their children grew up with little knowledge of the Hebrew language. The Bible was translated into Greek. This translation was called the Septuagint ("Seventy") because of the legend that seventy Jewish scholars, each working on his own, had produced seventy Bibles which agreed in every detail! The Septuagint was very important, for through it the ideas of Jewish teachers and prophets became known to the entire Greek-speaking world.

Under Greek rule

The teachings of Israel, however, did not blend well with the culture of Athens. The Greeks produced wonderful sculpture, but the commandment against graven images (idols) prevented faithful Jews from trying their hand at this art. Greek philosophy was fascinating, but it often thought of human life in a gloomy and hopeless way. These attitudes clashed with the Jewish belief that every person is basically good and can improve the world by positive action and righteous living. Advanced Greek thinkers taught that truth can be found only by a few people through long study, while Judaism said that truth is open to everyone in the Torah, the word of God.

Yet Greek culture appealed to many

Jews. Some were frankly willing to give up Judaism whenever necessary to enjoy the comforts of the Greek conquerors. Others tried sincerely, though with great difficulty, to put together the best features of the two cultures. But many Jews rejected Greek ways, finding them totally foreign to Jewish traditions.

The cruelty of Antiochus

If Jews found it difficult to deal with Greek culture, they found it even more difficult to deal with the Egyptian and Syrian successors of Alexander. Of these, the worst was Antiochus IV, who as king of Syria controlled all of Israel. He suffered from feelings of grandeur which bordered on insanity. He thought he was a god, and took the title *Epiphanes*, which means "the manifest God." His enemies, however, nicknamed him *Epimanes*—"the madman."

Antiochus taxed the Jews cruelly to pay for his many wars. Everything he controlled was for sale to the highest bidder. Even the sacred office of High Priest of the Temple was sold, to a Jew who had adopted Greek culture and the Greek name of Jason, and Jerusalem developed into a city more Greek than Jewish.

Antiochus dreamed of conquering Egypt but was prevented from doing so by the Roman armies. Frustrated and furious, he vented his anger on his Jewish subjects, first by robbing the Temple treasury and slaughtering those who rose up in protest, then by outlawing the practice of Judaism. Keeping the Sabbath was a crime. Circumcision was a crime. Honoring the God of Israel was a crime. Jews were required by law to offer sacrifices to the gods of Greece and were forced to eat pig. Punishment for disobedience was death.

The Maccabean revolt

For the first time in history a people fought for religious liberty. Revolt began when Mattathias, the elderly leader of the Hasmonean family and priest of the small town of Modin, killed a traitorous Jew who was about to offer a sacrifice to the Greek gods. With the cry "Those who are faithful to Law, follow me," he led his five sons and their many loyal followers into the hills to prepare for a Greek attack.

Antiochus was angered by this act of rebellion and sent a strong army with war elephants and chariots. The odds against the Jews were tremendous; but the third son of Mattathias, Judah, proved to be an extraordinary military leader. Carefully using his band of guerrilla fighters, he was able to drive the Greek armies away. Antiochus sent a stronger army with a better general, but Judah and his troops promptly disappeared into the hills. While the king's army searched for them in vain, they fell upon the camp that the Greeks had left unprotected—and destroyed it. Judah became known as MACCABEE, מַכַּבִּי —the Hammerer.

Judah Maccabee's forces were small, but with courage and determination they moved from victory to victory. After two years of fierce fighting, the rebels regained control of Jerusalem. There they cleansed the Temple, destroyed the statue of Zeus which had been worshiped there, and on the 25th of Kislev, 165 B.C.E., rededicated the building to the service of God. This great victory of human freedom is com-

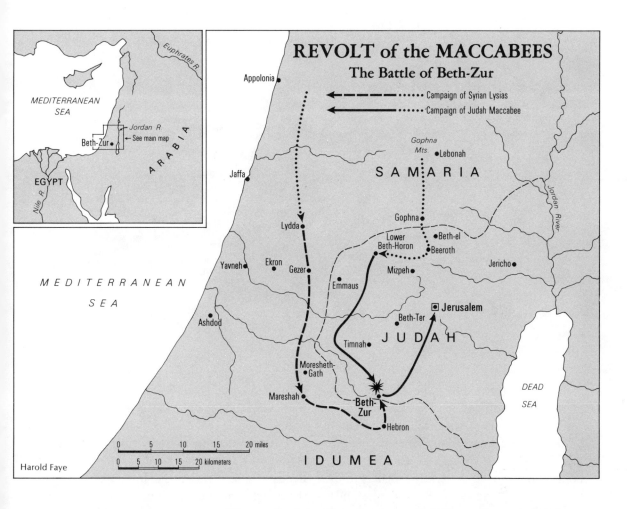

The revolt of the Maccabees began in 167 B.C.E. Two years of fighting passed before the forces of Judah Maccabee were able to defeat the armies of Antiochus and recapture Jerusalem. In one key battle, at Emmaus, Judah surprised the enemy troops, forced them to flee, and then destroyed their camp before a second Greek army could reach it. Judah's men then returned to the Gophna Mountains to await the next attack. A later battle took place at Lower Beth-Horon, and from there the forces of Judah Maccabee (solid line) took a roundabout route toward Jerusalem. They were met, outside Beth-Zur, by still another Greek army (broken line), this one commanded by a Syrian general named Lysias. Again the Maccabees outfought the Greeks, and from Beth-Zur the Jews went straight to the City of David. On the 25th of Kislev, 165 B.C.E., they rededicated the Temple—an act we remember today in the feast of Ḥanukkah.

The Maccabean revolt began when Mattathias killed a Jew who was about to sacrifice to a Greek god.

memorated today by the holiday of Ḥanukkah, the Feast of Lights.

From the end of the Exile to the celebration of the first Ḥanukkah, our people had faced many crises. At each turning point, however, a relatively small group had been willing to risk all to see the children of Israel survive. A minority returned to Israel from Babylon. A minority took up arms against the armies of Antiochus. Yet in each case their dedication and determination proved fully justified. After 400 years of rule by Babylonians, Persians, and Greeks, the Jews were again the masters of their own country.

SUMMARY *The period following the Babylonian exile was one of rebuilding. Though the details of the period are not always clear, its achievements are still with us. Thanks to religious leaders like Ezra and Nehemiah, Judaism was given a strength of purpose and institutions that survive to our own time. With the victory of the Maccabees over the armies of Antiochus, the Biblical Period comes to a triumphant conclusion.*

PART TWO

The Roman Empire

The Age of the Rabbis

The Age of the Rabbis is also the era of the Talmud, that vast and richly complex collection of laws, opinions, legends, sayings, stories, and debates — a glorious achievement of our people and one of the greatest monuments the human mind has ever produced. So deep and wide and replete with variety is the Talmud that it has been likened to a sea; students of its wisdom sometimes speak of having only dipped a foot into its oceanic depths, or refer to a master of the Talmud as one who has fully immersed himself in its waters and learned to swim about with ease.

If the Talmud is like an ocean in its vastness, in another sense it is like a mirror. We see in it, as people have seen in the Jews themselves over the centuries, the spirit of rational inquiry and relentless questioning, the thirst for logic and clarity and analytic truth. But at the same time we see in it a spirit of compassionate understanding in the face of human frailty, a spirit of brotherhood, and a spirit of humble

Romans and Jews

The story of the Romans and the Jews is also
a tale of two cities: Rome and Jerusalem. The
inset shows the Colosseum, where thousands of men
were killed in a single day just to satisfy the
Romans' thirst for spectacle. In the surrounding
scene we see the busy street life of Jerusalem,
where intrigues flourished and factions clashed,
but also where gentler spirits like Hillel
taught a moral way of life that has far
outlasted the brutalities of Rome.

---

acceptance before the will of God. Add to all these things the Rabbis'
calm and confident and unceasing love of everything Jewish, and
you begin to catch something of the spirit that breathes through
every syllable and every page of the Talmud.

The Rabbis of the Talmud used to say of the Torah: "Turn it, turn it,
everything is in it." They meant that the word of God as contained in
His Holy Scriptures was infinitely revealing; the more we study it,
the more we learn from it. Something similar might be said of the
Talmud itself: everything the Jewish people holds dear is explained
and clarified in this great work. To know who we are as Jews, we need
only look into the mirror which is the Talmud.

ABBA EBAN

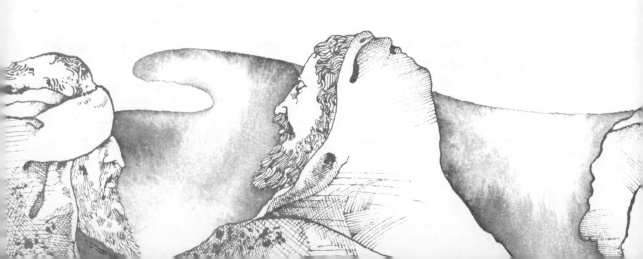

The destruction of Jerusalem was an event of historic importance
for Jews and Romans alike. Above, carvings on the Arch of
Titus in Rome show soldiers triumphantly carrying the spoils of the
Temple; below and right, Roman warriors prepare to beseige the
Jewish fortress at Masada.

The late Roman period witnessed a
rich outpouring of Jewish art.
The mosaic to the right, a picture
of Moses, comes from about 250 C.E.;
the decorated glass pieces were made
perhaps 100 years later. The mosaic floor
showing the signs of the Zodiac (below)
dates from the sixth century C.E., which
means it was made after the
Roman Empire had been divided.

5

INTRODUCTION TO PART TWO

The Roman Empire

Rome—a name known for grandeur and excitement.

Rome—the largest city of the ancient world, at one time the home of 2 million people.

Rome—the greatest empire the West has ever known, which brought peace to the Mediterranean lands for hundreds of years.

Rome—a nation whose history reeks with murder, bloodshed, and immorality.

Rome—the army that destroyed the land of Israel and sent the Jewish people into an exile which lasted nearly 2000 years.

Perhaps no nation has left us so much to admire and so much to detest. One can stand today in the Roman Colosseum, admiring the beauty and grandeur of the ruin. And then one imagines the brutal spectacles performed there: massacres of as many as 3000 people to provide the Romans with a single day's "entertainment."

From republic to empire

This love of bloodshed was part of a society dedicated to military expansion. Once the Roman armies began to occupy new territories, about 400 B.C.E., no force was able to stop their slow but steady advance. By 275 B.C.E. the Romans were masters of the entire Italian peninsula, and within another 100 years they had gained virtual control over Greece and the Western Mediterranean.

They then moved to extend their influence into Egypt—and, in doing so, became involved in Jewish history. In 168 B.C.E., as Antiochus Epiphanes prepared his armies to attack Alexandria, the Romans sent a messenger to order him to leave Egypt at once. Seeing his dreams of conquest collapsing, the king asked for time to decide what to do. The messenger drew a circle around him and told him to reach his decision before stepping out of it! The power

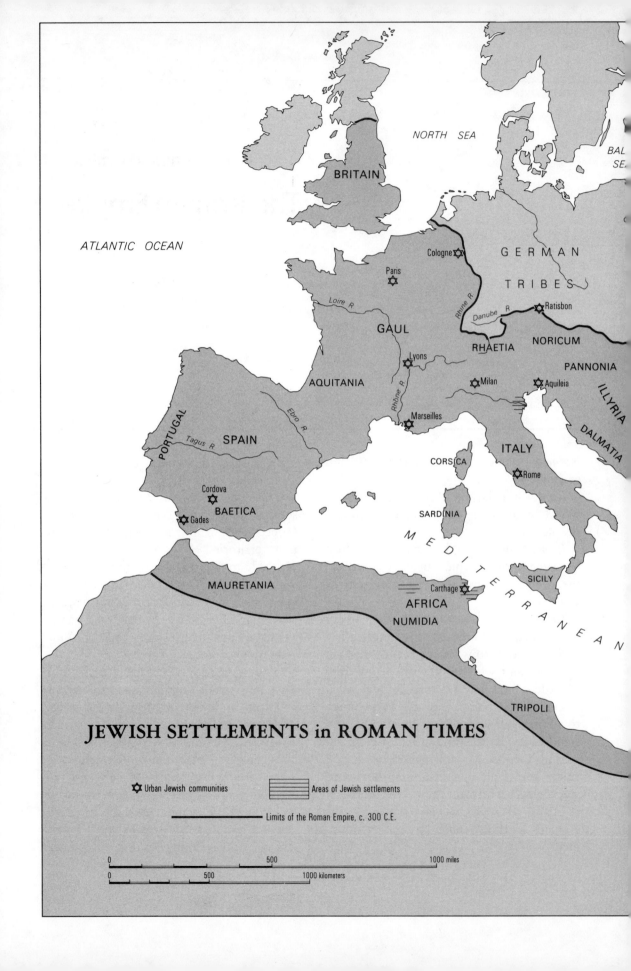

NORTH SEA

ATLANTIC OCEAN

BRITAIN

GERMAN

TRIBES

Cologne ✡

Paris ✡

Loire R.

Rhine R.

Danube R.

Ratisbon ✡

GAUL

RHAETIA

NORICUM

AQUITANIA

Rhône R.

Lyons ✡

Milan ✡

Aquileia ✡

PANNONIA

ILLYRIA

PORTUGAL

Tagus R.

SPAIN

Ebro R.

Marseilles ✡

ITALY

DALMATIA

Cordova ✡

BAETICA

Gades ✡

CORSICA

SARDINIA

Rome ✡

MEDITERRANEAN

SICILY

MAURETANIA

Carthage ✡

AFRICA

NUMIDIA

TRIPOLI

JEWISH SETTLEMENTS in ROMAN TIMES

✡ Urban Jewish communities

Areas of Jewish settlements

Limits of the Roman Empire, c. 300 C.E.

0   500   1000 miles

0   500   1000 kilometers

This map shows how widely dispersed Jews had become by the fourth century C.E. Note that by the year 300, Jews were already in Spain, France (then known as Gaul), and Germany; they would soon reach Belgium and Britain. Although many place names on this map should be familiar to you, some may seem strange. These unfamiliar names are the Latin words for Roman provinces and cities that have no direct modern counterparts.

HUNS

CASPIAN SEA

BLACK SEA

MOESIA

Danube R.

THRACE

ARMENIA

ACEDONIA

Constantinople

PONTUS

Salonika

BITHYNIA

GALATIA

Halys R.

GREECE

CAPPADOCIA

PERSIAN EMPIRE

Corinth

Athens

Ephesus

CILICIA

Tarsus

MESOPOTAMIA

ACHAEA

Antioch

Euphrates R.

Ctesiphon

CRETE

CYPRUS

SYRIA

Nehardea

Tigris R.

SEA

Damascus

Sura

PERSIAN GULF

PALESTINE

Cyrene

Jerusalem

Alexandria

ARABIA

LIBYA

Memphis

EGYPT

ARABIA

Nile R.

RED SEA

Harold Faye

The Names
of the Land

The territory on the east coast of the Mediterranean Sea has had many names. In the time of Abraham, it was called the land of Canaan. When the territory was conquered by the Hebrews, different areas became known for each of the Hebrew tribes: Judah, Ephraim, Benjamin, and so on. After Solomon's death, the area was split into two parts: the kingdom of Israel in the north and the kingdom of Judah in the south.

These kingdoms were destroyed and the Jews exiled. After the Jews returned, the entire territory was known as Judah. The Romans, who conquered it in 63 B.C.E., called the same land Judea. However, after the last Jewish revolt, in 135 C.E., the Romans decided to use a term that had no Jewish associations. They included the land in the province of Syria (which also included the present country of Lebanon and parts of modern Syria), and termed Judea "Palestinian Syria." "Palestine" was the name originally used by the Greeks in references to the Philistines, who dominated the Mediterranean coastline in the days of Saul. Palestine remained the name for the area until modern times.

Jews, however, continued to speak of the "Promised Land," the "land of Israel" (*Eretz Yisrael,* אֶרֶץ יִשְׂרָאֵל), and of "Zion," the mountain which became a symbol for Jerusalem. The modern movement of resettlement was called *Zionism* (צִיּוֹנוּת), and Zion was actually considered as a name for the modern Jewish state established in 1948. The final decision, of course, was to revive the name of Israel.

---

of Rome was already so great that Antiochus was forced to withdraw his armies, but he was angered by this disgrace and looked for some way to get revenge. It was then that he decided to force his Jewish subjects to adopt the Greek religion— only to suffer the worse humiliation of defeat in the Maccabean revolt.

Rome's successes in foreign wars were not matched with success at home—at least if success is measured in terms of peace and harmony. Class rivalries and civil wars were common. Successful generals would return from overseas and try to become dictators.

Two of the ablest generals were Pompey and Julius Caesar. Pompey's military and diplomatic victories came in the East— victories which included capturing Judah for the Roman Empire. Caesar's exploits were in the West, in what is now France. Eventually the two leaders came into conflict, and when they met in battle Pompey's forces were beaten badly. He fled to Egypt, where he was murdered, and Caesar returned in triumph to Rome.

As a hero without rival, he was able to govern with absolute power—and, on the whole, he ruled humanely. He pardoned many of his enemies, improved the governmental system, and provided work for the poor. He also treated his Jewish subjects very favorably, protecting their interests and freedom of worship. However, a group of Romans feared his one-man rule and, in an effort to restore the republic, killed him.

The civil war that followed left Caesar's legal heir, Octavian, sole ruler of the Mediterranean world. He took a new title—Augustus ("Revered One"). With this event, in the year 27 B.C.E., the Roman Republic came to an end and the Roman Empire began.

Triumph and decline

We need not trace the complex history of the Roman emperors. Some, like Augustus, were relatively enlightened. Others, like the mad and sadistic Nero, who murdered his own mother, have become symbols of evil.

Whatever one may say about individual emperors, however, the empire as a whole was a military, social, and technological triumph. It was enormous, extending at its height from Britain to Egypt, from Spain to the Persian Gulf. Moreover, within this huge territory there was remarkable order. The first two centuries of Roman rule are known as the *Pax Romana* ("Peace of Rome"). International travel was made safer and easier by Roman engineers who built 50,000 miles of roads, some of which are still in use today. Mail traveled more swiftly from London to Rome in the first century C.E. than at the beginning of the nineteenth!

About the year 200 C.E., the empire began to decay. Inflation, plague, a dizzying series of palace murders, political assassinations, and constant pressure from Germanic tribes on the European frontiers all were part of what historians later called the "decline and fall" of the Roman Empire. The government became unable to control all the Roman territories, and so the empire was split into Eastern and Western halves, each with its own ruler.

Rome, Christianity, and the Jews

One of the first of the Eastern emperors, Constantine, built a new capital which he named after himself—Constantinople. (It is now called Istanbul and is the largest city in modern Turkey.) Constantine was a very strange man. After fighting three civil wars to gain control of the empire, he murdered his son, brother-in-law, nephew, and wife in arguments as to who should follow him on the throne. But perhaps because of a vision before a battle, perhaps because of his love for his mother (who was a devout Christian), he converted to Christianity just before his death.

Christianity, which had once been persecuted by the emperors, soon became the official state religion. The religious leader (or bishop) of the city of Rome became the "Pope"—the head of the Church throughout the empire. The ideals of

The Romans were the greatest engineers of the ancient world. This bridge, the oldest in Rome, has been in use for over 2000 years.

monotheism were established in the life of Western civilization.

Unfortunately, while the Christian Church took many of its teachings from Judaism, it did not adopt the principle of toleration, least of all toward Jews. By 325 C.E., just twelve years after Christians had been granted toleration in the empire, Church councils were meeting to adopt openly anti-Jewish legislation. One item, small in itself, demonstrates the spirit of the Church leaders. They changed the date of Easter so that it would no longer be observed at the same time as Passover:

> . . . it appeared an unworthy thing that in the celebration of this most holy feast we should follow the practice of the Jews, who have impiously defiled their hands with enormous sin, and are, therefore, deservedly afflicted with blindness of soul.
> . . . Let us then have nothing in common with the detestable Jewish crowd.

Not until 1965 did the Catholic Church officially change its attitude.

An end—and a beginning

The division of the empire left the Western half—whose capital was still the city of Rome—at a severe disadvantage, since most of the wealth and resources were in the East. The government in Italy, ruined economically and unable to defend its borders, finally collapsed, and the West ceased to have an emperor in 476 C.E. The Eastern half survived for another 1000 years, but it became an oriental monarchy whose ruler was all but worshiped as a god. The Age of Rome was over.

We are all very much products of the Roman period. Roman concepts of justice are built into our system of laws. The very word "justice" is one of many that come from the language of the Romans—Latin. As Jews, we live in a Christian society that the Romans helped build.

Although Jewish national life was destroyed in 135 C.E. by the armies of Rome, the period under Roman rule was one of the most productive in the development of our religion. During this time the basic forms of Jewish law were developed under such great men as Hillel, Johanan ben Zakkai, and Akiva. Jewish life was reorganized, and rabbis replaced priests as the religious leaders of the Jewish community.

So much to admire. . . . So much to despise. . . . This is the complex but fascinating age that we will consider in the following chapters.

SUMMARY   *As Rome slowly developed from a tiny village to a huge empire, it became a state geared largely to military life. Its heroes were soldiers like Julius Caesar and Pompey; its entertainments were gory and destructive. Nevertheless, the Roman Empire provided the Mediterranean countries with two centuries of excellent government and gave the world concepts and institutions of permanent value. Roman treatment of the Jews varied from great generosity to great brutality. Yet, all in all, the Roman era was one of the most productive in Jewish history.*

6

The Emerging Tradition

The Roman general Pompey looked at the Jerusalem Temple with curiosity. The building's innermost chamber was the Holy of Holies, where no Jew dared enter except the High Priest, and he only on the most sacred day of the Jewish year, Yom Kippur. "How," wondered the soldier, "does the God of the Jews reveal Himself in that room?"

Calmly he strolled through the Temple. He reached the Holy of Holies, entered it, and found—nothing. There was no Ark of the Law—that had disappeared when the Temple of Solomon was destroyed. There was no priest or priestess claiming to deliver messages from the gods. There was not even an imposing idol before which one could offer sacrifices.

Pompey turned and left the building. Perhaps he thought it stupid for Hebrews to treat an invisible God with such respect. Perhaps he didn't really care about religious questions, and was thinking only of his power: he had violated the Temple of the Jews, and no one dared raise a hand to stop him.

Judea falls to Rome

Thus began a period of 200 years during which Judea was a province of the Roman Empire. How did this happen? How did the land of the brave Maccabees become the slave of Rome?

After defeating the armies of Antiochus, the Hasmoneans (the family of Mattathias) became the royal family of Judea. Unfortunately, these children of heroes rapidly forgot the principles of their fathers. Instead of supporting the belief in religious freedom—the very belief which had been basic to the Maccabean revolt—one of the early Hasmoneans, John Hyrcanus, conquered the country of Idumea to the south of Judah and forced the entire population, tens of thousands of people, to convert to Judaism.

Jews have often been the victims of forced conversion, but at no other time have we practiced it on others. As we shall see, this action had terrible results.

During the 100 years in which the Hasmoneans ruled, they wrecked the country and violated the ideals for which their ancestors had fought. There was a nine-year period of relief from civil war and murder when, for the only time in its history, Judea was ruled by a woman. Queen Salome Alexandra was a kind and gentle person who succeeded in bringing some unity to the country; but as soon as she died, her two sons began to battle for the throne.

Rather than begin a new civil war, the brothers decided to ask Pompey, who was in nearby Syria, to judge between them. The clever soldier immediately took advantage of the situation and seized Judea for Rome. This was in 63 B.C.E., and it was then that he was able to stroll, un- touched, into the holiest sanctuary of the Jewish people.

Herod the murderer

Roman rule might not in itself have been a misfortune, but the Romans gave day-to-day control of the country to a family from Idumea. These people were officially Jewish—hadn't they been forced to convert to Judaism by John Hyrcanus? But they were really pagans who had little respect for Judaism or the Jews.

Their loyalty to the Romans became clear when the throne fell to a man named Herod. He soon proved his devotion to the empire by going to Rome instead of Jerusalem for his coronation, and offering sacrifices to the Roman god Jupiter.

Herod trusted no one and killed those he suspected of disloyalty. He ordered the murder of the High Priest and of his own

When the Roman general Pompey strolled into the Temple and entered the Holy of Holies, no one dared to try and stop him.

wife and sons. Small wonder that the Emperor Augustus, who knew that Jews did not eat pig, said it would be safer to be one of Herod's swine than one of his children!

While thousands were dying at his command, Herod turned his attention to massive building projects, largely to serve his own purposes. He built fortresses to protect the land—but also to provide himself with places of refuge in case the people of Judea revolted against his oppressive rule. He rebuilt the Jerusalem Temple, making it more splendid than the Temple of Solomon—but largely to display his wealth and increase his prestige.

In fact, Herod cared so little for Judaism that he had a huge golden eagle mounted on the Temple gate. This was both a violation of the Second Commandment, which prohibits making statues of animals, and a sign of loyalty to Rome, since the eagle was a symbol of the Roman Empire. Jewish patriots tore the eagle down, so Herod had forty-two of them arrested and burned to death.

Zealots and Essenes—fight or flight?

This, then, was Judea at the beginning of the Roman period. In this insane world, right and wrong meant nothing and innocent people could be murdered at the whim of a king. The question of how to deal with the Roman oppressors split Jewish society into rival groups. Two of these groups, called the ZEALOTS (קַנָּאִים) and the ESSENES (אֶסִיִּים), shared the belief that extreme measures were needed.

The Zealots were revolutionaries whose goal was to expel the Romans and restore Judean independence. They used terrorism against the foreign enemy—and against those Jews who opposed their violent methods. Mixing in large crowds, they would stab to death their political opponents, thus earning the title of Sicarii (dagger men). "Courageous fighting conquered Antiochus," they reasoned, "and equal courage will defeat Rome."

The Zealots were brave, but they sadly underestimated the power of the Roman armies.

The Essenes were the "dropouts" of the age. Like the Zealots, they sought radical change, but not in politics—in themselves. They felt that society was too corrupt ever to be improved, so they withdrew from it, giving up the normal comforts of life to follow a strict pattern of prayer, work, and purification. Their regulations were so strict that until one had obeyed their rules for three years, one was not thought worthy to be a full member of the group. While some Essenes continued to live in the cities, others rejected normal society entirely and lived in the desert in a spiritual search for God.

The Essenes were a small group that, in the long run, had little effect on Judaism. However, certain Christian groups imitated their ideas and practices. Even today, some monks live in communities not unlike those of the Essenes near the Dead Sea some 2000 years ago.

Sadducees—party of the privileged

Unlike these extremists, some Jews enjoyed wealth and power under Roman rule. They were naturally eager to keep conditions as they were, so they formed a highly conservative political party. They were called the SADDUCEES (צְדוֹקִים), a name which may have come from that of Zadok, the first High Priest of the Jerusalem Temple. The group included a large number of priests. The Sadducees were opposed to change not only in political but also in religious affairs. They were especially strict in interpreting the laws of the Torah, insisting on applying old priestly traditions even in new and unusual cases.

This group was not very large, and it had few followers in the Jewish communities outside of Judea, such as Alexandria and Rome. Nevertheless, because of the wealth of its members, and the authority of the priests, the Sadducees enjoyed great power for many years.

Pharisees—party of the people

The real future of Judaism lay with the fourth and largest of the political parties. This was the party of the people, rich and poor, farmers and laborers, priests and commoners. They were called PHARISEES (פְּרוּשִׁים).

One is tempted to call the Pharisees the moderates of the age, but this might suggest that they protected themselves by staying in a "middle of the road" position. In fact, they were dedicated and creative people whose leaders willingly risked their lives for their beliefs. They rank with the great spiritual teachers of all time. In matters of religious observance they were extremely strict—the name "Pharisee," which means "separate one," shows their concern to separate themselves from evil and ritual impurity. In legal matters, however, they were flexible, realizing that many ancient religious laws had to be reinterpreted to give them meaning for their own age. This sometimes led them to make revolutionary changes in outdated practices, but it meant that Torah continued to be a meaningful force in Jewish life.

In addition to updating Jewish legal practices, the Pharisees tried to make the practice of our religion enjoyable for every family. To keep the home cheerful on the Sabbath eve, for example, they taught that the woman of each household should light extra lamps just before sundown on Friday. This became standard practice, and led to the modern ceremony of lighting candles to celebrate the beginning of the Sabbath.

The spirit of the Pharisees

The spirit of the Pharisees is perhaps best illustrated by the story of a poor woodcutter. He grew up in Babylonia with

One Roman in Ten When Pompey conquered Judea in 63 B.C.E., it was the home of about 3 million Jews. An additional 4 million Jews lived in other parts of the Roman Empire. Since the population of the entire empire was not greater than 70 million, no fewer than one of every ten Romans was Jewish. Never before or since have Jews formed so large a part of the known population of the Western world.

The Dead Sea Scrolls

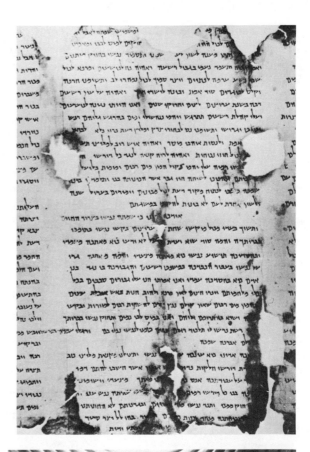

The Dead Sea Scrolls are a group of
2000-year-old manuscripts written in
Hebrew and Aramaic. They include
versions of the books of the Bible, other
texts from the Biblical Period,
commentaries, and the sacred writings of a
Jewish sect very much like the Essenes.
The scrolls were discovered in the caves of
Qumran (opposite page) in 1947. Then
they were carefully unrolled and
deciphered (above). Upper right, one of
the original manuscripts; lower right, the
"Shrine of the Book" in Jerusalem, where
some of the scrolls are displayed.

This scene may be legendary, but the characters in it are not.
Shemaia and Avtalion were outstanding scholars, and Hillel (center)
left his life as a woodcutter to become the greatest teacher of his time.

little education, but in time decided that he should learn the Law of God. So he traveled to Jerusalem to study with the leading teachers of the day, Shemaia and Avtalion.

The woodcutter worked hard to earn two pieces of silver each day. With one he supported himself and his family; with the other he paid the entrance fee for school in the evening. One Friday, however, he earned nothing. Rather than miss the lesson, he climbed onto the roof where, through a skylight, he could hear the words of his teachers.

It was a cold night, and snow began to fall. Too tired to move, or perhaps too intent on the lesson, the woodcutter was trapped under a three-foot drift. The next morning the teachers, noticing that the room was darker than usual, looked up and saw the shadow of the man on the skylight. Quickly they ran to the roof, rescued him from the snow, and brought him into the school. He was nearly frozen.

The man desperately needed to be warmed, but it was the Sabbath and the laws forbade a Jew to build a fire. Shemaia and Avtalion decided quickly: "This man deserves to have a Sabbath law broken." The fire was built, and the woodcutter's life was saved.

Hillel

This story tells many important things about the Pharisees. It shows how Jews from distant lands came to Judea to study with them. It shows, moreover, that the teachers were prepared to accept students from every walk of life. Most important, it shows how they were prepared to break or modify laws when necessary to serve, and especially to save, human life.

Furthermore, though the tale itself may be legendary, the characters in it are real. Shemaia and Avtalion were outstanding scholars, and the woodcutter who studied with them became the greatest teacher of his age, famous for his wisdom, his kindness, and his love for his fellow man. His name was Hillel.

Hillel, in his turn, set up a school where he followed the example of his masters by teaching living, meaningful Judaism. "Love peace and pursue peace," he taught. "Love all creatures, and bring them near to the Torah."

His patience was remarkable. The story is told that a pagan decided to have some fun at the expense of the learned men of Israel. First he went to the school of another leading teacher, Shammai. "Teach me the Torah while I stand on one foot," he said to the scholar, "and I will convert." Shammai was furious at the suggestion that the Torah could be mastered in a few moments, and drove him away. Pleased with himself, the non-Jew went to Hillel and made the same request. "What is hateful to you, do not do to your neighbor," said Hillel. "That is the whole Torah, the rest is commentary. Go and learn."

Thus Hillel stated the Golden Rule. And, according to the story, Hillel's patience so impressed the Gentile that he did convert to Judaism.

Heroes—false and true

Hillel, Shemaia, and Avtalion, like Pompey and Herod, lived in the first century B.C.E. To most people it would have seemed that the soldier and the king were the most important men of their era, while the teachers were of passing interest.

Pompey, however, returned to Rome only to be defeated by Caesar and murdered by an Egyptian assassin. Herod became so insanely cruel that he ordered his men to have all Jewish leaders killed as soon as he died, so there would be no rejoicing at the news of his death. His soldiers refused to obey this barbaric command, however. The anniversary of Herod's death became a day of celebration, and his chosen heir was overthrown by the Jewish people.

Hillel, on the other hand, left a family which provided the leaders of Judean Jewry for 400 years. More important, he and the other Pharisaic teachers established a living tradition of study, piety, and humanity which is still part of our heritage.

SUMMARY   *The decay of Israel under the Hasmoneans, the descendants of Mattathias, gave the Romans the opportunity to take control of the land. The authority they gave Herod, a great builder but a brutal murderer, brought further disorder. Amid this confusion, the people sought meaning and order in different ways. The Zealots fostered rebellion. The Essenes rejected society. The Sadducees tried to preserve their own privileges. But the Pharisees, led by great men like Hillel, taught an observant but humane Judaism that would form the basis of future Jewish thinking and Jewish life.*

7

The Last Days
of the Temple

The teachings of the Pharisees would become the mainstream of Judaism—but not until after the Zealots had brought revolution to Judea and destruction to themselves.

Tyrants of Judea

Julius Caesar and the Emperor Augustus were kind to their Jewish subjects. Jews were even freed from military service, since in the army they could not eat kosher food or observe the Sabbath. Unfortunately, this generous spirit was not reflected in the men who actually ruled Judea. We have seen how King Herod filled the land with brutality and bloodshed. After his death, Rome ended the monarchy and appointed its own governors, called procurators. In order to keep these procurators from becoming too rich and powerful, the emperors replaced them on a regular basis. The sad result was that each governor tried to steal as much as possible from the country before he was assigned to another location.

Of these procurators, one of the most bloodthirsty and corrupt was Pontius Pilate. He regularly ordered executions without even the form of a trial. He stole Temple funds and, when the Jews protested, sent disguised soldiers among them who massacred both demonstrators and casual onlookers. Even other Romans, who were certainly not squeamish about bloodshed, protested his unusual brutality.

Jesus of Nazareth

In the face of this suffering, many Jews prayed for miraculous deliverance. According to a tradition which dated back to the prophets, a descendant of King David would free his people from misery and reestablish the independent kingdom of Israel. He would be the perfect ruler, totally just and righteous, bringing peace and happiness to the world. Like a king, he would be anointed with holy oil—he would be called "the anointed." The Hebrew expression for this is מָשִׁיחַ, from which we get the English word for the miraculous king and savior—MESSIAH.

Some felt that the Messiah had already come when they met a young preacher from the town of Nazareth. He was called Joshua, but he is known to the world by the Greek version of his name: Jesus.

Few facts are known with certainty about Jesus of Nazareth. We do not have a single word written by him, nor by anyone who ever saw him. The information we do have comes from the books which Christians call the New Testament, whose authors were born as much as a hundred years after Jesus' death. Even they disagree in important areas. Moreover, they wrote not as historians but as spokesmen for the belief that Jesus was divine.

It is generally agreed that Jesus was a Jew of Galilee who shared the religious outlook and ethical ideals of the Pharisees. He differed, however, in his belief that the end of the world and the Kingdom of God were near at hand; because of this, he said, matters of family and community life were not very important. Jesus also taught the idea of passive resistance. If someone slaps you on one cheek, he said, you should turn the other cheek and be struck again; do not degrade yourself by resorting to violence, for you will have to account for it at the time of the Last Judgment.

The procurator was not interested in Jesus' beliefs. To the Romans the man was politically dangerous—a possible leader for a Jewish independence movement. Pilate had him arrested and executed him in the customary Roman manner: nailing him to a wooden cross and putting him on public display until he died.

From martyr to "Messiah"

Jesus' death was clear proof that he was not the earthly king for whom the Jews had been waiting. Most of our people continued to hope and pray for the Messiah (as Orthodox Jews do to this day), and Jesus might well have been forgotten except for the work of a man known throughout Christendom as Saint Paul. Paul believed that Jesus had come back to life to rule, not in this world, but in heaven. In this sense, he was still the king, "the anointed." And so Jesus became known as the Messiah in the Greek translation of the word: *Christos*—Christ.

Paul's claim raised many questions. Why was Jesus to be the ruler of heaven? Because he was the son of God. Why had he come to earth? To pay for the sins of mankind by his own death. Was it important to believe this? Yes. Only those who did so would be admitted into his kingdom of heaven. Thus Christianity developed as a religion based not on the beliefs *of* Jesus, but on beliefs *about* Jesus.

As Christian doctrines became more and more removed from those of Judaism, Christian teaching became more and more anti-Jewish. In the New Testament, for example, the brutal Pontius Pilate is portrayed as a sensitive man who wished to save the life of Jesus. Only "the Jews," bloodthirsty and merciless, prevented him from doing so. For sixteen centuries this story was used as an excuse for the persecution of Jews, "the murderers of Jesus." Finally, in 1965, the Roman Catholic Church stated officially that neither all the

Jews of Jesus' time nor any Jews of today should be held responsible for his
death.

Josephus and the "Jewish War"

When Jesus died, only a few people
had ever heard of him. To those who
learned of his execution, it probably
seemed just another senseless murder ordered by the cruel Roman procurator. But
as the number of such killings increased,
relations between Jews and Romans grew
more and more tense.

At this critical point, the position of
procurator fell to Florus, a man so wicked
he made those who came before him seem
kind and generous. He attempted to steal
what he could from the people, and at
last he demanded gold from the Temple
treasury for his personal use. Riots broke
out in which his soldiers massacred 3600
people.

This was the moment for which the
Zealots had been waiting. With the people
already up in arms, the Zealots took over
and led a rebellion against the Emperor
Nero.

The tiny country of Judea was challeng-
ing the world's mightiest empire. Amazingly, the Jewish rebellion lasted seven
years, from 66 to 73 C.E., and presented
the Roman army with one of the most
difficult campaigns in its history.

The Romans first marched through the
rich northeastern section of Israel, the
province of Galilee. The Jewish commander in the area was no hero, and when
he was besieged in the town of Jotapata
he tried to surrender the city. When this
failed, and the city was defeated, he went
over to the enemy. His fellow Jews re-

garded him as a traitor, but in an important
sense he did not desert his people. Under
the Latin name of Josephus (his real name
was Joseph ben Mattathias) he wrote major works giving a sympathetic account of
the history of the Jews. His book *The
Jewish War* is our best source of information about the period. He also was the
first person to prepare a detailed defense
of Judaism as a religion, which he wrote
in a brilliant reply to the words of an
anti-Semite from Alexandria.

Jerusalem besieged

Zealot leaders escaped from Galilee and
fled to Jerusalem, plunging the city into
civil war between those who wished to
continue fighting and those who wanted
to surrender. Many of the nobles and
Pharisees who opposed the war were
killed. Vespasian, the able Roman commander, conquered all the other parts of
the country, leaving the Jews in the capital
time to destroy each other.

Then, suddenly, he was called back to
Rome. The emperor Nero had committed
suicide, disgraced after years of violent
and immoral rule, and Vespasian was proclaimed the new emperor. He gave his son
Titus command of the Roman army in
Judea, and the new general quickly placed
Jerusalem under siege. At last the Jewish
citizens united for the common defense,
but it was too late. They held out for five
months, despite starvation and exhaustion,
before the Romans captured the gates of
the city. A last battle was fought in the
Temple courts, and the Sanctuary went up
in flames.

According to tradition, this event occurred on the ninth day of the Hebrew

Messianism and the
Jewish Spirit

Jesus was not the only Jew to be hailed by some as the Messiah. These were hard times for the Jews, and many wanted to believe that God would surely send a leader to save His chosen people. Within fifteen years after the crucifixion of Jesus, a man named Theudas claimed he could repeat the miracles of Moses. Many Judeans believed him; but in the end he failed, and like Jesus he was put to death by the Romans. Before the first century was over, at least two more false (or *pseudo-*) Messiahs would disappoint their followers.

This longing for a Messiah—for a leader who would bring signs that God had sent him to save the Jews—is called MESSIANISM. Messianism has through the centuries been a very important part of Jewish life. Of course, there are many different ideas as to what sort of person the Messiah would be and what kinds of things the Messiah would do. Some thought of him as a great warrior who would defeat the enemies of Israel on the battlefield. Others waited for a miracle-worker or a supernatural being, or a man so spiritually pure that by his words alone the Jewish people would be saved. All agreed, however, that the Messiah would come just when things were at their worst—and it was this belief that gave our people hope and courage at some of the most dangerous and desperate moments in our history.

---

month of Av. This was the date on which the Temple of Solomon had been destroyed by the Babylonians in 586 B.C.E.

The meaning of Masada

Small groups held out for a time in strongholds in the wilderness. The largest band headed south to the huge granite rock fortress called Masada in the desert near the Dead Sea, where they made their last stand against Rome. For two years, less than 1000 Zealots held off an army of 9000 troops and 6000 support personnel. At last the Romans built a huge ramp to the top of the mountain fortress so that they could march directly into the Jewish camp. When they smashed through the last walls of Masada, they were met by a strange silence—only two women and five children were alive to tell what had happened. The remaining 960 defenders, preferring death to captivity and slavery, had killed themselves.

The Jewish War was over. Vespasian minted coins to celebrate the victory with the inscription JUDEA CAPTA—"Judah Cap-

"While the Sanctuary was burning, looting went on right and left, and all who were caught by the Romans were put to the sword. . . ."

tured." Titus was given a hero's welcome in Rome, where a triumphal arch was erected in his honor. It stands to this day. On it one can still see the picture of victorious Roman soldiers carrying the sacred menorah from the Jerusalem Temple.

Looking back

Time plays tricks. The victor can become the defeated, the vanquished may triumph.

The arch of Titus stands among ruins, a reminder of the grandeur of an empire that disappeared centuries ago. The glory of Judaism and Israel live on.

Vespasian's victory coin, showing a proud Roman soldier beside a weeping widow, inspired a new coin issued by the State of Israel in 1958 to celebrate its tenth anniversary. On it a woman stands happily holding her baby in the light of freedom as her husband kneels to plant a tree in the ancient soil. Above their heads is the slogan ISRAEL LIBERATA—"Israel Freed."

Masada was recently excavated, bringing to light the remains of the years of Roman siege. As the site of heroic self-defense it has taken on special meaning for the embattled citizens of modern Israel, who swear that it will never again fall to an enemy.

The Western Wall of the Temple was

The Sanctuary
in Flames

Josephus watched from the Roman side as the Temple of Jerusalem was ransacked, looted, and burned. Earlier, as the Roman armies encircled Jerusalem, Josephus had conveyed the demands of Titus to the Jews trapped inside the city. The Jews, struggling for their lives, had good reason to hate Josephus and think of him as a traitor to his people.

But when he came to describe the destruction of the Temple in his famous history book The Jewish War, *Josephus painted a picture of Roman butchery and Jewish bravery which even today stands as a monument to the courage of the Jews. Even though he had chosen to become a Roman, Josephus could not forget his Jewish heritage. He knew full well what that terrible day meant for the future of the Jewish people.*

While the Sanctuary was burning, looting went on right and left, and all who were caught by the Romans were put to the sword. There was no pity for age, no regard for rank; little children and old men, laymen and priests alike were butchered; every class was held in the iron embrace of war. . . .

Through the roar of the flames as they swept relentlessly on could be heard the groans of the falling. . . . The entire city seemed to be on fire, while as for the noise, nothing could be imagined more shattering or more horrifying. . . . Many who were wasted with hunger and beyond speech, when they saw the Sanctuary in flames, found strength to moan and wail. . . .

The Romans, judging it useless to spare the outbuildings now that the Sanctuary was in flames, set fire to them all. . . . They also burned the treasuries, which housed huge sums of money, large quantities of clothing, and other precious things; here, in fact, all the wealth of the Jews was piled up, for the rich had dismantled their houses and brought the contents here for safekeeping. Next the Romans came to the last surviving colonnade of the Outer Temple. On this, women and children and a mixed crowd of citizens had found a refuge—6000 in all. . . . The soldiers, carried away by their fury, set fire to the colonnade from below. As a result, some flung themselves out of the flames to their death; others perished in the blaze. Of that vast number there escaped not one.

At Masada in 1968, archaeologists discovered a huge water storage area, cut from solid rock. If you look closely, you can see ancient Hebrew writing on the walls.

the only part of that building to survive. Though constructed by the despised Herod, it had been dedicated to God, and as the last remnant of what had been the center of Jewish religious life for more than 500 years, it was regarded as especially sacred by our people. Over the centuries, while Jerusalem was controlled by Romans, Christians, and Muslims, Jews were often forbidden to visit it, but when they could they came to offer prayers for the redemption of Israel. So many tears were shed there that Gentiles named it the "Wailing Wall." But in 1967, in the midst of the Six-Day War, it became the scene of inspired rejoicing when it was restored to the rule of the Jewish people.

Thus the very symbols of our worst defeat become the symbols of our triumph. While nations come and go ... AM YISRAEL ḤAI . . . עַם יִשְׂרָאֵל חַי . . . the people of Israel lives.

SUMMARY   *While most Jews in the Roman Empire were favorably treated, those who lived in Judea were not. The oppression and greed of the Roman governors who followed Herod pushed tensions to the breaking point. For some this expressed itself in a never-ending hope for the coming of an earthly king, the Messiah. (Early Christians changed the concept to refer to a heavenly king who, they believed, was Jesus of Nazareth.) For the majority of Jews, Roman oppression led to a struggle for national rights that burst into rebellion in 66 C.E. The Romans were victorious, destroying the Temple in 70 and the last pocket of Jewish resistance at Masada in 73. Yet the Jewish people survived, and today the very symbols of this defeat are symbols of the rebirth of modern Israel.*

8

New Times, New Heroes

One can tell a great deal about a nation from the people it most admires. Many countries have made heroes of their greatest warriors, their conquerors and kings. In this chapter you will meet heroes of a different and uniquely Jewish type. They were not young and handsome, warlike and strong. They were men of compassion, men of deep learning, men of God who had the vision and courage to sustain the Jewish people through the effects of two dreadful wars.

Johanan ben Zakkai

In the year 68 C.E., in the midst of the revolt against Rome, Johanan ben Zakkai realized that the situation in Jerusalem was critical. The Jewish people, hopelesssly divided by bitter rivalries, were quite unprepared to battle with the nearby Roman armies. Ben Zakkai was at least eighty—

some said nearly 100—but he still felt he had a critical role to play in saving the Jewish people.

His first step was to escape from the city. However, the Zealots would not allow any living Jew to leave, fearing that this would make the people lose hope. To outwit the Zealots, the aged teacher prepared a daring plan. He told his students to pretend he had died and to carry him to the city gate. There they told the armed guards they wished to bury their master in the cemetery outside the walls of Jerusalem. Had the truth been discovered, they would all have paid with their lives—but the trick worked. Once safe from capture, Ben Zakkai went directly to the Roman general Vespasian, of whom he made only one request: permission to teach Torah in the town of Yavneh. The enemy commander preferred Jews to devote themselves to study rather than war, and he readily agreed.

Johanan ben Zakkai escaped from Jerusalem by pretending to be dead
and having his students carry him outside the city gate.

The Academy of Yavneh

This seemed a small favor, but it was
enough to permit Ben Zakkai to save Judaism. He organized his school so that when
Jerusalem was captured and devastated,
in the year 70 C.E., the Academy of Yavneh
could become the new capital of the Jewish
religion.

Ben Zakkai and his students took on the
combined roles of judge, legislator, and
teacher. As the supreme religious authorities in the country, they settled the cases
which had formerly been directed to the
Jewish High Court in Jerusalem (the
Sanhedrin). As the source of Jewish law,
they revised practices to deal with the new
conditions. Ben Zakkai himself transferred
some ceremonies which had been performed in the Temple to the synagogues,
now the center of Jewish worship.

In adapting Judaism to meet current
needs, the scholars at Yavneh also determined the future course of the religion.
Judaism would not depend on priests—
indeed, the party of the priests, the Sadducees, slowly disappeared after the destruction of the Temple. Judaism would
be religion as it had been taught by the
Pharisees—pious yet open-minded, rever-
ent toward the sacred texts yet willing to
reinterpret them to keep them meaningful
for their time.

In fact, it was the scholars of the Academy who decided exactly what those
sacred texts were to be. All Jews regarded
the WRITTEN TORAH (תּוֹרָה שֶׁבִּכְתָב) text as
sacred, but not until about the year 100,

at Yavneh, was it finally settled which books should be included in the Hebrew Bible.

Role of the Rabbis

The students of Ben Zakkai were the first Jewish leaders to have the title RABBI (רַבִּי), a term which means "my master." They, and those who followed them, were the most respected leaders of the Jewish community for 400 years, and so the era of Rome is known to Jews as the Age of the Rabbis.

While this term is correct, it is also misleading. It may make us think of "Rabbis" as one identical group whose lives were filled with nothing but books. But in fact, the Rabbis were enormously varied and active individuals. They could not spend their whole lives studying—Rabbis received no salaries, and those without private means had to earn their own living. Hillel, as we have seen, was a woodcutter. His friendly rival Shammai was a mason. Ben Zakkai was a businessman, while others were tailors, blacksmiths, brewers, and so on. Even the notion that they read book after book is wrong. Aside from the Bible, they were concerned almost exclusively with the tradition that had been passed down by word of mouth from previous generations. This tradition is called the ORAL TORAH (תּוֹרָה שֶׁבְּעַל־פֶּה).

Despite their differences in age, personality, and profession, the Rabbis were united by their love for Jewish law and the belief that only by studying it could they learn to live in a righteous manner. They worked together as equals, examining each and every tradition, considering each different viewpoint and opinion. Final

decisions on points of law were reached in an orderly way, by majority vote.

Democracy and the Law

This use of the democratic process even in the most sensitive religious questions was extraordinary in ancient times, and even today is rare in religions. The Roman Catholic Church, for example, teaches that one man, the Pope, has final authority on questions of faith and morals. Our people, thousands of years ago, rejected the notion that any single individual could be God's only true representative.

The Rabbis, who often taught by telling stories, expressed their faith in the principles of democracy through a wonderful tale in which two students of Johanan ben Zakkai—Rabbi Eliezer ben Hyrcanus and Rabbi Joshua ben Hananiah—are the central characters.

Rabbi Eliezer, the story says, was arguing a point of law, but no matter how many arguments he made, he could not convince the other Rabbis. Finally, in exasperation, he pointed to a tree and said, "If I am right, may that tree move 100 yards." The tree promptly moved 100 yards, but the Rabbis were unimpressed. "What has a tree to do with a point of law?" Rabbi Eliezer called upon a canal to flow backward as a proof of his position, and, though the water turned about, the Rabbis were not one bit more convinced. "May the walls of this House of Study prove my point," cried Rabbi Eliezer, and the walls bent inward as if they would fall. Rabbi Joshua stood up and scolded the walls: "If the learned argue over a point of law, what has that to do with you?" So to honor Rabbi Joshua, the walls did not fall—though out of respect to

**In the Age
of the Rabbis**

If you were a boy in the Age of the Rabbis, you would be
doing just what you are doing now—going to school. From
about 100 B.C.E., education began to play a central role in
Jewish life, a role it maintains to this day. Each community
was expected to have its own school, usually in the synagogue,
and a class was to have no more than twenty-five pupils
for each teacher. If there were forty in a class, an assistant
teacher had to be appointed.

The classwork, however, was very different from ours. The
purpose of school was to prepare students for a life of
Torah, and particularly to teach the Oral Torah. There were
few books, and most of the time was spent memorizing laws as
they were recited by the teacher.

The teachers realized that blind memorization would not
interest students very long, so they spiced their lessons with
stories, questions, and discussions. Furthermore, they felt
it was their duty to prove the value of religious life by setting
an example of outstanding behavior. But this did not mean
they were meek. A boy who did not do his work might get a
sound beating.

Girls did not go to school; instead, they learned household
and religious duties from their mothers. Though lacking
in formal education, they were deeply involved in Judaism
through keeping the home and preparing meals in strict
accordance with Jewish law.

Relics from the Age of the Rabbis.
Top, an 1800-year-old mirror;
below, the tools of a scribe; right,
a Roman arrow used in battle
against the Jews.

Left, part of a synagogue at Bet Shearim, an important center of Jewish learning in the second century C.E. Below, children play beneath the remains of a Roman aqueduct in Caesarea.

Despite the pressures of school and housework, children found plenty of time for fun. Team games were frowned upon by Jewish leaders because they were often played by the Greeks and Romans in association with pagan rituals, but there was no objection to individual sports such as archery, fencing, and horseback riding. For quieter moments there were pastimes much like modern dominoes, checkers, and chess. During Sukkot, the most important of the harvest festivals, national leaders set a hilarious example with public dancing, acrobatics, and displays of their skill at juggling eggs, knives—or even eight burning torches!

Grain was still the principal food. Bread was such an essential part of the diet that no meal was considered complete without it. For this reason, the Rabbis decided that the main blessing over a meal should be the MOTZI (הַמּוֹצִיא), which praises God "Who brings forth bread from the earth."

Those who were too poor to buy grain were given a share of the crops, in accordance with Biblical law. Each community ran a public kitchen in which two meals a day were served. There was also a fund from which the needy received some money on Sabbath eve. These practices were the foundation of the formal systems of charity which have been part of Jewish life ever since.

Rabbi Eliezer they did not become quite straight either!

Finally, in desperation, Rabbi Eliezer cried out, "If I am right, let the heavens prove it." Then a heavenly voice said, "What have you against Rabbi Eliezer? His interpretation of the Law is always right." Again Rabbi Joshua rose: "We pay no attention to a heavenly voice. God gave his Torah to mankind, and decreed that we would interpret it for ourselves. The majority decides."

And, the legend concludes, God laughed with delight.

Thus the Rabbis showed their faith that God had given humanity not only His Law but also the ability to understand and apply that Law to the changing conditions of daily life.

Bar Kochba fights for freedom

The Rabbis were given only a generation to study the Torah in relative peace. Then they were forced to fight and die for their principles.

The destruction of the Temple in the year 70 did not bring an end to life in Israel. Cities such as Yavneh that survived the great war took on the functions that had once been centered in Jerusalem. Many believed that the Temple would soon be rebuilt.

This hope was spurred by a new emperor. Hadrian hoped to pacify his Jewish subjects and gave broad hints that their capital would be reestablished. It soon became clear, however, that he wanted to build a Roman city. The new Temple was to be dedicated, not to the God of Israel, but to the Roman god Jupiter. Hadrian also prohibited circumcision.

Again the land broke out in rebellion.

This time the Jews were able to unite behind a single leader. His real name was Simeon bar Kosiba, but he was known to many by the name BAR KOCHBA, בַּר כּוֹכְבָא ("Son of the Star"). He was a man of great strength, daring, and personal courage. Many believed he was the Messiah.

His armies freed Jerusalem and set up a government, issuing coins inscribed "Redemption of Zion" and "Freedom for Israel." Yet, despite this early success, the revolt was doomed by the limitless resources of the Roman Empire. Hadrian brought in 35,000 soldiers, conquered Galilee, and recaptured Jerusalem. Bar Kochba moved his forces to Betar, a hill town five miles southwest of the capital. The Romans built ramps to his camp from the surrounding valley, much as they had done at Masada, and smashed their way through the improvised defenses. Bar Kochba was among the dead.

Rabbi Akiva—fact and legend

Bar Kochba was a brave soldier who died fighting for principle against overwhelming odds—the stuff of which heroes and legends are made. Yet it was a totally different kind of man who truly captured the imagination of the Jewish people during this period. This man was indeed courageous, but he was also a person of great religious feeling and outstanding scholarship. He was a Rabbi—Rabbi Akiva.

Many stories have been told about Akiva, as they have about all heroes, and it is not easy to separate history from legend. For our purposes, however, the legendary elements in his biography are as important as the historical ones, because they show us what the Jewish people *wanted* their heroes to be.

Jews as Soldiers

Coin issued
by Bar-Kochba.

Since 1948 the armies of the State of Israel have had to fight four wars with Arab neighbors. Each time, Israeli soldiers have won worldwide admiration for their courage and skill. Even the enemies of Israel could not help but respect the bravery and resourcefulness of these Jewish fighters— men and women.

During the Biblical Period, Jewish soldiers were also famed for their fighting skills. You have already seen how Judah Maccabee defeated the army of Antiochus IV by mixing careful preparation with surprise attacks—the same tactic used by modern Israeli soldiers in commando raids some twenty-one centuries later. In Chapter 7 you read how the Jewish fighters of Judea, though greatly outnumbered, gave the Roman army one of its most difficult campaigns. Later, Bar Kochba was able to recapture Jerusalem and for a short time restore Jewish rule, until his army too was overwhelmed by the vastly more powerful Roman legions.

Here's a fact which may surprise you: as long ago as 600 B.C.E., the Babylonians hired thousands of Israelites to guard the southern part of Egypt against invaders from Ethiopia. (Ironically, only fourteen years later the Babylonians conquered Jerusalem.) These Israelite warriors were mercenaries; they fought for money and not for ideals or for self-defense. Jewish mercenaries were very much in demand throughout the Middle East after the success of Judah Maccabee. So the "People of the Book" could also be the "people of the sword"—then and now.

Akiva, according to tradition, was an ignorant shepherd. He worked for a wealthy Jew whose daughter, Rachel, recognized in the poor worker signs of greatness, and married him on condition that he would become learned in Torah. Her father disowned her, yet she willingly supported herself in poverty while Akiva was away studying with the great disciples of Johanan ben Zakkai. When Akiva returned to his wife many years later, he had become a leading scholar.

He was also a man of action. He journeyed widely to help Jewish communities in and out of Judea. As Roman laws became oppressive, he traveled to Rome with a group of Rabbis to protest to the emperor. When all efforts at a peaceful solution failed, he supported rebellion, and was one of those who thought Bar Kochba was the Messiah.

During this period he continued to teach publicly, though Roman law threatened death to anyone giving instruction in the

Torah. When asked why he deliberately put himself in danger, he gave this answer: A fox came to a river and suggested to the fish that they escape from the fisherman by coming onto dry land. But the fish replied, "If we are in danger in the water, which is our element, what will happen to us on land?" In the same way, said Akiva, if there is no safety for us in the Torah, which is our home, how can we find safety without it?

The Romans captured Akiva and decided to kill him with a ghastly torture—tearing off his flesh with red-hot pincers. Akiva smiled in the face of his executioners. He had lived more than eighty years, but only now could he be sure he had fulfilled the SHEMA's command:

וְאָהַבְתָּ אֵת יְהוָה אֱלֹהֶיךָ בְּכָל לְבָבְךָ
וּבְכָל נַפְשְׁךָ וּבְכָל מְאֹדֶךָ:

And you shall love the Lord your God with all your heart, with all your soul, and with all your might.

And so he died, reciting the words of the prayer.

Keeping Judaism alive

Following the death of Akiva and Bar Kochba, the Romans turned on those who had supported the revolt. Five hundred thousand Jews died or were sold as slaves, and not a single village in the southern half of the country was left with any sign of Jewish life. Such actions succeeded in destroying the spirit of rebellion. From the fall of Betar in 135 C.E. until the twentieth century, no Jewish forces would take up arms to fight for independence in the land of Israel.

Hadrian also wanted to destroy the Jewish religion—but this part of his plan failed completely. He killed large numbers of our people for teaching and practicing Judaism, yet others refused to let our tradition disappear. The next emperor, Antoninus Pius, repealed most of Hadrian's anti-Jewish laws. Students of Akiva opened a new school, and Jewish studies revived.

Judaism had survived the worst the Romans could offer. Ennobled by heroes of learning, courage, and piety, it was now stronger than ever before.

SUMMARY *Johanan ben Zakkai escaped from the Roman siege of Jerusalem and founded a school in Yavneh. This became the center of Jewish life in Palestine after the destruction of the Temple. Far-reaching decisions made there enabled Judaism to continue and develop. Moreover, here were trained the first in a series of great Rabbis that would be the leaders of Judaism in the coming centuries. Outstanding among them was Rabbi Akiva, a participant in the Bar Kochba rebellion and a martyr to the cause of Jewish freedom and the Jewish religion.*

9
The Rabbis
Triumphant

Though the Roman persecution ended after the death of Hadrian, it had proved to the Jewish people how fragile their tradition really was. The Bible was safely preserved in manuscripts, but the rules derived from it—the Oral Law—existed only in the minds and hearts of the Rabbis. If a new dictator were to massacre a single generation of these scholars, the chain of Jewish tradition would be broken and a thousand years of learning would be lost forever.

The Oral Law had to be put into permanent form. The task was massive, but a man appeared whose scholarship and position made him the ideal choice for this critical undertaking.

Judah ha-Nasi

His name was Judah. He was born at the time—some said on the very day—that Akiva died, and those who knew Judah thought that the genius of the older Rabbi had been passed directly to the younger. He was also a descendant of the great Hillel, and so was heir to the position of Nasi (נָשִׂיא)— leader of the Jewish community in the land of Israel.

Judah ha-Nasi was a man of extraordinary learning and piety. He dedicated his life to Jewish scholarship and used his wealth, which was very great, to support young Jewish students. Within his household he insisted on the use of the purest form of Hebrew, and his example succeeded in bringing new life to the language as a spoken tongue. (Another Semitic language, Aramaic, had been commonly spoken in the land of Israel since the destruction of the First Temple.) Rabbi Judah also knew something of European language and culture, and by talking directly with Roman leaders he was able to improve conditions for the Hebrew people.

Rav and Rabbi   The scholars of the Babylonian academies generally bore the title "Rav," but always as part of their names, such as "Rav Huna." Abba was *the* Rav. Similarly, the title "Rabbi" was given to the scholars of the Holy Land, but only Judah ha-Nasi was honored by being called simply "Rabbi." He was *the* Rabbi of the land of Israel.

Talmud: Mishnah and Gemara

His greatest achievement, however, was editing the Oral Law. Rabbi Akiva, among others, had begun to sort and organize it, but Judah ha-Nasi was able to get the cooperation of all major scholars in preparing a final, authoritative version of the verbal tradition. This work is called the MISHNAH, מִשְׁנָה ("Study"). It may originally have been intended only as a guide for students, but in a short time it was regarded as second only to the Torah as a sacred book of Jewish law.

No sooner was the Mishnah completed, about 200 C.E., than discussions began over how to apply the rules and precepts contained in it. These discussions are called the GEMARA, גְּמָרָא ("Completion"). The Mishnah and Gemara combined form the TALMUD, תַּלְמוּד ("Learning"), the massive work which became the lifeblood of Jewish thought.

Actually there are two Gemaras (and, consequently, two Talmuds).

The older, the "Palestinian" or "Jerusalem" Gemara, was produced in the land of Israel between 200 and 400 C.E. During these years the Jews were living under increasingly difficult conditions. Roman taxes were unbearable. In the fourth century, Christianity became the state religion, and new pressures and restrictions were brought on Jewish life. All this resulted in a serious decline in the size and importance of the Palestinian community, and in the authority of its Talmud.

The second Gemara was produced under very different conditions. In the Persian empire a million of our people enjoyed toleration and prosperity. They were the descendants of those who had been exiled to Babylonia after the destruction of the First Temple—indeed, they were still referred to as "Babylonian Jewry" even though the kingdom of Babylon had long since been conquered by the Persians. And it was these Jews who, between 200 and 500 C.E., compiled the "Babylonian Talmud"—*the* Talmud.

At the time of the Mishnah, however, the Persian community lacked the key element for a great intellectual life—fine schools. Its best students traveled to the land of Israel to study, settle, and teach.

This was changed by two followers of Judah ha-Nasi: Abba and Samuel.

Abba and Samuel

Abba and Samuel were good friends who shared a common love for Judaism

THE DEVELOPMENT OF JEWISH LAW

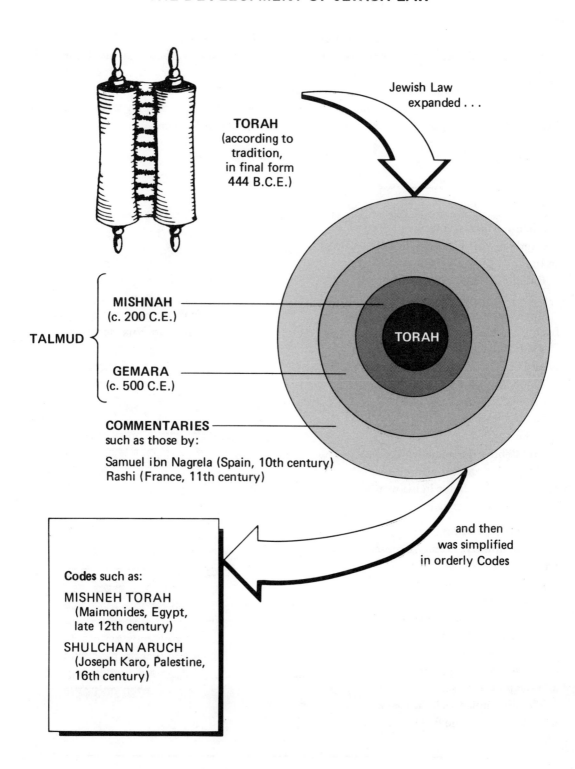

TORAH
(according to
tradition,
in final form
444 B.C.E.)

Jewish Law
expanded . . .

TORAH

TALMUD

MISHNAH
(c. 200 C.E.)

GEMARA
(c. 500 C.E.)

COMMENTARIES
such as those by:

Samuel ibn Nagrela (Spain, 10th century)
Rashi (France, 11th century)

and then
was simplified
in orderly Codes

Codes such as:

MISHNEH TORAH
(Maimonides, Egypt,
late 12th century)

SHULCHAN ARUCH
(Joseph Karo, Palestine,
16th century)

The Wisdom of the Fathers

Down through the centuries, the most popular part of the Talmud has been the book called Pirke Avot ("Chapters of the Fathers"). Unlike the other sixty-two books of the Talmud, the Avot has in it no halachah. It is made up altogether of aggadah—favorite teachings and sayings of the Rabbis, as well as stories and legends about them. We also find in the Avot, as in the other books of the Talmud, how much the Rabbis disagreed. Of course they were not arguing just for the sake of arguing, but as the Avot says, "for the sake of Heaven."

THE TRUE PATH

This story is told of Rabbi Joḥanan ben Zakkai and his students.

Rabban Joḥanan said to them: "Go out and see which is the right path in life for a person to follow."

Rabbi Eliezer answered: "A good eye."

Rabbi Joshua answered: "A good friend."

Rabbi Yose answered: "A good neighbor."

Rabbi Simeon answered: "Seeing the end of a thing at the start."

Rabbi Eleazar answered: "A good heart."

Said Rabban Joḥanan ben Zakkai to them: "I prefer the answer of Eleazar ben Arach, for in his words your words are included."

אָמַר לָהֶם:
צְאוּ וּרְאוּ אֵיזוֹ הִיא דֶרֶךְ טוֹבָה
שֶׁיִּדְבַּק בָּהּ הָאָדָם.
רַבִּי אֱלִיעֶזֶר אוֹמֵר עַיִן טוֹבָה,
רַבִּי יְהוֹשֻׁעַ אוֹמֵר חָבֵר טוֹב,
רַבִּי יוֹסִי אוֹמֵר שָׁכֵן טוֹב,
רַבִּי שִׁמְעוֹן אוֹמֵר הָרוֹאֶה אֶת הַנּוֹלָד,
רַבִּי אֶלְעָזָר אוֹמֵר לֵב טוֹב.
אָמַר לָהֶם:
רוֹאֶה אֲנִי
אֶת דִּבְרֵי אֶלְעָזָר בֶּן־עֲרָךְ מִדִּבְרֵיכֶם,
שֶׁבִּכְלַל דְּבָרָיו דִּבְרֵיכֶם.

FOUR KINDS OF STUDENTS

There are four types among those who sit in the presence of the Sages: the sponge, the funnel, the strainer, and the sifter.

The sponge soaks up everything.

The funnel takes in at one end and lets out at the other.

The strainer lets pass the wine and retains the dregs.

The sifter holds back the coarse flour and collects the fine flour.

אַרְבַּע מִדּוֹת בְּיוֹשְׁבִים לִפְנֵי חֲכָמִים:
סְפוֹג וּמַשְׁפֵּךְ מְשַׁמֶּרֶת וְנָפָה.
סְפוֹג שֶׁהוּא סוֹפֵג אֶת הַכֹּל.
וּמַשְׁפֵּךְ שֶׁמַּכְנִיס בְּזוֹ וּמוֹצִיא בְּזוֹ.
מְשַׁמֶּרֶת שֶׁמּוֹצִיאָה אֶת הַיַּיִן
וְקוֹלֶטֶת אֶת הַשְּׁמָרִים.
וְנָפָה שֶׁמּוֹצִיאָה אֶת הַקֶּמַח
וְקוֹלֶטֶת אֶת הַסֹּלֶת.

When Abba taught at the Academy of Sura, thousands of students came to hear him. Years earlier, he had been a pupil of Judah ha-Nasi.

and belief in the future of the Babylonian Jews. For this reason, after studying in the land of Israel, they returned to their homeland in the Persian empire. There they directed schools which were destined to change the course of Jewish history and learning.

Samuel must have been a fascinating teacher, for he was both an expert in Jewish law and a scientific genius—a brilliant astronomer and a skilled physician. He was unusual for his time in prescribing cleanliness, a regular routine, and avoidance of extremes of weather as aids to health. In addition, he maintained excellent relations with the civil authorities and was friendly with the king of Persia.

Abba was regarded as the greater scholar, however. While Samuel became the head of an existing school in his home town of Nehardea, Abba created a new academy in the previously uneducated town of Sura and, through his own genius, turned it into the intellectual center of world Jewry. Twice a year, thousands of Jews journeyed there to hear the lectures of this man who was both intellectually and physically a giant. Abba became known as Rav, רַב ("The Master").

Never had a Jewish community outside of the land of Israel been so excited by Jewish studies. Other schools developed until Babylonian scholars could finally learn the Law in their own communities.

The ultimate result of the work begun by Rav and Samuel was the Gemara of the Babylonian Talmud.

Teachings of the Talmud

What is the Talmud like?

As we have said, it is made up of Mishnah and Gemara. The Mishnah is customarily clear, brief, and concise. In one short passage, for example, it warns against hurting the feelings of others with harsh or thoughtless words.

The Gemara, on the other hand, is the detailed and unpredictable discussion of the Rabbis based on this general theme. First, they consider the statement itself and use Biblical quotations to prove that the warning is valid. Then they try to find good examples to show how serious it is to violate this law. Rav is quoted as saying that it is better for a man to throw himself into a fiery furnace than to shame his neighbor publicly.

But it is not only one's neighbor who must be protected from embarrassment. One must give special attention to one's wife. This leads to a discussion of the role of women. "One must always observe the honor due a wife," says one Rabbi, "because blessings rest on a man's home only because of his wife."

Suddenly the discussions break off and we are told a story. It is the legend that we read in the last chapter: how Rabbi Eliezer failed to convince the other rabbis of his opinions, even when he performed miracles. The point of the story is the thoughtful manner in which Rabbi Akiva treated Eliezer after his humiliating defeat.

Finally, this part of the Gemara concludes by warning against insulting a convert by reminding him that he and his parents worshiped pagan gods. One must always be thoughtful to the stranger and the foreigner because, as the Bible tells us, the Hebrews "were strangers in the land of Egypt."

Aggadah and halachah

The section we have just described is a sample of the Talmudic material known as AGGADAH (אַגָּדָה), material which includes sayings, moral instructions, and especially stories and legends. Two-thirds of the Babylonian Talmud, however, deals with legal material, known as HALACHAH, הֲלָכָה ("the rule by which to go"). Here the Rabbis consider such technical questions as: How is ownership of real estate determined? What rights does a wife have if her husband mistreats her? The halachah

---

Aggadah   The Hebrew word AGGADAH means "to tell, relate." In the Talmud it refers to all nonlegal material—tales, sayings, and so on. The Passover prayerbook is called the HAGGADAH (הַגָּדָה) because in it we "tell" the story of the Exodus.

also deals with matters of ceremonial law, such as: What actions are permitted or forbidden on the Sabbath? May a sick person eat on Yom Kippur?

Using the two approaches of halachah and aggadah, the Rabbis of the Gemara covered just about every phase of Jewish life. Their work was huge: the Talmud contains 2½ million words which fill twelve large volumes—thirty-five in the standard English translation! Yet it was remarkably complete, a vast reservoir of knowledge such as the world had never known.

Judaism in daily life

The Rabbis felt that Judaism showed how truly noble every individual could be, and they were determined to try to live up to that standard.

This might not mean a life that was simpler or more practical. It might, for example, mean cutting into one's profits—Samuel forbade merchants to make more than a one-sixth profit on a sale.

It might mean showing mercy to criminals. The Rabbis felt that life comes from God and that only God should end life, and so they all but abolished capital punishment.

It might mean losing sleep. Rav said that those who wake early to study a chapter of sacred text bring a special blessing on the people of Israel.

It might mean discomfort. Since animals were to be treated with the utmost consideration, their master was required to feed them before he had his own meal.

It might mean forcing yourself to adopt a viewpoint broad enough to include every

living soul. The Rabbis taught that non-Jews were to be accorded full rights. "Before the throne of God there is no difference between the Jew and the non-Jew," said Samuel. "There are good and noble men among all the nations of the world."

But there was one thing it did not mean: it did not mean accepting an official set of beliefs. While leaders of other religions engaged in bitter debates over doctrine, our Rabbis insisted that such matters be left to each individual. They concentrated on developing practical rules for daily life, so that every phase of it—from doing business to eating a meal—could be conducted with justice and decency, purity and kindness.

The prayer book

The constant examination of Jewish law might have led the Rabbis to think of God as an impersonal force, a distant Lawgiver and Judge. Actually, the opposite happened. The Rabbis thought of the Torah and Talmud as precious gifts, given to the

An oil-burning lamp from the fourth century C.E. The handle of the lamp is shaped like a menorah.

people of Israel by a loving Father and Friend.

They looked for a way to express these feelings in worship. And so the Rabbis developed the SIDDUR (סִדּוּר)—the prayer book which, in its basic form, is still in use today. Our prayer services begin with an expression of wonder at the magnificence of God's universe, move on to consider the special relationship between God and Israel, and conclude with an opportunity for our most private and personal requests.

The Rabbis did not write all the material in the prayer book, of course. Rav, for example, used a verse from the Bible (Zechariah 14:9) in a new prayer which today brings our worship to its triumphant conclusion. In it, he voices the hope for a messianic age:

> We hope in You, O Lord our God, that we may soon behold the glory of Your might, when You will remove evil from the earth. . . . When You will help the wicked of the earth to turn to You. . . . For the Kingdom is Yours, and to all eternity You will reign in glory, as it is said: "The Lord shall be King over all the earth.

בַּיּוֹם הַהוּא יִהְיֶה יְיָ אֶחָד וּשְׁמוֹ אֶחָד.

On that day the Lord shall be One, and His name shall be One."

A new day dawns

In the fifth century the Persian empire began to decline. As so often happens in failing nations, its rulers became oppressive. While this helped spur the Jewish people to complete the Talmud, it did nothing to preserve the Persian kings. A new age and a new empire were about to sweep over the world.

At about the same time, the Western half of the Roman Empire was collapsing. Old nations were disappearing—but the Jewish people and religion were strong. Jews had seen the destruction of their homeland and the murder of some of their most revered leaders, but they now felt secure. They now possessed the world's greatest body of religious wisdom and literature: the Bible, the Talmud, and a prayer book. Armed with these documents, Judaism would rise above the ruins of Rome and Persia and enter a new and magnificent era.

SUMMARY *The period following the death of Akiva saw the Oral Law developed and put into written form. Leaders in this were Judah ha-Nasi, who edited the Mishnah, and Abba (Rav) and Samuel, whose teachings were the foundation of the Babylonian Gemara. The Mishnah and Gemara combined are the Talmud, the great storehouse of Jewish knowledge and tradition. The Rabbis also created the basic form, as well as some of the material, of our prayer book. Thanks to their work, Judaism emerged from the Roman era stronger than ever, prepared to move on to another great period in our history.*

PART THREE

The Empire of Islam

The Golden Age

In Parts One and Two, I emphasized how much the Biblical Period and the Age of the Rabbis are alive today. Strangely, the Golden Age of Spain, which is much more recent, does not seem so contemporary.

There are several possible reasons for this. It is hard for us to imagine a world in which the great centers of learning and power were in Muslim Spain, North Africa, and the Middle East, and not for the most part in Europe. Spanish Jews may also seem remote because they left behind few stories and legends about themselves, but rather expressed their thoughts and feelings in works of philosophy and poetry, which are somewhat more difficult to understand.

Yet we really should be more familiar with the Spanish Golden Age, for a number of reasons. First, the situation of the Jews in Spain — a respected minority in a non-Jewish state — was a bit like the situation

of Jews today who live in the lands of the Western Diaspora, and
especially in the United States. Second, the culture created by the
Jews of the Golden Age, during those periods when conditions were
relatively tolerant, was one of the richest and most brilliant in the
whole history of our people.

The Spanish experience is therefore instructive: it shows how fruitful
and interesting life in a mixed society can be. But the story of the
Spanish Jews also teaches us a negative lesson, for it is a story with a
tragic ending. From the heights of achievement made possible by
tolerance and friendship, the Spanish Jews were cast into the depths
of persecution and near-despair. For a people without a homeland of
its own, this was an ever-repeated and ever-bitter fact of existence.

ABBA EBAN

Today we honor Maimonides as a scholar and teacher, but in his own time he was recognized as the greatest doctor in the world. Below, Maimonides at the Sultan's bedside (you can read Maimonides' own description of his medical practice on page 106). On the opposite page (clockwise from upper right), three manuscripts: a page from a copy of the *Mishneh Torah,* a beautiful drawing from the Lisbon Bible, and a recipe for cough medicine from an Arabic text.

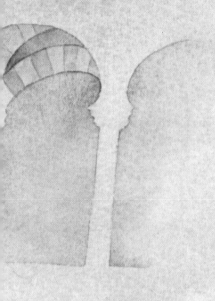

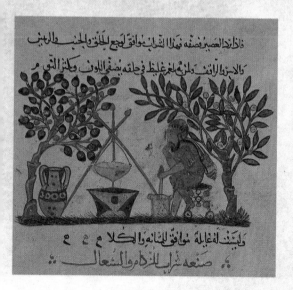

Not much Jewish art from Spain survived the centuries of persecution that followed the Golden Age. One of the few items we have is a seder plate (above) from about 1450, when the Golden Age was already over. The masterpiece of Jewish art in Egypt is these carved wooden synagogue doors (right). They were made in the twelfth century near Cairo, in Fustat, where Maimonides lived.

10

The Empire of Islam

The Arabian Peninsula is an unlikely place to cradle revolutionary movements. It is filled with deserts so huge and so desolate that they could blanket the entire United States east of the Mississippi River. Nevertheless, long before this seeming wasteland was identified as one of the world's greatest sources of oil, it proved to be one of the world's greatest reservoirs of human energy. Time after time, Arabian nomads burst from their homeland to change history. Such a group was the original Semitic people whose descendants included the Babylonians, Canaanites, Phoenicians, and, of course, the Hebrews.

And Arabia was the birthplace of one of the most important of all religions and one of the most splendid of all empires.

Until the seventh century, life in Arabia continued as it had since earliest times. Most of the Arabs were nomads, moving from oasis to oasis with their goats, sheep, and camels, living on little more than milk and dates.

Among the few cities on the livable edge of the peninsula, the most important was Mecca, where, about the year 570, Muhammad was born. He was orphaned by his sixth year and had no formal education—he never did learn to read—so he worked at odd jobs until he became a camel driver for a wealthy widow. He traveled with her goods throughout Arabia, then north as far as the Byzantine Empire, the surviving eastern half of what had been the empire of Rome. These trips brought him into contact with Jews and Christians, whose ideas very much impressed him.

The birth of Islam

When he was about forty, Muhammad began to have visions which convinced him that he was the last and greatest in the line of prophets including Adam, Noah, Abraham, Moses, and Jesus. Upon these visions he based a new religion which he

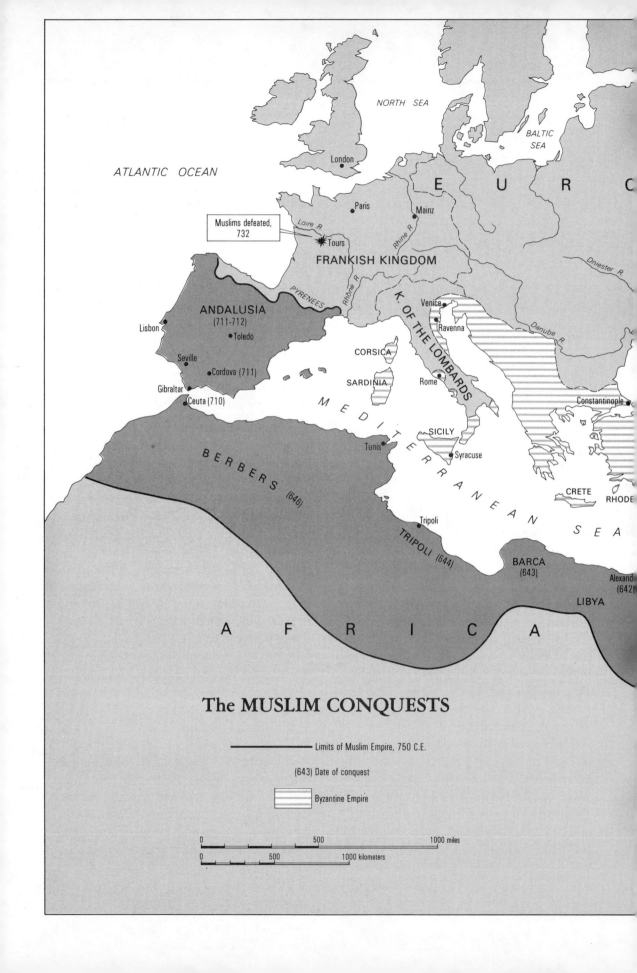

NORTH SEA

BALTIC SEA

ATLANTIC OCEAN

London

E U R O ... C

Paris

Mainz

Muslims defeated, 732

Loire R.

Rhine R.

Tours

FRANKISH KINGDOM

Rhône R.

PYRENEES

Dniester R.

ANDALUSIA
(711-712)

Venice

Danube R.

Lisbon

Toledo

Ravenna

K. OF THE LOMBARDS

CORSICA

Seville

Cordova (711)

SARDINIA

Rome

Gibraltar

Ceuta (710)

Constantinople

M E D I T E R

SICILY

B E R B E R S *(646)*

Tunis

Syracuse

CRETE

R A N E A N

RHODE

Tripoli

S E A

TRIPOLI *(644)*

BARCA
(643)

Alexand
(642)

LIBYA

A   F   R   I   C   A

The MUSLIM CONQUESTS

Limits of Muslim Empire, 750 C.E.

(643) Date of conquest

Byzantine Empire

0   500   1000 miles

0   500   1000 kilometers

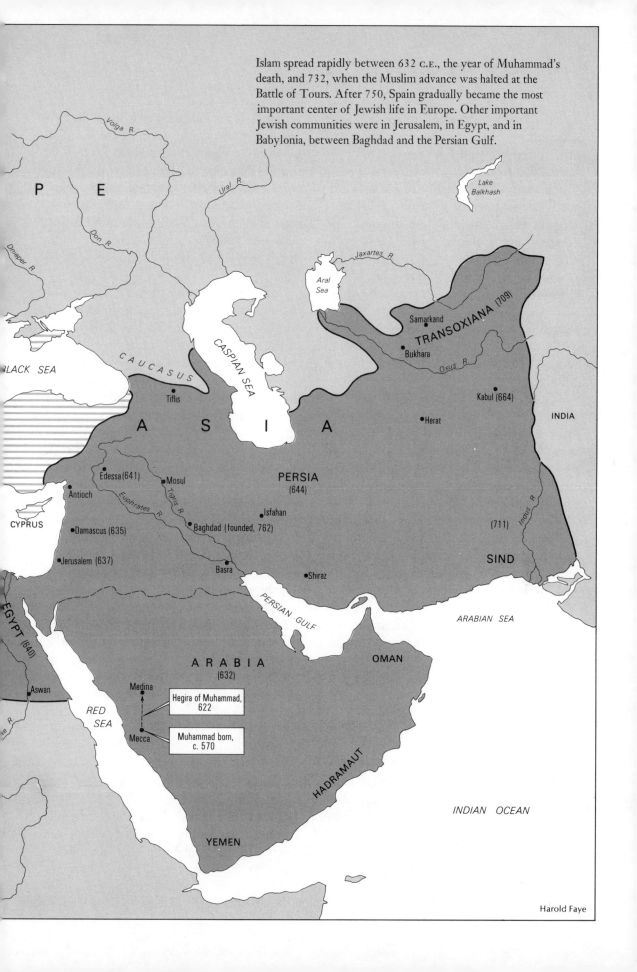

Islam spread rapidly between 632 C.E., the year of Muhammad's death, and 732, when the Muslim advance was halted at the Battle of Tours. After 750, Spain gradually became the most important center of Jewish life in Europe. Other important Jewish communities were in Jerusalem, in Egypt, and in Babylonia, between Baghdad and the Persian Gulf.

Volga R

P E

Ural R

Don R

Dnieper R

Lake Balkhash

Jaxartes R

Aral Sea

Samarkand

TRANSOXIANA (709)

Bukhara

Oxus R

C A U C A S U S

CASPIAN SEA

Tiflis

A S I A

Kabul (664)

Herat

INDIA

BLACK SEA

Edessa (641)

Mosul

PERSIA (644)

Euphrates R

Tigris R

Antioch

Indus R

CYPRUS

Isfahan

Baghdad (founded, 762)

(711)

Damascus (635)

Jerusalem (637)

Basra

SIND

Shiraz

PERSIAN GULF

ARABIAN SEA

EGYPT (640)

OMAN

A R A B I A (632)

Aswan

Medina

Hegira of Muhammad, 622

RED SEA

Mecca

Muhammad born, c. 570

HADRAMAUT

INDIAN OCEAN

YEMEN

Harold Faye

called *Islam*—"submission to God." (His accounts of these visions were collected after his death and became the bible of Islam, the *Koran*.)

Muhammad drew many of his ideas directly from Judaism. Central to his new religion was the belief in one absolute God (ALLAH, the Arabic word for God, is related to the Hebrew word אֱלֹהִים). He taught that all believers were equal in the eyes of the Lord and that the rich should share their wealth with the poor. He asserted that man's destiny is in God's hands and that the righteous and wicked would receive reward or punishment on a final Judgment Day.

While these ideas had been part of Judaism for centuries, they were revolutionary in the Arab world. Arab paganism had taught that death was the end of all things, that wealth was the standard of true achievement, and that Allah was only one of many gods.

New religious ideas usually appeal most to the poor and uneducated. Muhammad found support among the lower classes— and was threatened with death by the well-to-do. He managed to escape from Mecca and fled to the town of Medina, some 200 miles to the north. This journey is known by the Arabic word *hegira* (flight), and it is this event in 622 C.E. which Muslims (believers in Islam) regard as the beginning of the Islamic era.

Muhammad and the Jews

In Medina, Muhammad gained both political and religious control. And his new power soon brought him into conflict with Jews.

Jews had lived in Arabia since the destruction of the Second Temple, when refugees from Roman persecution fled to Yemen, at the southern tip of the Arabian peninsula. Their descendants may have founded the city of Medina; certainly Jews were rulers of that city for many years. Muhammad adopted some Jewish practices, such as the fast of Yom Kippur and facing Jerusalem during prayer, and he confidently expected the Jews to convert to Islam.

But the Jews reacted with scorn. For them, Muhammad was no prophet at all, and his teachings seemed like a bad copy of the truth that had been revealed to the people of Israel. Jewish courts, for example, had long offered mercy to lawbreakers. But Muhammad ruled that a guilty thief should have his hand chopped off.

Seeing that the Jews would not convert, Muhammad set out to develop his Islamic community among Arabs. Yom Kippur was replaced with a month in which fasting was practiced during all daylight hours. While the Jews prayed toward Jerusalem, Muslim prayers were said facing the Kaaba, a shrine in Mecca where Arabs had long worshiped.

The mixture of Jewish teachings and Arab nationalism was explosive. When Muhammad learned that the Jews had been in contact with his enemies in Mecca, he let his followers cut off the heads of all Jewish men in Medina. Some 600 were executed, and their women and children were enslaved.

"Holy war"—the Arab conquest

Thus the sword became a religious weapon. Muhammad taught that war fought in the name of Islam was holy. His followers were told that success in

The holiest shrine of Islam, the Kaaba in Mecca, was a holy place for Arab peoples centuries before the birth of Muhammad.

battle would bring them riches, while death in a holy war would win them immediate entrance into a paradise filled with every delight. The first troops of Islam were little more than religious bandits who would attack caravans, stealing booty and offering the survivors the choice of Islam or death. Yet these forces had fantastic success—by Muhammad's death in 632 they controlled Arabia and were ready to attack the heartland of Western civilization.

In the next 100 years, the Arab troops moved from victory to victory with astounding speed, conquering the territory from the Holy Land to the borders of India and China in the East, and across Northern Africa into Spain in the West. Not until 732 were the Arabs finally halted. When the European armies led by Charles Martel stopped the armies of Islam at the Battle of Tours, the Muslim banners were only 150 miles from the city of Paris.

Blessings of toleration

In time, Islam split into sects, some of which were fanatically opposed to any beliefs other than their own. For the most part, however, the Muslims were very tolerant of the traditions of their new subjects. Paganism was not permitted, but Judaism and Christianity were accepted as true examples of monotheism. Although members of both religions had to pay special taxes, they were able to practice their religions with a large degree of freedom, and Jews and Christians took part actively in Islamic society, holding many important positions.

This was a special blessing for the Jews. The last Persian rulers were cruel and oppressive. Early Christian Europe was intolerant and uncivilized. (The era of Islamic conquest was the period in Europe we now know as the Dark Ages.) Jews who had been forced to hide their religion were suddenly welcomed by an exciting new civilization—a civilization using a Semitic language related to Hebrew and based on monotheistic beliefs that the prophets of Israel would not have despised. The Jews huddling fearfully in the cold, cruel, and still savage Christian kingdoms of the north could rejoice at what was happening in the lands of Islam.

It was the dawning of the Golden Age.

SUMMARY   *Islam, the second great stepchild of Judaism, was born in Arabia in the seventh century through the visions and organizing skills of Muhammad. His mixture of monotheism and Arab nationalism inspired a powerful fighting force that conquered the Arabian Peninsula in his lifetime and an empire stretching from Spain to the border of India in another century. Though the early phase of Islam involved the murder of Jews, and though the Muslim Empire imposed special taxes on Jews, the arrival of the Arab armies brought welcome release from oppression to most of our people, who then used the freedom granted by their new rulers to create the Golden Age.*

11

Under Islam

The creative powers of the Jewish people were released under the Muslim policy of toleration. From the Atlantic Ocean to the Euphrates River, Jewish learning and culture made amazing progress.

In the Holy Land

The community in the land of Israel won back much of its leadership of world Jewry. While the academies in Babylonia still held authority in legal matters, the Holy Land became the center of a new kind of Bible study.

This new work arose from the fact that the Bible, like all ancient books, could only be copied by hand. Scribes had to write out each word letter by letter, and in this long and difficult process, errors would creep into manuscripts. The thought that the words of God might have been garbled by scribes was very disturbing; and so Jewish scholars began checking every available version of the Bible, considering each difference until they established an edition they thought matched the original.

But this was not their only worry. Problems were caused by the fact that ancient Hebrew was written without vowels. (Torah scrolls are still written that way.) This can cause confusion not only about the pronunciation of a word but also as to its meaning. To fix the correct readings permanently, systems of vowels and punctuation were made up, and marks were provided for the entire Bible.

The gigantic task of preparing a definitive text with vowel markings began well before the Arab conquest but was completed under Muslim rule during the seventh and eighth centuries. The finished work is called MASORA, מָסוֹרָה ("Tradition"), and to this day the standard version of the Hebrew Bible is the Masoretic text.

By the ninth century the Diaspora included not only Jews in Muslim and Christian lands; there were even Jews in China. This scene is based on a sixteenth-century Chinese sketch of a synagogue.

To the people of that time, however, far more important than the return of Biblical scholarship to Palestine was the return of the Jewish people to the city of Jerusalem. For the first time since the persecutions of Hadrian, Jews were permitted to live in the ancient capital, though in limited numbers. They were supported by gifts sent from men and women all over the world who saw in the rebirth of the Jerusalem community proof of the unbreakable ties of Judaism to its ancient homeland.

In Northern Africa

Across Northern Africa, from Morocco to Egypt, other Jewish communities thrived, growing both in size and as centers of learning. Of these the most important was the city now called Cairo, whose key location near the crossroads of Africa and Asia made it the key link between the Jews of East and West.

Thanks to a chance discovery, the Cairo community also became a key link between the Islamic period and our own era. Jewish law prohibited the destruction of documents containing the name of God, so when any text was no longer needed it was stored in a remote part of the synagogue known as the GENIZAH, גְּנִיזָה (hiding place). The Cairo genizah was forgotten for many centuries, then accidentally rediscovered in modern times. In it were found more than 200,000 pages. Thanks to the dry Egyptian climate they were still in good condition, though the oldest had been lying there for 1000 years! Among them were priceless treasures: original Hebrew versions of books which had been known only in translation, a wealth of letters that gave us our first real knowledge of some of the history of the period, and manuscripts written by one of the great Jews of the era, Moses Maimonides.

The Geonic Period

Though Jewish communities grew both in Palestine and Africa, the center of our religion remained, for much of this period, in the Babylonian academies set up by Rav and Samuel. The president of each of these schools held the title of GAON, גָּאוֹן (the plural is GEONIM, גְּאוֹנִים), or "Excellency." Thus, the four centuries from 600 to 1000 are often called the GEONIC PERIOD of Jewish history.

Messengers from every corner of Jewry came to Babylonia with questions for the Geonim and gifts to support the Babylonian schools. To each question the Gaon provided a written reply. These answers, known as RESPONSA (in Hebrew: תְּשׁוּבוֹת) were later collected and published, adding much valuable material to Jewish law. The custom of bringing problems to outstanding Jewish authorities continues, and responsa are still written by rabbis today.

Most of the geonic responsa were brief legal decisions, but others were of quite a different nature. The first known complete prayer book was compiled by a Gaon in the ninth century at the request of Jews living 3000 miles to the west, in Spain.

Saadia versus the Karaites

Meanwhile, a new split was threatening the unity of the Jewish world. Jews based in Palestine, who called themselves the KARAITES (קְרָאִים), rejected the Talmud, arguing that the Rabbis had distorted the meaning of God's Law by their interpretations. The Karaites wanted to return to the Bible itself and to work out all Jewish practice from it.

The great Jewish scholar to deal with this problem was Saadia who, in 928, became Gaon of the academy at Sura. Saadia was an Egyptian, and as a foreigner he would not normally have been invited to head a Babylonian academy. However, he had already shown such learning that the Jewish leaders hoped that by choosing him they would bring renewed glory to the school.

Saadia pointed out that any law must be applied to particular problems and that the Karaites were interpreting just as much as the Rabbis had. The difference, said Saadia, was that the Karaite interpretations destroyed the wise practices established in the Talmud. For example, the Karaites read in the Torah that one may not light a fire at home on the Sabbath and decided that all fires had to be put out. For them the Sabbath was a day of darkness and gloom. How much wiser the Rabbis had been, said Saadia, in permitting us to burn lights that had been kindled *before* the Sabbath so that the holy day could be one of warmth and joy.

One by one, Saadia answered and attacked the Karaite beliefs. Although the movement continued to exist—there are 10,000 Karaites today in the State of Israel —Karaism lost its power in the face of the Gaon's arguments and never again threatened the unity of Jewish life.

Reason and belief

The entire Islamic period was one of remarkable achievement in medicine, astronomy, and mathematics. Then, as now, people were troubled by what they saw as a conflict between science, which was based on reason, and religious faith.

Saadia tried to answer this problem in his *Book of Beliefs and Doctrines*. To Saadia, the solution was simple: the Torah does not oppose reason but aids it. It teaches us the very ideas that a thinking person would discover for himself by using his own mind. For example, said Saadia, a person who studied the universe through science would find that behind the world of nature was a single creative force. This is precisely the meaning of the story of creation.

How then is the Torah important? In two ways. First, it gives us answers which it might otherwise take mankind centuries to discover through reason alone. Second, it tells us that those answers we find which agree with the teachings of Judaism are truly correct.

But what of those places in the Bible which seem to contradict reason? What are we to make of statements which refer to God as if He had a face and hands? Again, taught Saadia, there is no problem. Any such idea must be recognized as poetic, helping us to understand what we could not otherwise imagine.

The Book of Beliefs and Doctrines was only one of Saadia's outstanding works. He began the scientific study of the Hebrew language, wrote commentaries on the Bible, and translated the Bible into Arabic, since that was the language many Jews understood. His translation is still in use in Arabic-speaking lands.

Spain under Islam

Saadia was the greatest of the Geonim. After his death the Babylonian schools began to fade away, and despite some moments of excellence, they passed out of

---

The Holy Land in the Golden Age

The fall of the Roman Empire and the rise of Islam brought new life to the Jewish communities in the Holy Land. But just as the Golden Age was reaching its peak (about 1100 C.E.), the Jewish settlement in Eretz Yisrael was nearly destroyed. For four centuries the Jewish population there was at a historical low point, with few if any Jews in Jerusalem.

What caused this change? A series of wars and invasions in the Holy Land, beginning with the arrival of Christian warriors from Europe—the Crusaders—in 1099. From then on, each time the Jewish community in Palestine began to grow, some new invader came and wiped it out. Small wonder that few Western European Jews risked the long journey to Palestine.

Fortunately, soon after the expulsion from Spain, conditions in the Holy Land became more favorable. Then not only Jerusalem but also Tiberias, Hebron, and especially Safed became key centers of Jewish life and learning.

The Tránsito Synagogue, built in fourteenth-century Toledo, is one
of the few Jewish buildings left from the Golden Age in Spain.

existence in the eleventh century. Fortunately, the flame of Judaism was already
burning brightly in the land of Spain.

Jews had lived in Spain since the Roman
era, but by the year 700 they had fallen
on very hard times. The Visigoths, the
Germanic tribes that ruled the country
after the fall of the Roman Empire, were
violently anti-Jewish. Judaism was out-
lawed. Adult Jews were enslaved and given
as gifts to Christians, and their children
were placed in Christian homes so that
the Jewish religion could be erased.

Before the Muslims invaded Spain in
the year 711, not a single Jew there could
openly show his religion. Small wonder
that our people greeted the Arab armies
with open arms. The Muslims were very
pleased with this welcome, gave weapons
to the Jews, and placed them in control of
such important cities as Cordova, Granada,
Toledo, and Seville.

Jewish life in Spain

In 756, after a lengthy period of conquest and civil war, the Muslims of Spain broke away from the rest of the Arab Empire and set up an independent state. They openly declared a policy of toleration for the Jewish community, beginning an era of growth and well-being for our people. Jews soon won fame as physicians, scientists, writers, politicians, even as soldiers. At the same time, they found new joy in being able to practice their religion openly and, on the whole, without restrictions. The special taxes and regulations placed on them did not prevent Spanish Jews from building beautiful homes, synagogues, and fine schools, nor from producing a flood of books on a great many subjects.

Most of the Jewish writings were in Arabic, the language of the Islamic Empire, but there was also a new interest in Hebrew. There were not only scholarly books—Hebrew dictionaries and grammars —but also large numbers of original compositions, including an outpouring of the finest Hebrew poetry since Biblical times.

Islamic Spain remained a secure home for the Jewish people for more than three centuries, until anti-Jewish feelings began to erupt among various Muslim sects. At about that time, however, Christians began to reconquer the Spanish peninsula. For many years they were tolerant of Judaism, and so Arabic-speaking Jews who were forced to leave the Muslim south often found acceptance in the Christian north. In this way Spain continued to remain a center for world Jewry until the Catholics too became intolerant, driving all Jews from the country in 1492.

But this is far ahead of our story. The centuries of toleration in Spain were very long indeed, and the achievements of those days were glorious. In the next chapter we will meet some of those Spanish Jews who made the period one of the most remarkable in our 4000-year history.

SUMMARY   *Under Muslim rule, Judaism flourished brilliantly. Centers of important activity were located in the land of Israel, including a newly restored community in Jerusalem, and throughout North Africa. Intellectual leadership remained in the Babylonian academies from 600 to 1000, the age of the Geonim. Of the Geonim, the greatest was Saadia. After his death, Spain became the leader of world Jewry and the site of a long and brilliant period in our history.*

12

Some Men
of the Golden Age

The country—Spain. The year—950.

The caliph considered his officials. There were many good men among them, men whose ability had brought his country power and wealth. But now he needed a person of outstanding skill and wisdom to handle the most important duties in his government.

At last he reached a decision: he selected his court physician. This choice was not unusual, since doctors of that day were often given government responsibilities. What was unusual was that this new leader was a Jew: Ḥasdai ibn Shaprut. Jews had enjoyed liberty in Spain for nearly 200 years, but never before had one risen to the very height of fame and power in a Muslim country.

Ḥasdai ibn Shaprut

Ḥasdai responded to the challenges of his new office and played an outstanding role in international diplomacy. During his time in office, Spain enjoyed years of great wealth. Cordova, its capital, became the most splendid city in Europe.

Nor did fame lead him to neglect the needs of his people. Ḥasdai used his office to protect them. He set up Jewish schools in Spain and brought in scholars from the East to teach them, starting a tradition of Jewish study in his native land. This helped to free Spanish Jewry from the legal rulings of the distant Geonim. But Ḥasdai also remembered the ancient academies, and he sent rich gifts to support the schools of Babylonia.

Ḥasdai's most exciting moment came when he learned that there was a Jewish state in what is now southern Russia. It was a huge country, larger in area than Texas, California, New Mexico, and Arizona combined, and was ruled by a people called the Khazars. Some 200 years earlier, their king had learned of the Jewish religion, become convinced of its truth, and converted. He had made Judaism the official religion, but had granted freedom of worship to both Muslims and Christians. This tolerant policy had been followed by all his successors on the Khazar throne.

Ḥasdai was thrilled to hear this. From his position in court he was all too aware that the Jews of Spain were guests in a foreign land who could be expelled at the whim of a Muslim ruler. He exchanged letters with the king of the Khazars and considered moving to their land in order to live with and be ruled by Jews. Just nine years later, however, Russian troops attacked and overran the Jewish state. With the fall of the Khazar kingdom, Jewish independence and religious toleration were both eliminated from Russia. They have not been restored.

Samuel ibn Nagrela

Ḥasdai ibn Shaprut earned his eminent position in the caliph's court through normal promotions. Samuel ibn Nagrela, the next great Jewish politician of Spain, came to power in such an extraordinary manner that his biography reads more like fiction than history.

Samuel was born to a wealthy family of Cordova in 993, some twenty years after the death of Ḥasdai. He received a fine education and looked to a bright future until a wave of African Muslims invaded Spain and destroyed his native city. The promising young man suddenly found himself a penniless refugee, reduced to selling spices in a shop in Málaga.

Yet even in the marketplace his genius did not remain hidden. He was a master of Arabic penmanship, an art the Arabs valued highly. His skill became known to

a slave of the vizier of Granada, who used him to pen some important letters. These letters, in turn, came to the attention of the vizier. He asked to meet the man who had written them, and he was so impressed by Samuel that he made the Jew his assistant.

Shortly thereafter the vizier died, and Samuel was awarded his master's position. In fact, he was king in all but name because the actual ruler of the great city-state was a pleasure-loving man who left Samuel to handle government affairs. The new vizier brought the country to even greater glory and wealth. Amazingly, he became the nation's greatest military hero. Through almost twenty years of constant war, this Jewish general led the Muslim armies into victorious battle.

Needless to say, Samuel impressed his fellow Jews. They chose him to head their community, and as their NAGID (נָגִיד), or prince, he brought Spanish Jewry to its peak of learning. He was a fine scholar: his introduction to the Talmud is still used today. As a poet he celebrated life in Spain in joyous Hebrew verse. (He was probably the only Jew ever to write poems on the glories of war.) But despite his love for his native country, he felt himself torn by a deep longing for Zion. He sent gifts to support the Jews of Jerusalem and expressed in his poetry a heartfelt yearning for the homeland of our people.

Solomon ibn Gabirol

If the statesmen Ḥasdai and Samuel were wise and tolerant, the poet Solomon ibn Gabirol was proud and stubborn. Not only that: he was also poor, chronically ill, and ugly. He wanted to devote his life to philosophy and poetry, yet found it difficult to stay on good terms with the wealthy people who would have supported him. Samuel ibn Nagrela was his patron for a time, but as Solomon insisted on criticizing the vizier's own poetry, their friendship ended in quarreling.

In spite of all his unpleasant qualities, Solomon ibn Gabirol was a poetic genius. Even as a teenager he was able to find the words to express his feelings beautifully in verse. Solomon found comfort in knowing that, though his tortured body was on earth, his mind could reach to heaven:

Early will I seek Thee,
God my refuge strong;
Late prepare to meet Thee
With my evening song.

Though unto Thy greatness
I with trembling soar—
Yet my inmost thinking
Lies Thine eyes before.

What this frail heart dreameth
And my tongue's poor speech,
Can they even distant,
To Thy greatness reach?

Being great in mercy,
Thou wilt not despise
Praises which till death's hour
From my soul shall rise.

Gabirol died in his thirties, but in his short life he produced works that became a model for later Jewish poets. Several became permanent parts of the High Holy Day service.

In addition, Gabirol wrote works of philosophy. One of these was translated into Latin and studied enthusiastically by Christian thinkers in the Middle Ages.

The growth of Toledo

When Samuel ibn Nagrela died, he was succeeded as vizier by his son. Unfortunately, Joseph ibn Nagrela did not have his father's charm and wisdom, or his ability to cool the anger of Muslims who objected to being governed by a Jew. Moreover, he unwisely involved himself in a palace plot and was murdered in 1066. This event unleashed simmering anti-Jewish feelings, and a raging crowd of Arabs massacred the Jews of Granada. This was the first Muslim persecution of Spanish Jewry—but similar events followed in other parts of the country.

A few years later, in 1085, the Christians of Europe took a major step in reconquering Spain: they captured the city of Toledo. The Jews who lived there were allowed religious freedom; and other Arabic-speaking Jews, impressed by this toleration and fearing persecution in the Muslim south, resettled in towns that were under Christian control. Though Jews did continue to prosper in some areas where Arabs ruled—in Seville they were notable as physicians, courtiers, astronomers, and viziers to the Moorish kings—Toledo became the most important Jewish community in Spain.

Judah ha-Levi

Among the Jews of Toledo at the time of the Catholic conquest was a ten-year-old boy who had already shown an unusual gift for languages. He grew up to be a well-known physician, but his special love was always writing, and he proved to be the finest Jewish poet since the Biblical period. His name was Judah ha-Levi.

In the Golden Age   The Golden Age was the only period before modern times in which Jewish girls had a chance for any real education. The opportunities were far more limited than those for boys—the male population was exceptionally well educated—but some classes for girls did exist, and on occasion a woman became a teacher. Blind scholarly men were highly prized because they could instruct girls without being distracted from their lessons!

The subjects taught went beyond the traditional disciplines of Torah and Talmud to include Hebrew language and grammar, a serious examination of the later parts of the Bible, and secular topics such as mathematics, astronomy, medicine, and the natural sciences. Arabic and Arabic penmanship were also studied.

Needless to say, not every child was a willing pupil. This is one of the concerns expressed by Judah ibn Tibbon, a famous scholar and physician, in the following excerpts from his "Ethical Will." The "Ethical Will" was a uniquely Jewish type of document, in which a father expressed the spiritual values and heritage he wished to leave to his children:

My son! Thus far you have relied on me to rouse you from laziness, thinking that I would live with you forever! You did not bear in mind that death must divide us. Who will be as tender to you as I have been? You are still young, and improvement is possible, if Heaven but grant you a helping gift of desire and resolution.

Therefore, my son! stay not your hand when I have left you, but devote yourself to the study of the Torah and to the science of medicine. But chiefly occupy yourself with the Torah.

My son! I command you to honor your wife with all your might. She is intelligent and modest, a daughter of distinguished family. She is a good housewife and mother, and no spendthrift. Her tastes are simple, whether in food or dress. If you give orders or correct her, let your words be gentle. It is enough if your displeasure is visible in your looks—let it not be vented in actual rage.

Never refuse to lend books to anyone who has not means to purchase books for himself, but only to those who can be trusted to return the volumes. Cover the bookcase with rugs of fine quality; and preserve them from damp and mice, and all manner of injury, for your books are your good treasure.

May He who gives prudence to the simple, and to young men knowledge and discretion, give you a willing heart and a listening ear!

The story of this document has a happy sequel. Judah's son, Samuel, became a scholar in his own right. His most famous work was a translation of Maimonides' *Guide for the Perplexed* from Arabic into Hebrew, a project undertaken with the approval and guidance of Maimonides himself.

A seder in Spain. The artist has based this picture on a drawing in a manuscript from the Golden Age.

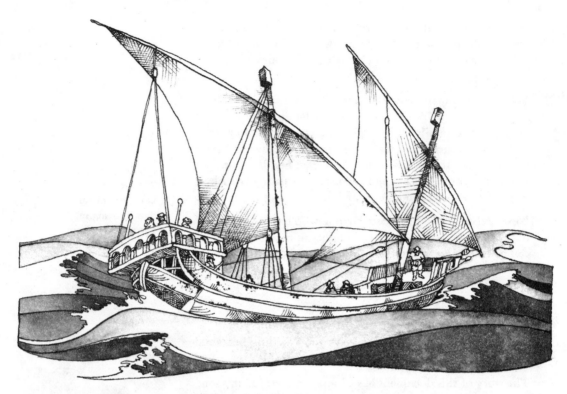

Judah ha-Levi sets sail for Zion. We know that Judah got at least as
far as Egypt, where he was greeted warmly. But we do not know
whether the author of "Ode to Zion" ever actually reached Jerusalem.

Judah wanted throughout his life to return to the Promised Land, and he often
gave expression to this in his Hebrew
poetry. In his famous *Ode to Zion* he cried
out:

Would I were wandering in those places
  dear
  Where God revealed Himself in ages
  past
Showing His light to messenger and seer!

And who will make me wings that I may
  fly,
  That I may take my broken heart away
And lay its ruins where thy ruins lie?

Prostrate upon thine earth, I fain would
  thrust
  Myself, delighting in thy stones, and
  lay
Exceeding tender hold upon thy dust.

However, his prose masterpiece, known
as *Kuzari* (כּוּזָרִי), was set in another
Jewish state: the kingdom of the Khazars.
It tells how the king of that land decided,
after a long search, to convert to Judaism.

Much of Judah's story is a dialogue between the king and a rabbi. The king asks
the very questions that were troubling
Spanish Jews, who, as a minority ruled by
Muslims and Christians, had begun to have

doubts about their own religion. The rabbi gives a solution to each problem the king raises.

In this way, the book gave answers to Jewish readers who were in doubt. It also reminded them that the larger religions were based on the teachings of Israel, and that a real king, seeking with an open mind into the three great faiths, had found that Judaism was the truest of all.

Thus Judah ha-Levi helped restore the faith of the Jewish people in themselves and their religion—but he was not fully happy. Even in his old age he continued to yearn for the land of Israel. At last he left his home, his only daughter, and his grandson and headed East. He was greeted warmly by the Jews of Egypt, who urged him to stay with them, but his love for Zion drove him on. There is no certain record of what became of him, but a tradition says that he did reach Jerusalem and that, as he was singing his *Ode to Zion* before the ruins of the Temple, he was ridden down by an Arab horseman.

Moses Maimonides

"From Moses to Moses, there arose no one like Moses." For 700 years this has been a saying of the Jewish people. After Moses the Lawgiver there was no one like him until Moses Maimonides.

What sort of man could win such praise? A man who gave his entire life to helping others who were sick in body or spirit, a man of brilliance in many fields; above all, a man who brought order to the great body of Jewish law and, in that sense, restored it to the Jewish people.

Maimonides was born in Cordova in 1135, just six years before the death of Judah ha-Levi. At that time, religious warfare was rapidly bringing the Golden Age to a close. Christian armies were step-

What's in a Name? Until relatively recent times, few people had family names. A man was simply known as "the son of" his father, as in David the son of Jesse. Living in many lands and using many languages, Jews have had many ways of saying "the son of." The Hebrew word is "ben" (as in the modern name David Ben-Gurion). The Aramaic word is "bar," which we have met with Bar Kochba. (BAR MITZVAH, בַּר מִצְוָה , means "son of the commandment.") The Arabic term is "ibn," as in Solomon ibn Gabirol. Greek adds the ending "-ides," so "Maimonides" means "the son of Maimon." Some great rabbis were also known by names made from their initials. So Maimonides, whose Hebrew name was Rabbi Moshe ben Maimon, was also called RAMBAM.

Genius at Work   *Suppose you were Moses Maimonides: what would your day have been like? In 1199, in a letter to Samuel ibn Tibbon, who was then living in France, the great sage described his daily routine:*

I dwell in Fustat and the Sultan resides in Cairo; these two places are 4000 paces distant from each other. My duties to the ruler are very heavy. I must visit him every day, early in the morning, and when he or any of his children, or any of the women in his harem are sick, I dare not leave Cairo. . . . Even if nothing unusual happens, I do not return to Fustat until the afternoon.

Then I am almost dying with hunger. . . . I dismount from my animal, wash my hands, . . . and eat some slight refreshment, the only meal I take in twenty-four hours. Then I go forth to attend my patients. Patients go in and out until nightfall, until eight o'clock or even later. I talk with them and prescribe for them while lying down on my back from sheer fatigue, and when night falls I am so tired I can hardly speak.

Therefore no Israelite can speak with me except on the Sabbath. On that day the whole congregation comes to me after the morning service, when I instruct them as to their doing during the whole week; we study together until noon, when they depart. Some of them return and read with me after the afternoon service until evening prayers. . . . I have related to you only a part of what you would see if by God's grace you were to visit me.

Maimonides at his writing desk. RAMBAM wrote some works in Hebrew, others in Arabic.

ping up their effort to recapture Spain,
and the frightened Muslims called in rein-
forcements from Africa. Across the Strait
of Gibraltar came the Almohades, fanatics
who not only fought Christians (and Muslims who did not accept their extreme
views) but also turned on every Jew they
could find with the choice of Islam or
immediate death. When he was about thirteen, Moses and his family had to flee from
one of these attacks. They left Spain and
traveled from place to place until they
were at last able to find a safe home near
the city now called Cairo.

There Maimonides became the greatest
physician of his day. He already had a huge
practice among Jews and Arabs when he
was appointed physician to the vizier of
the Sultan Saladin. Somehow he managed
to find time to treat his master and his
household plus all his regular patients, to
be the leader of the Jewish community of
Egypt, and still to write the two works
which rank him as the great philosopher of
his age.

The philosophy of Maimonides

In the book called *Guide for the Perplexed* (מוֹרֶה נְבוּכִים), the philosopher
tried to prove that the Torah could fit
well with science and philosophy. Like
Saadia before him, he taught that there
was no real conflict between them. For
example, when the Bible states "God commanded" or "God spoke," we should
realize that this means "through the words
of Moses and the other prophets." We are
not supposed to believe that the voice of
God was actually heard. Translated into
many languages, the *Guide* also helped
Christian thinkers who tried to match sci-

ence and reason with the teachings of their
own religion.

Even more important for Jews, however, was his earlier work, *Mishneh Torah*,
מִשְׁנֵה תּוֹרָה (literally, "The Repetition of
the Torah"). Knowing that few people
could cope with the entire Talmud,
Maimonides took the legal material from
it, summed up and rearranged what he
found, and presented his summary in a
clear way that was easy to use. This was
a gigantic project, but through it he hoped
to allow Jews to understand the Oral Law
without studying the whole Talmud. Like
the first Moses, he brought the teaching of
God to the people of Israel in a way they
could appreciate, absorb, and through
study, love.

Lessons of the Golden Age

In this chapter we have had space to
mention only a few of the famous Jews
of Spain. Many other famous people could
be described. And, of course, there were
hundreds of thousands of "ordinary" men
and women whose names have been forgotten but who nonetheless played a key
role in building a cultured and creative society.

Even though our look at the Golden
Age has been brief, we can still say several things about it—judgments which suggest much of importance about the nature
of Jews and Judaism.

First, it is sometimes said that Jews lose
interest in Judaism when they are free
and cling to it only in times of persecution.
The Age of Islam shows that this is not
true. For more than three centuries our
people were allowed to practice their religion as they wished and were permitted

A letter written and signed by Maimonides in the year 1173.

Second, despite their great success, many Spanish Jews felt a strange lack. They were loyal to Spain and served it well, but they wanted to be part of a Jewish state. This was not merely a desire to be safe from attack—if anything, this longing was felt most deeply by those whose lives were secure, like Ḥasdai ibn Shaprut and Judah ha-Levi.

Third, and perhaps most important for our time, is the realization that the Golden Age of Judaism was also the Golden Age of Islam. The period of real fellowship between Muslims and Jews produced an era of unmatched splendor for *both* peoples.

The collapse of their working relationship marked the beginning of the end of Muslim rule in Europe. How tragic that Arabs and Jews, whose cooperation brought such great success, and who are so close in ancestry, language, and history, should still face each other as enemies, when the combined resources of both peoples might bring about a new Golden Age in the Near East.

to enter professions in which they gained fame and wealth; yet, at the same time, they remained devoted to Jewish religion and Jewish culture.

SUMMARY *During the Golden Age, Judaism produced men of extraordinary talents: diplomats like Ḥasdai ibn Shaprut and Samuel ibn Nagrela, poets like Solomon ibn Gabirol and Judah ha-Levi, and the physician-philosopher Moses Maimonides. Widely varied, yet united in their unending loyalty to Judaism, they were men of remarkable achievement. Yet this period of toleration and cooperation also included the greatest flowering of Arabic culture—a lesson whose meaning has yet to be realized by modern Arab leaders.*

13

Christian Europe
During the Golden Age

We now skip back in time to see what Europe was like outside of Spain between the end of the reign of the last Roman emperor in 476 C.E. and the victory of the Catholic armies at Toledo in 1085. For Islam this was the great epoch which included the birth of Muhammad and the creation of a huge empire. For Jews it was the Golden Age, leading from the completion of the Talmud through the Geonic Period into the brilliant world of Spain.*

But for Christians in Europe it was the time of an extremely backward and primitive civilization.

The Dark Ages

Following the fall of the Roman empire, the society of Western Europe came

apart. The entire area became a battleground for Germanic tribes who fought against each other and against the Christian Church. The tribal kings seldom had the power to control or protect their subjects, so most people organized into local units within which they tried to raise everything needed for survival. They did not bother to keep an educational system —even kings and nobles could not read or write—so the scientific skills of the Romans were forgotten, and farmers were soon able to scratch only a bare living from the soil. Little if anything was left over to sell to others, and the cities, which had been trade centers, all but disappeared.

Small wonder that these centuries, which lasted approximately from 500 to 1000 C.E., have been called the Dark Ages.

Only once during this period did the light of civilization begin to shine, though dimly. Charles Martel—whose army stopped the Muslim advance into Europe at the Battle of Tours (see Chapter 10)—

* The great era which Judaism enjoyed under Islam continued past the period covered in this chapter: Judah ha-Levi lived until 1141, Maimonides until 1204. The Christian world in this later period is described in Section Four.

had a grandson who became king of a Germanic tribe called the Franks. He too was named Charles, and he soon became known as Charles the Great, or Charlemagne.

Charlemagne

Charlemagne did not have the military brilliance of his grandfather, but he lacked nothing in skill and firmness. He reigned for forty-six years. During that time he built a huge empire that included most of what is now France, Germany, and Italy, as well as much of Eastern Europe.

He was truly interested in improving education—in part because there were not enough educated men to help govern his kingdom! His efforts had some success, but when you realize that while Charlemagne was learning to write his name, the scholars of Muslim Spain were studying hundreds of thousands of manuscripts in the libraries of Cordova, you can see that Christian Europe was a very primitive place indeed.

Still, Charlemagne did control almost the same area that had once been ruled by the emperors of Rome. In recognition of this (and as part of some complex political plots), the Pope crowned him "King of the Romans" in the year 800. Thus was founded the Holy Roman Empire. As a later writer pointed out, nothing about it was holy, it was not Roman but German, and after Charlemagne died it was never much of an empire. Still, it stood for the dream of recreating the glory of Rome— a dream which was not officially given up until 1806. And in the twentieth century, when Adolf Hitler called his government the Third Reich—the Third German

Kingdom—it was the Holy Roman Empire which he thought of as the first. (The government which ruled Germany during World War I was the second.)

Jews in Christian Europe

Following the death of Charlemagne, his empire was split and his efforts at education collapsed under a flood of attacks from the Vikings of Scandinavia. These were great sailors—they reached North America about the year 1000—but it was their cruelty which became legendary. The story is told of one warrior who was scorned by his fellows because he would not join in their sport of throwing live babies into the air and catching them on the points of their spears.

Jews were one of the few civilizing elements in the midst of these horrible conditions. Jewish education, though limited, was still vastly superior to that of the Gentile world. Nearly all Jewish men were literate and could both read and understand the Hebrew Bible and prayer book.

This was one of several things which helped Jews become successful in the field of international trade. Another was the fact that while Christendom and Islam were deeply opposed to each other, Jews lived in both worlds without being too close to either. They were therefore ideally suited to serve as "middlemen" in commerce between the great powers. Moreover, Jews could work out contracts with other Jews in any country because all shared the same language and the same system of law. For all these reasons, Jews were often in demand as leaders in overseas commerce; by the ninth century, Hebrew

The CHANGING FACE of EUROPE

600 C.E.

NORSEMEN
NORTH SEA
CELTS
ANGLES AND SAXONS
JUTES
DANES
BALTIC SEA
ATLANTIC OCEAN
London
SAXONS
SLAVONIC PEOPLES
BRETONS
Paris
Mainz
FRANKISH
KINGDOMS
Vienna
AVARS
SLAVS
CASPIAN SEA
VISIGOTHIC
Toledo
KINGDOM
Cordova
Rome
BYZANTINE
MEDITERRANEAN SEA
BLACK SEA
Constantinople
EMPIRE
Athens
PERSIA

900 C.E.

K. OF NORWAY
FINNS
SCOTLAND
K. OF SWEDEN
ESTONIANS
LIVONIANS
NORTH SEA
IRELAND
WALES
ENGLAND
K. OF DENMARK
BALTIC SEA
LITHUANIANS
PRUSSIANS
PRINCIPALITY OF RUSSIA
ATLANTIC OCEAN
London
POLES
Paris
Mainz
Troyes
GERMAN STATES
BOHEMIA
KHAZAR EMPIRE
BRITTANY
FRANCE
BURGUNDY
Vienna
MAGYARS
PATZINAKS
CASPIAN SEA
K. OF LEON
K. OF NAVARRE
PROVENCE
VENICE
K. OF ITALY
EMIRATE OF CORDOVA
Toledo
Cordova
SERBS
BLACK SEA
Constantinople
K. OF BULGARIA
Rome
MEDITERRANEAN SEA
BYZANTINE EMPIRE
CALIPHATE
CALIPHATE
Athens
Harold Faye

Just a glance at these two maps tells you that enormous changes took
place in Europe during no more than 300 years (to see even further
changes, look back at the map of the Roman Empire on pages 44–45).
Notice how many more names of countries and kingdoms there are on
the map of Europe in 900 C.E.; you probably recognize quite a few
of them. Do you think this is evidence that Europe was growing more
civilized? Of particular interest to us as Jews is the Khazar
Empire, on the map in the year 900. A map of Europe in 1000 would
not show this empire, however, for it was conquered in 965.

was the language used in trading between points as widely separated as Paris and Baghdad.

As the Western world began to develop a taste for spices, silks, and other luxuries of the Orient, the rivers of Central Europe became busy routes of trade and Jews settled along their banks. The two most important of these settlements were in two German towns: Mainz on the River Rhine, and Regensburg (also known as Ratisbon) on the Danube. Both were starting points for trade trips to the East.

Many rulers welcomed the talented Jewish merchants, lowered their taxes, and gave them other privileges. One of the leading German kings—legend says Charlemagne himself—went so far as to com-

---

Jews Under Christian and Muslim Rule

Part of a folding Haggadah which could be carried— or hidden—in a coin box.

Was it better to live among the Christians or among the Muslims?

The Church taught that no Jew could rule over a Christian. This meant that Jews could not have Christian servants, hire Christian workers, or command Christian troops. In Muslim lands it was different. Samuel ibn Nagrela led Spanish Muslim armies into battle for twenty years. Jews played a major part in Islamic political and business life and were, by and large, free from the terrors and persecution that might strike anywhere and anytime in Christian Europe.

However, Jews did not share in Muslim society as equals. Just as in Christian Europe, Jews living under Islam were forced to wear special badges and costumes. Conversion to Judaism was strictly forbidden by Christians and Muslims alike. Muslim "toleration" was just that—the Muslims thought the Jews inferior, but "generously" allowed them to live in Muslim countries. This was, of course, better than the medieval Christian hatred of Jews as "Christ killers" and infidels.

What made living in Christian lands worse in the end was the power of the Church. There was no power like it in Muslim lands, where the laws were enforced loosely in many towns and provinces. Though there were pockets of "toleration" in Christian lands, the Church worked hard to have its teachings followed throughout Christendom. And even when these teachings did not threaten Jewish lives or Jewish livelihoods, they almost always limited the hopes of our people.

mand certain Jews of northern Italy to settle in Mainz. They were members of the Kalonymos family, a group which during the next four centuries gave German Jewry many of its best-known rabbis, teachers, poets, writers, and communal leaders.

Ashkenazim and Sephardim

Where the Jews lived changed the way they practiced their religion. Slowly the life and culture of the Jews of Christian Europe (and especially Germany), who were known as ASHKENAZIM (אַשְׁכְּנַזִּים), became very much different from that of the Jews of Muslim lands (and especially Spain), who became known as SEPHARDIM (סְפָרַדִים).*

Some of these differences were minor. For example, the Ashkenazim, who remained in close touch with the Holy Land, followed the practice of the Palestinian teachers who considered it proper for a man to go bareheaded even during worship. The Sephardim, on the other hand, were directly in touch with the academies of Babylonia, where some teachers recommended covering the head as a mark of special piety. (Gradually the Babylonian custom spread to Spain and, much later, to the rest of Europe. It only became a matter of debate in modern times, when Reform Judaism did away with the head covering.)

Similarly, differences developed in the use of the Hebrew language. Modern Hebrew is a combination of the two tradi-

* Ashkenaz and Sefarad are two place names mentioned in the Bible, which the Jews of this period incorrectly identified with Germany and Spain.

In Rashi's time, Jews practiced many skilled trades. Later they were forced out of most fields, until peddling was one of the few jobs Jews could do.

tions: Ashkenazic script and Sephardic pronunciation.

Far more important was a basic difference in outlook brought about by the world in which each group lived. The Sephardic Jew in Spain lived a busy life with only limited time for Jewish studies. The greatest work of Sephardic scholarship was a clear guide to Talmudic law —Maimonides' *Mishneh Torah*—written especially for those who could not spend hours studying the entire Talmud.

The Ashkenazic Jew saw life in a very different way. The secular world around him held little interest, since it was so far inferior to his own, and so the Jew of Christian Europe had both the time and the desire for learning. During the

Dark Ages, such study was not on a very advanced level; but as general conditions began to improve, a teacher appeared who was able to raise the standard of scholarship among the Ashkenazim.

Rabbenu Gershom

This man was Gershom ben Judah, who came from what is now eastern France to settle in the city of the Kalonymos family —Mainz. There he received students from many parts of the continent who in turn became teachers of European Jewry. He was commonly known as ME'OR HA-GOLAH, מְאוֹר הַגּוֹלָה ("The Light of the Exile") or, more affectionately, RABBENU, רַבֵּנוּ ("Our Rabbi") Gershom.

Gershom was concerned with the practice of Judaism, particularly in the area of women's rights. He forbade divorce in cases where the wife did not agree. He also forbade Jews who were busy in international trade from keeping families in more than one country. For many centuries, monogamy (having only one wife or husband) had been usual in Europe, but Rabbenu Gershom made it the law.*

Another of his teachings shows the frighteningly insecure position of the Jewish people. Many were still subject to persecution, and some converted to Christianity to save their lives. When such people wished to return to Judaism, Gershom ordered that they be welcomed and never reminded of their temporary faithlessness.

* His decree was not known, much less accepted, by Oriental Jews, some of whom even today take more than one wife.

Rashi

Gershom's pupils established schools in the communities of the Rhineland, and to them came a young Frenchman who had been born in 1040, not long after Rabbenu Gershom's death. At the age of about twenty-five he returned from Germany to his native town of Troyes, 100 miles southeast of Paris, to work in the rich vineyards of the Champagne district. His name was Rabbi Shlomo ben Isaac, but he was universally known by the word formed from his initials—RASHI (רַשִׁ״י).

In Troyes he opened a school. This was not to make money—for he did not believe in profiting from Jewish scholarship—but to allow him to share his knowledge of the Law with others. He continued to support himself by growing grapes and making wine, while teaching so brilliantly that his fame soon spread throughout France, Germany, and Italy.

Rashi had a remarkable ability to understand and explain the Bible and Talmud. He examined every sentence of these books, writing comments on them in a style that was simple and clear. He explained the meaning of difficult passages, often with just a few words, and his Talmud commentaries became a necessity for students. In his commentary on the Torah he also dealt with passages that were simple to understand, illustrating them with examples and stories (MIDRASHIM, מִדְרָשִׁים) which made Rashi's writings easy to read and highly popular. Proof of its lasting appeal is the fact that when printing was invented, the first Hebrew work to come from the press was Rashi's commentary on the Torah. Even today,

Rashi taught his three daughters, who became famous for their learning.
Their sons wrote further commentaries on Talmud and Torah.

scholars still turn to his writings for valuable help in understanding the Bible.

Among Rashi's students were his three daughters, who became famous for their knowledge. (It was said that he discussed Torah and Talmud with them to find out what questions would trouble a student, and that he wrote his answers so simply even his children could understand.) Their sons, in turn, were among those famous scholars who wrote further commentaries on the sacred texts which are called TOSA-FOT, תּוֹסָפוֹת (additions).

A delicate balance

Thus the Biblical and Talmudic traditions continued to develop among the Ashkenazim. This loyalty to Judaism is all the more remarkable when one remembers how tiny the Jewish communities of Northern Europe were. The average town had no more than 200 Jews, while Rashi's own city of Troyes had less than fifty Jewish families. Nevertheless, each group kept its Jewish identity, as well as an active and often scholarly Jewish life.

And so, by 1085, our people had developed two very different patterns of Jewish life. The Sephardim produced universal geniuses, physicians, scientists, and statesmen who remained pious and observant in the midst of wealth and glory. The Ashkenazim developed a deeply devout Jewish population. Jewish study and practice were the most important parts of their lives.

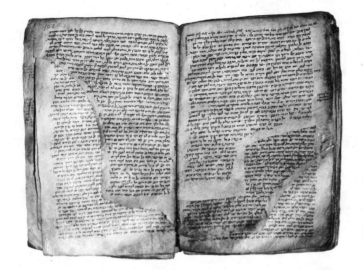

This copy of the Bible, with Rashi's commentaries, dates from about 1250. The commentaries were first published separately, but they were later printed in the spaces surrounding the Biblical text.

The rise of Ashkenazic Jewry occurred in an age when Christendom was weak and therefore willing to trade peacefully with the world of Islam. Because the Jew was a go-between in international trade, he was, more often than not, allowed to live his religious life in peace. This working partnership between the three faiths entered its most fruitful phase about the year 1000, but it did not last to the end of the century. When Rashi died in 1105 he had seen Christian Europe grow strong enough to challenge the Muslim powers, with German Jewry trapped between the opposing giants.

How all this came about will be seen in our next section.

SUMMARY *The backward conditions of Europe during the period from 500 to 1000 led the Jews of France and Germany to develop a unique life-style. This was Ashkenazic Judaism, which contrasts with the Sephardic Judaism of Spain. Ashkenazic studies of the Bible and Talmud reached their height under Rabbenu Gershom and Rashi in the eleventh century. In their secular lives, many Jews worked in international commerce, forming a link between the Christian and Islamic worlds—and many were invited to the Rhineland to aid German economic expansion. However, Jewish life was soon to undergo a radical change.*

PART FOUR

The Middle Ages and the Renaissance

Persecution and Expulsion

In this section we have to describe many horrible events and tell sad stories many of us would rather forget.

Why tell them at all?

An important thinker once said that those who do not learn from history are condemned to repeat it. Unless we try to make sense of the past, we cannot hope to shape our own future.

The history of the Middle Ages and Renaissance, a history of persecution and hatred, helps to explain many modern events. The same France that expelled all its Jews in the fourteenth century helped assemble Jews for extermination during World War II. The same Catholic Church that passed anti-Jewish laws during the Middle Ages still has not established diplomatic relations with the State of Israel. In Germany and in Eastern Europe, anti-Semitism has been a recurring theme from the Middle Ages up to the latest anti-Jewish campaign in today's Soviet Union.

The Sephardim

The Golden Age ended in torment and heartbreak for the Sephardim, the Jews of Spain and Portugal. First they were forced to convert to Christianity. Then, when some of these "New Christians" were found to practice Judaism in secret, they were tortured by the Inquisition. This scene, painted by Pedro Berruguete, shows an auto-da-fé ("act of faith") in which Jews were stripped and then burned at the stake. The artist was asked to do the painting by the Grand Inquisitor himself, the infamous Tomás de Torquemada.

But if history tends to repeat itself, we would be wrong to think that it always repeats itself in exactly the same way, or that it is a clear and simple process. Sometimes nations and peoples can and do change their ways. Since 1965, for example, the Catholic Church has sought a new dialogue with Jews and with the Jewish state. West Germany has paid millions of dollars in reparations to individual Jews who suffered during the Nazi period, and has helped Israel establish links with the European community.

The facts of history, then, are complex — which is all the more reason for us to know them. I promised in Chapter 1 to tell you the facts. Here are some which are little discussed, but which are crucial for an understanding of Jewish history and of the world we live in.

ABBA EBAN

Expelled from Spain and Portugal, many
Sephardim fled to the Netherlands.
Above, a Rosh Hashanah plate from Delft;
below, the *Jewish Philosopher* by the
great Rembrandt, who often used Jews as
his models. Right: the Portuguese
Synagogue in Amsterdam, painted about
1680 by Emanuel de Witte.

The Ottoman Empire, which included Palestine, also welcomed the exiled Sephardim. As Jews returned to the Holy Land, Safed (in what is now northern Israel) became a major center of Jewish learning. Top and bottom left, Safed's sixteenth-century "ARI" synagogue; below, a manuscript drawing of a Jewish woman "at home" in Turkish dress.

Dona Ebrea in Casa

14

INTRODUCTION TO PART FOUR

Middle Ages and Renaissance

The world we know was born about the year 1000.

No great event took place in that year. Trends which were to prove of lasting importance had begun decades earlier; others would begin decades later.

But by the year 1000, life in the West was clearly moving in a new direction.

During the previous 500 years, as we have seen, Christian Europe was much more primitive than the Islamic world—and it was far behind the splendid cultures of Mexico, India, Southeast Asia, China, and Japan. During the next five centuries, however, the changes in Europe would be so startling that by 1500 its culture could rival the finest. Its artists and thinkers would include geniuses like Michelangelo and Leonardo da Vinci, and its explorers would open the gates to the riches of the New World.

The Italians of the 1500's looked at this magnificent new civilization and saw in it the rebirth of Europe. *Renaissance*—which means "rebirth"—became the name for the period from about 1450 to 1520.

When the people of the Renaissance thought about the culture of the previous thousand years, on the other hand, they felt nothing but scorn. To them the only type of civilization worth considering—the type they tried to recreate—was that of the ancient Greeks and Romans. The years between the fall of Rome and their own time were to them wasted centuries, which they called simply "Middle Ages." (The Latin term is *medium aevum*, from which we get the English word "medieval.")

This section deals with:	
500–1000	Dark Ages (also called Early Middle Ages)
1000–1450	High Middle Ages
1450–1520	Renaissance

Christopher Columbus (left) surveys the ships that will carry him to the New World. His voyage in 1492 was largely supported by Jews, and Columbus himself may well have been a secret Jew, or Marrano.

The High Middle Ages

In the nineteenth century, when the classical world was no longer used as the only standard of culture, people saw things in a somewhat different light. While they recognized that what we have called the Dark Ages (500 to 1000) were truly backward, they saw that the period from 1000 to 1450 was special in its own way, and called it the "High Middle Ages" to distinguish it from the earlier period.

This was the era of knights in shining armor, huge castles, Robin Hood—and of savage warfare, widespread ignorance, and the burning of "witches." Most important,

in the long run, it was the time that kings began to gain real control over large areas of land. By 1500 they had changed England, Spain, and France into centrally controlled national states, much as they are today.* Once having united their countries, rulers and citizens began to look for new territories to conquer. In 1521 a group of Spaniards conquered the Mexican kingdom of the Aztecs, leading Europe into an age of overseas conquest which would affect every part of the globe.

* Germany and part of Italy were supposedly united in the Holy Roman Empire. In fact, they were divided into so many rival states and kingdoms that neither country was unified until the nineteenth century.

The power of the Church

During the years between 1000 and 1520, the Roman Catholic Church enjoyed tremendous power. The control of religion over the money as well as the mind of the population can still be seen in the magnificent cathedrals which rose all over Europe in the newly wealthy towns. The leader of the Church, the Pope, was at times the most powerful man in Europe. In 1076 he was able to remove the Holy Roman Emperor, who could regain his crown only by standing in the snow for three days until he was permitted to beg the Pope for forgiveness.

In addition to directing the Church, the Pope ruled a large part of central Italy— and so his throne promised both influence and riches. The post was often held by power-hungry men who might or might not have deep religious feelings but who were excellent politicians. Pope Julius II, who commissioned Michelangelo to paint the ceiling of the Sistine Chapel, was also a soldier who led his own troops into battle.

Some things about this period may seem strange to us. But the Middle Ages and the Renaissance produced a remarkable culture whose politics, art forms, and ideas continue to play a major part in our lives.

The Jewish people entered this period with great hopes. We have seen how they developed well-to-do communities in Germany, France, and Christian Spain. Individual Jews had become important in business, and Rabbenu Gershom and Rashi had already brought European Jewry to scholarly renown.

What became of these hopes is the subject of the following chapters.

SUMMARY   *Europe began to emerge from the Dark Ages about the year 1000, and gradually evolved both the national divisions and the desire for international power which are a part of the modern world. At the same time, in the periods which are known as the High Middle Ages and the Renaissance, Europe developed a magnificent culture. The age was dominated by the power of the Catholic Church—a fact which had great consequences for the Jewish people.*

15

Catholic Europe
Versus the Jews

This chapter is as hard to write as it will be shocking to read.

One would like to write that the Jews became full partners in the European society whose trade and welfare they had done so much to promote.

But this is not true.

One would like to write that the brilliant culture of the High Middle Ages and Renaissance was joined with a brilliant regard for justice and humanity.

But this is not true.

One would like to write that the period of Catholic rule led to a civilization built on the gentle teachings of Jesus.

But this is not true.

The truth is that no individual, group, or nation has ever persecuted the Jewish people so often and so brutally over so many centuries as has the Roman Catholic Church; and this persecution was given its official and classic form during the Middle Ages and the Renaissance, the very time when the Church had its greatest power

to control, for good or evil, the minds and hearts of Europe.

Nor can all this be ignored as "ancient history." The anti-Jewish attitudes taught by the Church helped create a European society in which the Holocaust was possible. Indeed, some of the anti-Semitic laws of the Nazis came directly from laws of the medieval Church.

These are heavy charges, made with sadness, but the history which we must now tell will bear them out.

At first, Germany seemed to offer the Jews their greatest opportunity. It was, for example, the local archbishop who invited our people to settle in Speyer "to increase the honor of the town a thousandfold." The emperor approved of this, and as late 1090 he granted the Jews a charter which guaranteed freedom of travel, the right to own property, permission to deal with lawsuits between Jews in their own courts, and protection against the forcible conversion of their children to Christianity. The fact that he made a special point of offering such basic human rights proves that our people would not have enjoyed them under ordinary circumstances. Still, his royal decree seemed to offer real safety for the present, and the hope of even better conditions in the future.

But only six years after the Jews of Speyer received this pledge of protection, their hopes—and the hopes of all medieval Jews—were destroyed. Their lives became a target for attack and persecution which continued for centuries in the name of the Church of Rome.

This sudden change came with the First Crusade.

The First Crusade

The Crusade was supposed to be a religious war to free the Holy Land from Muslim control. Many people were ready to fight simply for this purpose, but others entered the campaign for very different reasons. To Pope Urban II it was a chance to show his leadership over European Christendom. To the nobles, a war in the East offered the chance for adventure, booty, and conquest. To the merchants of Italy, it meant reopening the trade routes in the Near East which had been blocked by the Muslims. Thus, the armies of Europe were united for the sake of religion, power, and greed; and with these strangely mixed motives, the first horde of Crusaders left for the Holy Land in 1096.

They traveled East through the Rhineland, where they came upon communities of Jews. Suddenly these soldiers of the cross, who were pledged to travel thousands of miles to fight Muslims, realized that

they had "infidels" in their own lands. Why spare the "murderers of the Lord"? Ferociously the Crusaders attacked the Jewish sections of town after town: Cologne, Speyer, Worms, Mainz. . . . They left behind them charred ruins and the bodies of some 5000 massacred men, women, and children.

At last, the Christian armies did capture Jerusalem. The date was July 15, 1099, a day the soldiers went on a wild rampage of destruction, rape, and slaughter. The entire Jewish population was crowded into the chief synagogue and the building was set on fire. The Jewish community of the City of David was burned alive.

The Crusaders controlled Jerusalem for less than a century—in 1187 it was recaptured by the Egyptian Sultan Saladin. (This is the man in whose court Moses Maimonides was physician.) Such Muslim triumphs led to the calling of new Crusades, but the European armies which marched to Palestine were weak, and in 1291 the last Christian troops were expelled from the Holy Land.

Slanders against the Jews

The later Crusades brought fewer direct attacks to the Jews than the First had; or, more correctly, the Christian world no longer waited for wars before attacking the Jewish people. In 1144 the notorious "Blood Libel" was invented in England. This was the fantastic charge that murder of Christians was a part of Jewish law and ritual, and that Christian blood was a necessary ingredient of Passover matzah. This notion was sheer nonsense. (In fact, the Blood Libel was first used by the Romans against the early Christians!)

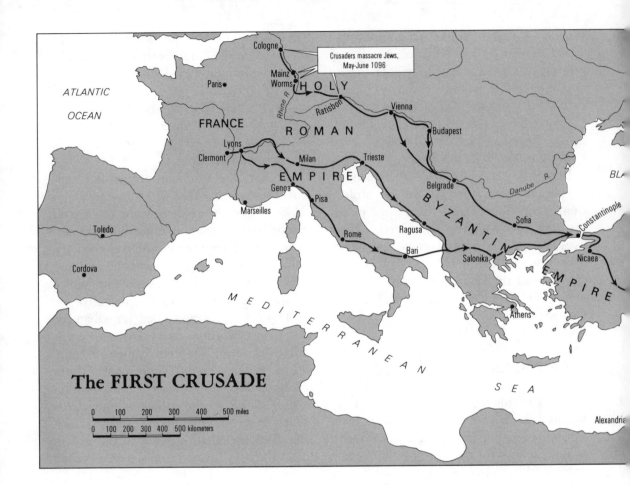

The **FIRST CRUSADE**

Nevertheless, this idea was picked up and repeated on the European mainland. The "guilty" Jews were massacred, their property taken, and the goods given to the local church. More than a few parishes gained sudden wealth from such attacks.

Another slander of slightly later origin was that of "desecrating the Host." The Host is a wafer of unleavened bread which, according to Catholic belief, becomes the body of Jesus during their religious service. Jews were accused of stealing the wafer and torturing it. It was even said that they had been able to force the blood of the suffering Jesus to flow from it! Silly as all this sounds, it was given as a reason for waves of violence that in one case alone resulted in attacks on 140 Jewish communities.

If the Jews could be made to suffer for events which had never taken place, they were certain to be blamed for any real disaster. When wells went bad, for example, Jews were blamed for poisoning them. Thus, for our people, every calamity struck twice: the event itself, and the punishment for having caused it.

The most widespread example of this injustice occurred when the Jews were named as the cause of the Black Death, a plague which killed about a third of the population of Europe in 1348 and 1349.

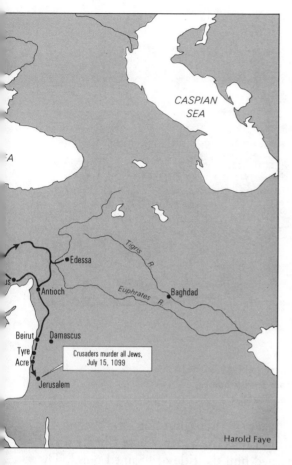

CASPIAN
SEA

Edessa

Tigris R.

Antioch

Euphrates R.   Baghdad

Beirut   Damascus

Tyre

Acre   Crusaders murder all Jews,
July 15, 1099

Jerusalem

Harold Faye

This map shows the main routes of the First Crusaders, who traveled from west to east between 1096 and 1099 c.e. Altogether, at least 5000 Jews in Germany, plus the whole Jewish population of Jerusalem, were murdered by the Crusaders. Here are two things to consider: (1) Today you can fly from Cologne to Jerusalem in less than five hours, yet it took the Crusaders over three years to finish the trip. Why? How did the Crusaders travel? What enemies did they meet? (2) Follow the main Crusade routes with your finger. From the cities you see, can you figure out the current names of the countries the Crusaders passed through? In particular, you may notice that the name "Germany" does not appear on the map. During this period, all of what we now call Germany and most of Italy were included in the Holy Roman Empire. The Empire also contained part of France and all of the lands which now make up Austria and Czechoslovakia.

The Jewish people, because of their superior knowledge of health and medicine, did have a somewhat lower death rate than the Christian community, but they too suffered heavy losses—clear proof that they had not set out to infect Christians. Nevertheless, many Jews were murdered—even in healthy towns which hoped that by killing their Jews they could escape the dread disease.

Anti-Jewish laws

Some Popes argued against the worst excesses of the Christian communities, especially the Blood Libel, but their words had little effect—in part because Church laws were themselves anti-Jewish. At the Fourth Lateran Council, a meeting of Catholic officials in 1215, Pope Innocent III announced measures designed to keep the Jews in a permanent state of humiliation. His goal was to break the soul of the Jews and force them to baptism or, failing that, to reduce them to a condition which would prove that the Lord hated those who refused to worship Jesus as the son of God.

According to the new laws, Jews were to be totally isolated from the Christian world. Jews and Christians were forbidden to live in the same house. No Jew was to

Twenty-four wagon loads of Talmudic manuscripts were publicly burned
in Paris in 1242. The sacred books had been taken from Jewish homes
by French police while the Jews were in synagogue on Shabbat.

be appointed to any office which gave him control over a Christian. Jews were forbidden to leave their buildings or even to open their shutters on Easter, to make sure that they would not "insult" Christians on that holiday.

Finally, to make sure that no Christian would accidentally become friendly with an unbeliever, Jews were required to wear a special hat or badge whenever they appeared in public. Like the Blood Libel, this anti-Jewish practice survived to modern times: Jews were again forced to wear distinctive badges by the Nazis.

Attacks on Jewish learning

Beyond this, the Christian world tried to destroy Jewish scholarship. In France a wave of book-burning was begun by King Louis IX, a man whose Christian zeal earned him the title of "Saint Louis." The Talmud was tried for blasphemy as if it were a person, found guilty, and sentenced to be burned. In 1242, twenty-four wagon loads of Talmudic manuscripts were fed to a huge bonfire in the streets of Paris. Persecution such as this had a disastrous effect on Jewish scholarship, and the academies that had grown up in northern France since the time of Rashi were closed.

The French example was followed elsewhere in Europe. In the following years and centuries more than twenty public burnings of the Talmud were held in Rome, Barcelona, and other cities.

On top of that, an effort was made to bring the teachings of Judaism into public scorn. The method used was the "disputation"—a formal discussion of the teachings of Judaism and Christianity between spokesmen for each religion, conducted by a government or Church official. These were supposed to be fair debates. In fact, the Jews were placed in an almost impossible position: a weak defense of their religion would be a disgrace, but a strong defense that could be interpreted as critical of Christianity was punishable as a crime.

The most famous disputation was held in Barcelona in 1263 in the presence of the king of Aragon and his court. The Jewish spokesman was a sixty-nine-year-old scholar and physician, Rabbi Moses ben Naḥman, also known as Naḥmanides. He asked for and was promised the right of free speech during the debate, and freedom from prosecution for what he might say. Nevertheless, after arguing his position with strength and skill, he was forced to leave Spain.

The Jew as "Shylock"

In these ways the Christian world attacked both the body and soul of the Jew. One more target was left: his livelihood.

In the Early Middle Ages, Jews were found in every sort of occupation: agriculture, dyeing, silk-weaving, silver- and gold-working, glass-blowing, commerce, and many others. Thanks to their education and skills, they were a key element in many branches of European life. During the High Middle Ages, however, Christians learned many of these profitable trades and then forced our people out of areas where they offered competition. Jews were forbidden to farm. They were kept out of the new craft unions (guilds). They were even forced out of interna-

tional commerce, a trade they had sustained for so long.

One field was left open to them: moneylending. In any growing economy, businessmen need to borrow money for new projects. When they make profits, they repay their loans, plus an additional percentage in interest as payment for use of the money. Today, bankers who provide such funds are a respected part of the business world, but in medieval times lending money at interest was regarded by the Church as the sin of "usury" and forbidden to Christians. The need for loans remained, however, and so Jews were invited—then forced—to become the moneylenders of Europe.

Thus, the Jew found himself in a neces-

The Jewish moneylender (seated) performed an important job, but was often hated for it.

Nahmanides (left) was promised the right of free speech during the Disputation of Barcelona, held before the king of Aragon. But the king had him exiled anyway, after demands from Christian fanatics.

sary but hated profession, maintaining the flow of cash into the pockets of Christian princes. He had to face not only the usual risks of lending—what if the borrower is unable to repay his loan?—but also dangers connected with his insecure position. Ordinary borrowers might accuse him of ritual murder or desecrating the Host, organize a riot, and kill him. Kings might simply refuse to pay, threatening the "infidel moneylender" with imprisonment or death. Under such conditions, when large losses were common, interest rates had to be very high. This fueled the hatred of the masses, who were convinced that the Jews were geting rich by bleeding poor Christians.

In this way, the stereotype of the crafty, money-mad Jew was born. This idea has poisoned Jewish-Christian relations ever since. The most famous example dates from late in the sixteenth century: Shylock in Shakespeare's *The Merchant of Venice*. Even today some dictionaries define "to jew" as "to get the better of in bargaining, as by sharp practices."

Actually, the Jews did not even control the dangerous and degrading field of

A Letter from Jerusalem

Forced to leave Spain, Nahmanides made the hard and danger-ous voyage to Palestine in 1267. By then Jerusalem had en-dured over a century of fighting between Christians and Mus-lims; and only a few years before, the Tatars, a warlike people from Asia, had sacked the Holy City. Finding himself at last in Jerusalem, Nahmanides wrote this emotional letter to his son in Spain:

I write you this letter from Jerusalem, the Holy City, for, thank God, I arrived safely in Jerusalem on the 9th day of Elul and shall remain there till the day after Yom Kippur, at which time I intend to visit Hebron, where our forefathers are buried, in order to pray at their graves and prepare a burial site for myself.

What shall I relate about the conditions in the land? There is large-scale destruction and ruin; in sum, the holier the site, the more severe the damage. Jerusalem is the most decimated of all the cities in Palestine, and Judah is more blighted than Galilee. Nevertheless, Jerusalem is very fine; its inhabitants number almost 2000, of whom 300 are Christians, refugees from the ruler's sword. The Jews fled from the Tatars or were killed by them, so that only two Jewish brothers, clothes-dyers, remain. . . .

We encouraged them by acquiring a destroyed house whose pillars and beautiful dome remained untouched, which we converted into a synagogue. We were able to acquire it because the houses of the city were abandoned and anyone who wished could claim them. We each donated funds to its restitution, and we have dispatched messengers to Shechem to return the Torah scrolls which were sent there from Jerusalem for safekeeping during the Tatar onslaught. A synagogue will be erected there and services conducted, for many Jews continually arrive from Damascus and Mesopotamia and the other regions of Palestine. They come to see the Temple site and mourn over it. May He who has granted us to see Jerusalem in its ruin, allow us to witness its restoration. . . . May you, my son, and your brothers and all my household be permitted to see the good of Jerusalem and Zion's comfort.

Nahmanides' emotions must have been much like those felt by the ancient Hebrews as they returned from exile in Babylon some 1800 years earlier. They too beheld Jerusalem in ruins— and they too set about to restore it to its former glory.

The Jews and the Popes

The first Popes, like the earliest Christians, were born Jewish. In medieval times, there was at least one Pope who came from a Jewish family. His life may have given rise to a popular medieval legend about a "Jewish Pope." Add to this the fact that, during the High Middle Ages, Popes often had Jews as their personal physicians and you can see that history sometimes works in very curious ways. And few things in history are more curious than the ties between the Popes of Rome and the Jews of Europe.

The pattern was set by Gregory I (also called "Gregory the Great"), who was Pope from 590 to 604. First he said that no Jew could ever be the social superior or even the equal of any Christian. But he also said that Jews were protected by Church law from being physically hurt. This may not sound like much, but it was more than some later Popes—and many other Christians—were willing to admit.

Strangely enough, European Jews began to think of the Pope as a source of help for our people. In fact, a tradition grew up that when the Messiah came, he would personally come to see the Pope and convince him to allow the Jews to return to the Holy Land. In 1524 an African Jew, a false Messiah named David Reubeni, tried to do just that. (One historian has actually called Reubeni "the first Zionist.") He grandly entered Rome on a white horse, hoping to talk the Pope into approving a Catholic-Jewish mission to recapture Palestine. Of course, the scheme fell through—Reubeni later was burned at the stake—and the cause of Zionism had to wait another four centuries.

Would a Pope help the Jews? This Jewish delegation (right) called on Martin V in 1417 to find out.

Pictures in medieval Christian religious books often contained crude anti-Jewish propaganda. Here Isaiah announces the coming of the Messiah—which to Christians means Jesus—to a group of Jews who are either asleep or refuse to listen.

moneylending for very long. Clever Christians found ways to get around the usury laws, and once they had established themselves in the profession, they forced the Jews out of it.

This meant that Jews were no longer needed in the only trade they had been allowed to practice. They could be looked on as totally useless members of society. King after king breathed a sigh of relief as he freed himself of the "Jewish problem" by the simplest of all means: complete expulsion.

SUMMARY *The seeming progress which Jews were making as members of medieval society ended abruptly with the Crusader massacres of 1096. The centuries that followed were filled with horrors: attacks on the life and property of Jews, sometimes growing out of absurd superstitions like the Blood Libel; attacks on the Jewish soul by anti-Jewish laws, book-burning, and disputations; and attacks on Jewish professional life. When all efforts to convert the Jews failed, and and when they could be eliminated from their key roles in the economy, they were expelled.*

16

In the Lands
of Western Europe

In the last chapter, we saw the general pattern of Jewish life during the Middle Ages and the Renaissance; but the Jews did not, of course, live in a "general pattern." They lived in certain countries under certain conditions. Each land of Western Europe was different from the next, presenting its Jewish citizens with different opportunities and different problems.

Italy

Italy was by far the most tolerant of the Western lands. It is strange that, during centuries of Catholic oppression, Jews were safest in the country which held the throne of the Roman Church. There were several reasons for this odd situation.

First, the Italian peninsula was broken up into independent territories and rival city-states; under such conditions, no unified anti-Jewish policy could have been either set up or enforced. The area south of Rome, moreover, had been in touch with the Muslim world. There, through the 1200's, Jews were granted many of the rights they enjoyed in Spain. By the time the government in the south became oppressive, the northern city-states needed moneylenders and so permitted Jewish settlement.

Second was the power of the Popes, some of whom did speak out against anti-Jewish violence and the Blood Libel.

Last was the mood of the Italians themselves. The people who were to give birth to the ideals of the Renaissance had little taste for religious oppression. There were anti-Jewish uprisings, and the Blood Libel did appear in Italy, but the damage was small. Even the badge laws were hardly enforced until after the Renaissance. This seeming safety led to a small-scale Golden Age. Original scholarship thrived, and

Italy became the center of Hebrew printing.

German-speaking lands

Unlike the Jews of Italy, Jews in German-speaking lands did not have the tolerant people or the sometime help of the Popes, but they did have even greater political disorder. While one ruler might permit riot, libel, massacre, or expulsion, there was always another eager to welcome the Jews—at least until they had boosted the economy of his land. Then he too might take their property for himself and

send them to find new homes. The situation has aptly been called "a sad merry-go-round," but it kept a large number of Jews in German-speaking territories.

England

In England the Jews enjoyed a rapid rise and, after just two centuries, an equally rapid fall.

In 1066, when Norman armies sailed across the English Channel and overcame the Saxon troops, William the Conqueror became king of England. He soon called in Jewish moneylenders from France

In Italy, the most tolerant of the Christian lands, Jewish art, music, and scholarship flourished. How many scenes and characters can you recognize on this beautifully decorated seder plate?

to provide credit for his political and trade projects. As far as we know, these Jews were the first ever to enter the British Isles.

Others followed. Within a few generations, our people were taking part in British trade, lending money to the general population, and, above all, supplying funds to the crown. By the year 1200, the Jewish community numbered only 2500 families, one-tenth of 1 percent of the population—yet it paid one-seventh of the taxes of the entire kingdom! These facts show both the importance of our people to English society and the unfair tax rates they had to pay.

At first, the Jewish population seems to have been well received, but things had begun to worsen by the middle of the twelfth century. In the last chapter we mentioned that the Blood Libel first made its appearance in England. In 1189, at the beginning of the reign of king Richard I ("Richard the Lion-Hearted"), a wave of violence broke out against the Jews. The king issued an order protecting them; but he soon left Britain on the Third Crusade, and new riots began not much later. The worst was in York, where the Jews were trapped in the royal castle. They defended themselves as long as possible, and then followed the example of their leader, Rabbi Yom Tov, in taking their own lives. Those few who did not do so were killed by the Christian mob.

Finally, when Christian moneylenders arrived from Italy, the Jews lost all protection. The ruler at the time was Edward I, whom a popular modern history book describes as "all that a king should be . . . a good and honest man." In 1290 this "good and honest man" expelled all Jews from the country and seized the property

they were forced to leave behind. No Jews were allowed to settle in England for over 350 years.

France

The territory that is now France was, in the Middle Ages, divided into several parts. The area in the southeast, Provence, had rulers who were quite independent of the French king and who ruled over one of the happiest and wealthiest Jewish communities in Christian Europe. As late as the thirteenth century, Jews continued to enjoy the right to own property and carry on a trade. The Jewish physicians of Provence were famous throughout Europe, its Jewish financiers were active in government, and it was a center of Jewish learning.

Yet it was the broadmindedness and tolerance that were to prove the ruin of Provence. Certain Provençal Christians, who could see the faults and corruption of the Church, rejected Catholicism and preached their own form of Christianity. Pope Innocent III—the same man whose Fourth Lateran Council placed such severe restrictions on the Jews of Europe—launched a crusade against these Christian heretics, and against the Jews of Provence as well. When the country fell to Rome in 1215, the Jews of Christian Europe had lost their final outpost of opportunity.

The situation in the rest of France was more complex. Between 1182 and 1322 the Jews were expelled on five separate occasions, but each time they were recalled when their skills were needed. Then, in 1361, the French king John II was captured by England, and the Jews were requested by France to raise his enormous

As the centuries passed, more and more Jews were forced to wear
special clothes and badges like the ones in this French law code.

Since discovery could mean death, Marranos had to pray in secret.

ransom. In 1394, however, there was a new order of expulsion, and for the next two centuries hardly any Jews were allowed to live in areas under the French crown.

Christian Spain—"New Christians" and Marranos

Most tragic of all was the fate of the Jewish community in Christian Spain.

At first, the young Catholic states were happy to have the aid of Jewish skills. But as those new lands became stronger and stronger, the Gentile attitudes changed. The lot of the Jews became worse and worse, until in 1391 an anti-Jewish campaign by a fanatical priest resulted in riots all over Spain which lasted for several months. When they were over, 50,000 Jews had been killed and another 100,000 converted by force to Christianity.

The outcome of these forced baptisms was not what the Church had in mind. Catholic law stated that once a Jew was baptized, however unwillingly or insincerely, he was for all time a Christian and free from the restrictions of anti-Jewish legislation. The "New Christians," as the forced converts were called, soon took advantage of these conditions and succeeded in all areas of business and government— even in the Church! Many became committed to their new faith, but many others remained Jewish at heart and practiced Judaism in secret. Catholic Spaniards, who hated these people for their dishonest attitude toward Christianity and were jealous of them for their professional success, called them MARRANOS—swine.

When, in 1478, some "New Christians" were found celebrating Passover, Spanish Catholics demanded that all false converts be found and punished. In response, the

Church created a new organization—the INQUISITION—which was given the power of life and death over anyone thought to hold heretical beliefs. Judges could use any type of torture to produce a confession, though the prisoners were not allowed any real defense. Once having confessed, the "guilty" person could be banished, flogged, or burned at the stake. Punishment was often made into a public spectacle called an AUTO-DA-FÉ ("act of faith"). These mass executions were presented as entertainments in Spain and Portugal on more than 2000 occasions.

The Inquisition continued to exist until 1834, but by then new victims were hard to find. When it was abolished, the Inquisition had brought 400,000 people to trial in the name of the Roman Catholic Church, and had burned more than 30,000 of them at the stake.

Edicts of expulsion

Not satisfied with persecuting Marranos, the first Grand Inquisitor, Tomás de Torquemada, proposed in 1492 to expel all Jews from Spain. This plan appealed to the reigning queen, Isabella, and was accepted by her husband, King Ferdinand. Thus, the edict of expulsion was signed. There was opposition from her chief financial adviser—a learned Jew, Isaac Abravanel, who tried everything in his power to get the edict withdrawn. All he won was a two-day postponement of the edict. Strangely enough, the new date was the Jewish fast day of Tisha b'Av, the memorial of the destruction of the First and Second Temples.

That same day, three small ships set sail from the Spanish port of Cádiz heading west, on an expedition largely supported

---

The Underground Hero

The Jews have had a long history, and many heroes. Judah Maccabee was one—he defeated the armies of Antiochus IV and rededicated the Temple of Jerusalem. Johanan ben Zakkai was another—he had himself smuggled outside the walls of Jerusalem so he could keep the Jewish tradition alive through his teaching at Yavneh. While Judah Maccabee fought the enemies of Israel directly, Ben Zakkai defeated the Romans through cleverness and wisdom. Two different kinds of hero—two different types of heroism.

Were the Marranos heroes? Certainly they did not fight their Christian oppressors directly, like some Jews in the Middle Ages. Instead, they called themselves "New Christians" and observed their Judaism "underground." Their resistance was not dramatic, not what we usually think of as heroic—but they did resist. Against great odds, the Marranos kept their Judaism alive. In short, they survived as Jews. And through centuries of darkness, Judaism survived with them.

Tisha b'Av 1492 marked the official date of expulsion for all the Jews of Spain. On that day, or near it, a scribe copying a Biblical manuscript in Toledo stopped his work and wrote on the page you see before you: "May salvation come speedily. . . ." The manuscript was finished five years later, in Turkey.

by Jews and Marranos—not, as legend would have it, by Queen Isabella pawning her jewels. Thus began the voyage of Christopher Columbus, en route to the land that would one day hold the world's largest Jewish community.

Spain had been a "new Jerusalem" for more than 700 years. Now the Jewish community was wiped out in a few months. More than a quarter of a million people were affected, and although some did convert to Christianity to avoid exile, the vast majority—including Isaac Abravanel—remained true to the Jewish faith and chose to leave Spain.

Some went to Portugal, but the fanatical Spanish queen demanded that they be forced to leave. The Portuguese ruler, Manuel I, gave in to her wish and in 1496

issued an edict of expulsion; but before it was put into effect, he ordered that all children between the ages of four and twenty be taken from their parents and converted to Christianity. Later he forcibly baptized most of the remaining adult Jews as well. Many managed to escape, but before long "New Christians" were forbidden to leave the country, and the Inquisition began its bloody work of searching out and punishing those who remained loyal to Judaism.

The fate of the Marranos

For those Marranos who remained in Spain and Portugal, life was dangerous indeed. To be found observing a Jewish ritual would mean certain imprisonment, probable death. Nevertheless, they secretly observed the most important holidays, especially the Sabbath, Passover, and the Day of Atonement. Jewish wedding services were held privately after a compulsory Catholic ceremony.

Children were not told of their true identity until they were old enough to keep the dangerous secret—usually Bar Mitzvah age. Imagine living for thirteen years as a Catholic, learning from your friends that Jews were horrible monsters, only to discover that *you* were Jewish and were expected to risk your life to learn about Judaism! Next day you would have had to return to your friends, never letting them know that anything had happened to you—though your whole life was suddenly different.

Most Jewish teaching was done at home by women, who often became the spiritual leaders of the Marrano communities. Of course, in the absence of books and schools, much knowledge was lost—even basic Hebrew was forgotten—but Jewish life was preserved with whatever bits of learning and tradition the people could remember.

We shall speak of those who found new homes in Section Five, but a word should be said of the fate of the Marranos. For a long time it seemed that the Inquisition had destroyed them all. Early in this century, however, Marrano colonies were discovered in villages of Portugal. Poor and mostly uneducated, these secret Jews had preserved their religion for more than 400 years. Though no longer in danger of the Inquisition, they continued to practice Judaism in hiding, preserving the traditions of secrecy which had so long preserved them. Even today, they still practice Judaism in secret.

Recently, a descendant of a New Christian family established a synagogue for his community, but even so the special form of Judaism developed by the Marranos may soon disappear. Young people have moved from the villages—a few to the land of Israel. Most of the Jews of Spain and Portugal today are those returning from other lands, for Jewish resettlement was permitted long before Spain officially abolished the edict of expulsion in 1968. Nevertheless, that some Marranos managed to survive, despite constant and deadly persecution, must be regarded as one of the most remarkable achievements of the Jewish spirit.

SUMMARY   *Conditions in the lands of Western Europe differed. Italy was the most tolerant country. Germany, though intolerant, was too divided politically to impose a large-scale anti-Jewish policy. Lands which were better organized expelled the Jews: England in 1290, France in 1394, Spain in 1492, and Portugal in 1496 (forced conversion followed in 1497). The Marranos, who remained secretly loyal to Judaism in Spain and Portugal, were hunted relentlessly by the Inquisition; but some managed to survive and retain their distinctive identity to the present day.*

17
Jewish Resistance

Our ancestors used every available way to resist the attacks against them.

When their communities were invaded, the Jewish people fought back with all their strength. One account tells how the Jews of Mainz resisted the Crusader attack of 1096. They had bribed the bishop, hoping he would give them the protection of his palace and his soldiers:

> With fluttering banners the [Crusader] army drew up before the bishop's castle. But the sons of the holy covenant [the Jews] knew no trembling in the face of these mighty numbers of the enemy. All of them, strong or weak, put on armor and girded on swords. Rabbi Kalonymos ben Meshullam led them. . . . Cruelly the combat raged . . . our enemies prevailed against us and streamed into the castle. The bishop's men, pledged to help us, fled and delivered us into the hands of the wicked.

The Jewish communities were simply too small to defeat the rioting Christian hordes. Jews in town after town met destruction and death.

Kiddush ha-shem and tzedakah

But death was not what was most feared by the medieval Jews. If they were captured, they would be commanded to say that Jesus was the son of God, and would be tortured until agony forced them to do so.

Judaism teaches us the value of life, and Jewish law states that death is to be avoided whenever possible—but not at the cost of profaning the name of God. Many of our people tried to avoid this problem by killing themselves before they could fall into Christian hands.

Such a sacrifice was known as KIDDUSH HA - SHEM, קִדּוּשׁ הַשֵּׁם ("sanctifying God's name"), and it became all too common in the Middle Ages. The record of the attack on Mainz describes what kiddush ha-shem was like in heartrending detail:

> The women . . . slew first their sons and their daughters and then themselves. Many men, too, plucked up courage and slew their wives and their children and their servants. . . . Girls and young men and women who were betrothed looked out of the windows and cried, "Behold, O God, what we do to sanctify Thy holy Name and to avoid being forced to acknowledge the Crucified!"

To protect themselves, the members of the Jewish communities tried to help each other. The rich were remarkably generous to the poor. Of course, care for the poor has always been basic to our religion, so much so that the Hebrew language unites the concepts of "righteousness" and "charity" in a single word: TZEDAKAH (צְדָקָה). Kindness of this type had a special meaning in medieval times, when a rich man of to-day might easily be begging for help by tomorrow.

Abraham ibn Ezra

The Jews who were forced to leave their homes by the many orders of exile could count on help when they reached other Jewish communities. But the most remarkable of these homeless wanderers was not a victim of persecution. He had grown up during the Golden Age of Spain along with men like Judah ha-Levi and could have lived out his days in the comfort of Toledo. Nevertheless, when he was fifty years old he became deeply troubled —we are not sure why—and left his home forever. For the remaining twenty-four years of his life he traveled through the world, visiting France, England, Italy, and,

according to some, Israel and India. His name was Abraham ibn Ezra.

To the Jews he visited, he was like a messenger from another world, for he could translate the Arabic learning of Spanish Jewry into the Hebrew they could understand. They were already suffering from the Crusades, but the learning of Spain offered them wisdom and hope.

Ibn Ezra was not merely a translator of other people's words. He was a fine scholar who wrote many books—not easy to do while traveling constantly. His studies cover a great number of subjects, from Biblical commentary and Hebrew grammar to astronomy and mathematics. In addition to these accomplishments, he was a poet and physician.

Moreover, beyond the knowledge he taught, this marvelous man gave hope to others. Listening to his words, more than one person must have thought of the prophet Elijah, who had promised to return to earth dressed like a homeless beggar to announce the coming of the Messiah.

Difficult choices

Instead of the Messiah, however, the Jews of Europe found conditions which became ever worse. Some, unable to fight persecution any longer, agreed to be baptized. Certain converts actually turned against the Jews. The trial which led to the first burning of the Talmud in Paris was brought about by a convert. The Catholic spokesman in the disputation with Naḥmanides was a convert who had shown his zeal for his new religion by adopting the name Pablo Christiani. Another attack was led in Germany in 1509 by Johannes Pfefferkorn, a Jewish butcher who had

צרה שם קביר עזיאל אשופר עה י רבנצבין שם קוהר רי בן מהרין בן מהריין י ישׁ שׁם כתיפ ופיס ופה
ואם קל בתיוכו, וכל הנלילות ההם הולכם שם ומעואיב נדרים ונדבות   וזה עארת אמקים י

הרך החו י שד קבור אהרן הכהן עז י א כמע ה מנרהנעשו עליזכ יֶ ת נאן ישׁם מ
אוה שוח   וני פילין על קברו ואין מוש להם ותי שמעלים תופסים איך בכבוד בדל י
שד י איש   בות הנביא התרמה ההט ההט למרעה יהוא חמקום א
ה נחרשם להמפיל י ושׁ שֹׁם אילן בדול נוברי שׁ   חי
ונו נמלכוי שֹׁ וכשה לכו לחתבו לתן קם   פולה לבלו אתל י

Some Jews were able to escape persecution in Europe by leaving for the Holy Land. One such pilgrimage is recorded on this parchment scroll from sixteenth-century Italy.

converted to Catholicism to avoid being jailed as a thief.

In this last case, the Jews were defended by a renowned Christian scholar, Johannes Reuchlin. That a Christian had both the knowledge and the desire to defend Jewish literature gave the Jews hope for a time. But in 1520, Pope Leo X ruled against Reuchlin and the Jews and in favor of Pfefferkorn.

It is not surprising that, when faced with torture and other persecutions, some of our people deserted and even betrayed Judaism. Far more remarkable is that the great majority stood by their religion. For these millions, the best hope was to escape from the lands of persecution—but escape was not a simple matter. Travel was uncertain and dangerous at best, and new homes offered no guarantees of real safety. Most

of the Jews who were forced from England, for example, fled to France—and only a century later, France exiled their descendants.

In addition, the Jews of Europe were often forbidden to move from their homes. Though they were hated and despised, their skill in business made them valuable property. The nobleman who gained from their skills and tax payments was unwilling to lose them until he had taken all the Jews had.

A famous escape attempt was that of Meir of Rothenberg, a leading rabbi of Germany. In his old age, he tried to lead a group to the Holy Land; but their journey had hardly begun when they were captured, and the rabbi was thrown into prison. The German Jewish community was prepared to raise a lot of money to pay his ransom, but the rabbi refused to let this be done. He was afraid that if the emperor succeeded in squeezing huge sums from the Jews simply by imprisoning one of their leaders, every leader would become a victim and every community would be bled to bankruptcy. He stayed in prison for the remaining seven years of his life, still writing responsa, legal rulings, and poems.

Kabbalah

When all physical forms of resistance had been tried, when battle was useless and escape impossible, the Jews still had an unconquerable weapon: the mind. Though life became hopelessly dark, though persecution seemed endless, they could try to force their thoughts beyond the horrors of the ordinary world. If the people could only bring their spirits into direct contact with God. . . .

The effort to rise above ordinary thinking to a feeling of oneness with God is called mysticism. Jewish mysticism of the High Middle Ages was given the name KABBALAH, קַבָּלָה ("Tradition"). The person who practiced Kabbalah, the KABBALIST, gave much of his time to prayer and meditation in the hope that these would bring him a greater sense of the nearness of God.

He also searched for hidden meanings in the words of the Bible and in Jewish ritual. Kabbalah has in it much that is noble and beautiful, but also many strange and superstitious ideas, some of them from non-Jewish sources. Among these ideas was the belief that the letters of the Hebrew alphabet have magic powers. Some Kabbalists tried to use these powers to protect the community from misfortune and to hasten the coming of the Messiah.

This may not seem to make "sense," but Kabbalah was not supposed to meet standards of logic. Even seemingly meaningless ideas and practices could be used by the mystic in his attempt to arrive at a state of holiness.

Message of the "Zohar"

The key work of the Kabbalah is called the *Zohar*, זֹהַר ("Brilliance"). This was supposed to be the work of Simeon ben Yoḥai, a rabbi of the second century C.E. who, while hiding in a cave for thirteen years to avoid Roman persecution, was said to have spent his time meditating. Most modern scholars agree, however, that the *Zohar* was really written in the late thirteenth century by the Spaniard who said he found it—Moses de Leon.

What meanings do you see in this mazelike pattern? To the Kabbalist Moses Cordovero, it meant the way by which God rules the world.

In the Middle Ages

A medieval synagogue was not only a place where men went mornings and evenings for services; it was also a community center for meetings and parties, a hospital for the sick, and a rooming house for Jewish travelers. Moreover, the synagogue served as the Jewish schoolhouse. In fact, this function was so important that the Yiddish word for "synagogue" is *shul*—school.

The Ashkenazim, unlike the Sephardim, restricted school-work to religious subjects. For them the purpose of education was to teach knowledge of the Torah, strict observance of the laws of Judaism, and a dedication to God and Israel so complete that one was prepared, if necessary, to face martyrdom.

This did not mean that the lessons themselves were grim. On the contrary, special devices were invented to make studying attractive. For example, when a boy began studies at age five, Hebrew letters were written on his slate and then covered with honey, which he was permitted to lick off. This treat was intended to make his first day of school a joy, and to teach him that learning is sweet.

The educational system was unusually successful. The

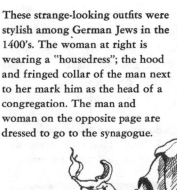

These strange-looking outfits were stylish among German Jews in the 1400's. The woman at right is wearing a "housedress"; the hood and fringed collar of the man next to her mark him as the head of a congregation. The man and woman on the opposite page are dressed to go to the synagogue.

Ashkenazim were famous for their piety and knowledge. Few
males did not know Hebrew, and learned Jews preferred
to speak Hebrew rather than Yiddish.

Girls did not attend school, but the average woman could
read, if not write, and knew many Hebrew words and much
Jewish lore. Moreover, she was thoroughly familiar with the
laws and customs through which homemaking became a
religious act. In short, she was likely to know more Hebraic
culture than today's better-educated Jewish woman. She was
as devoted to Judaism, and at least as willing to give her life
for her people, as the males around her. In addition, she might
well be familiar with business matters and have a firm hand in
her family's financial affairs.

Jews of the Middle Ages, as in most periods of our history,
dressed like the non-Jews among whom they lived. Often
(but not always) bearded, a Jewish man looked just like his
Christian neighbor. It was for this reason that the Church
required Jews to identify themselves with a visible sign—the
oddly pointed "Jewish hat," or a yellow circle on their
clothing (see page 139).

The *Zohar* teaches that God and man need each other—man's righteous acts bring God's presence into the universe. It also deals with the nature of God, the meaning of the Sabbath, and hidden meanings in the words of Torah. This combination of help, hope, and mysticism was quickly believed by the Jewish communities, and the *Zohar* soon ranked as a sacred text to be studied along with the Bible and the Talmud. For four centuries it brought comfort to those who could otherwise find neither sense nor hope in the world around them.

Jewish practice—our strongest weapon

The medieval Jew's strongest weapon of resistance was not Kabbalah or superstition or even study. It was the daily practice of what one might call "normal" Judaism. The Jewish calendar gave life meaning, rhythm, and variety. The very beginning of the service for the New Year brought even the most oppressed community a new glow of confidence and optimism: "With an everlasting love have You loved your children Israel, O our God." The High Holy Days continued with grandeur and ceremony, to be followed by the festive beauty of Sukkot. The long winter months were brightened with the joy of Ḥanukkah and the simple gaiety of Purim. The spring was highlighted by the celebration of Pesach, the festival of freedom and hope, and then by Shavuot, when the synagogues were decorated with leaves and flowers and the gift of the Torah was recalled with joy.

Each new moon was a special occasion. Each day had its own prayer services; but most important was the Sabbath, with its

The Rashi Synagogue at Worms, built more than 900 years ago and rebuilt in 1961. The yearly cycle of home and synagogue observance was—and is—the Jew's strongest weapon against oppression.

A Jewish Wedding in the Middle Ages

How old will you be when you get married? Twenty? Twenty-five? Perhaps older? If you were a woman in the Middle Ages, you might well be married by the age of fourteen and have several children by the time you were twenty. The marrying age for men was not much later—usually about eighteen, and sometimes as young as fourteen. One reason for such early marriages was that lifetimes were much shorter then. Another reason was the uncertainty of Jewish life. Why wait to get married until you had "made your fortune" when times might get worse and not better, and you might never make a fortune at all?

Of course you will want to marry a person you love. But the idea of marrying for love is a new one. In the Middle Ages, couples might not meet each other until they were already engaged. Marriages were arranged by parents; and from the twelfth century on, matches were usually made through the SHADCHAN (שַׁדְכָן), or "marriage broker." One important part of the marriage had to do with money: how much of a dowry, or wedding present, the bride would bring to her new husband was spelled out in the KETUBAH (כְּתֻבָּה), or "marriage contract."

Like the modern wedding, the medieval ceremony was a very happy affair. The celebration often started on a Friday and lasted for another seven days. A parade with fine musicians would lead the bride and groom to the synagogue. The wedding ceremony might be performed indoors or in the synagogue courtyard, and the couple would be married under a canopy (ḤUPPAH, חֻפָּה), a tradition since Rabbinic times. But a new tradition arose in the Middle Ages which we still hold to today—the wedding ring, which was introduced about 1200 years ago.

A medieval wedding
procession, with
ḥuppah (canopy)
and musicians.

weekly message of peace and rest. The world around the medieval Jews may have had little of the order and goodness pictured in the first chapters of the Torah, but with steady faith they stopped all work and joyfully honored the anniversary of the completion of God's creation.

New traditions were added to old. The Bar Mitzvah ceremony became a regular part of Jewish life during the medieval period. The Kol Nidre tune which opens the service of Yom Kippur eve was created in the Middle Ages.

In these last chapters we have pointed out a number of ways in which our lives were changed by the events of the Middle Ages and the Renaissance. No one of these, however, is as important as what we can learn from the period as a whole. The overriding fact is that our people survived a period whose horrors we really cannot imagine, while holding to a belief in generosity and humanity that we would do well to follow. Hopelessly weak in numbers, forced to bear every form of physical abuse, Jews still made their lives examples of spiritual strength and beauty.

The lesson is simple and clear, and yet remains hard for us to learn. Our people may win fame and fortune in many professions, and at times may enjoy wealth and renown. The real strength of the Jew, however, comes from none of these things. It comes from deep loyalty to Judaism, and to the Jewish people.

SUMMARY   *The Jews of the Middle Ages used every available means to resist oppression. Worldly responses included battle, martyrdom, escape, and in some cases conversion. Spiritual resistance was notable for the development of Jewish mysticism—Kabbalah. The greatest strength of the Jewish people came, however, from a steadfast commitment to the lasting forms and values of Jewish life.*

PART FIVE

Reformation and Enlightenment

The Age of the Ghetto

In Part Three we encountered a world in which the Jewish spirit had reached new heights of intellectual brilliance and accomplishment: the world of the Spanish Golden Age.

The world we are about to enter now is in some ways the complete reverse of that earlier time. In Spain, Jews had lived in relative friendship and prosperity among their neighbors. In the early modern period in Eastern Europe, by contrast, Jews were isolated in ghettos or in Jewish villages called shtetls. Relations between Jews and non-Jews were not common, and they were certainly not cordial. While a tiny few achieved economic success and political influence, most Jews lived in direst poverty.

Yet the amazing fact is that, in conditions so utterly different from those of the Golden Age, and so hostile to creations of the spirit, our forebears in Eastern Europe did indeed fashion a culture that was fully equal to its predecessor. Eastern Europe too had its poets, its thinkers,

The Ashkenazim

Poverty, isolation, persecution—the Ashkenazim endured for centuries the worst hardships the Christian world could inflict upon them. Yet in Germany and the lands of Eastern Europe, the Ashkenazim produced art and literature that wonderfully expressed the strength and joy of being Jewish. This eighteenth-century menorah, a masterpiece of ceremonial art, is now in the Jewish Museum in New York City.

its religious dreamers and mystics. And in later years it had its revolutionaries as well — Jews who saw through the degradation and impoverishment of their people to the unquenchable spark of national feeling that still burned within.

The ultimate expression of Eastern European Jewish culture was the language in which it was created, the language of Yiddish. Yiddish began as a language of commerce and the marketplace, a language of the home; it became a language of instruction in school and synagogue, and soon it became the language in which great works of art were created — that marvelous Jewish literature which has done so much to shape the way we Jews think about our immediate past.

In my introduction to Part Three, I noted that the world of the Golden Age seems very remote to us today. The world of the Eastern European Jews is not remote at all. It is the world of our own parents and grandparents, the Jewish world of yesterday.

ABBA EBAN

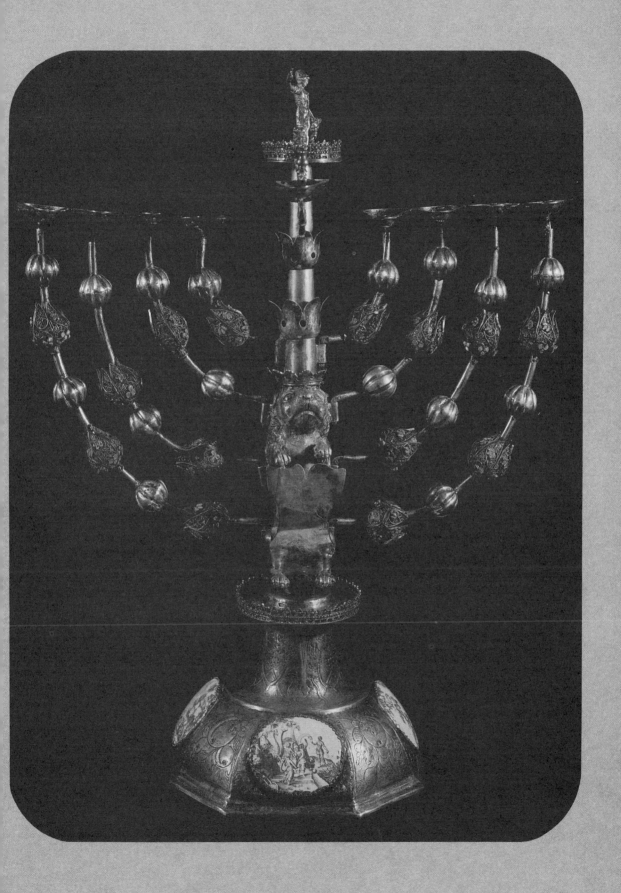

Jews first settled in Prague about 900 C.E., and Ashkenazic culture thrived there until the Holocaust. Right, the interior of the Alt-Neu (Old-New) Synagogue; below, an eighteenth-century ghetto scene.

The synagogues and ceremonial art of
Prague: (1) and (2) Torah ornaments
from the eighteenth century; (3) a
Torah cover from around 1800; (4) a
gilded Torah crown of the modern era;
(5) a modern synagogue in Spanish
style, built after World War II.
The Pinkas Synagogue (6), built during
the sixteenth century, has been
remodeled as a war memorial; its walls
bear the names of more than 77,000
Czechoslovak Jews killed by the Nazis.

3

1

4

2

5

6

These three photographs show the growth
of German Jewish art from simple, charming
drawings to astonishing heights of
detailed craftsmanship. The odd-looking
figures at right come from the *Birds'
Head Haggadah*. The birdlike faces were
probably used to avoid what the fourteenth-
century artist feared would be a violation
of the commandment to make no "graven
images"; note that each figure wears the
"Jewish hat" required of Jews by Christian
authorities. Below, from a slightly later
period, a Jewish schoolmaster drills
his pupil the hard way. You can see (at
bottom right) how brilliant Ashkenazic
art in Germany had become by the 1700's;
these ceiling panels from a synagogue in
Horb are now at Jerusalem's Israel Museum.

18

INTRODUCTION TO PART FIVE

Reformation and Enlightenment

The unity of Christendom was shattered in 1521. The direct cause of the Christian revolution was the work of one man, a moody, unpredictable German monk named Martin Luther.

Even as a young man, Luther had been troubled by the power of the Roman Church. He was one of many who spoke out against pleasure-loving Popes, ignorant and greedy priests, and the immoral actions of the people. Luther, however, also opposed some basic teachings of Catholicism. The Church ordered Luther's writings burned, excommunicated him, and had him declared an outlaw.

The Reformation and the Counter-Reformation

But it was impossible to stop his ideas from spreading. Many Germans had already been swayed by Luther's ideas, and many others were tired of seeing their religious lives controlled by Italians. Luther became a German hero, the champion of all protests against Catholicism and all demands for religious reform. This was the beginning of the *Protestant Reformation.*

One German state after another declared itself independent of the Church of Rome, and other nations soon followed. By 1581, just sixty years after Luther's break with Catholicism, England, Scotland, Switzerland, Denmark, Norway, Sweden, the Netherlands, and much of Germany were officially Protestant, and large Protestant minorities could be found in every country of Western and Central Europe except Spain, Portugal, and Italy.

The Roman Church met this challenge by holding fast to every idea that Luther had rejected, while at the same time re-

---

This section deals with:
    1521–1648   Reformation and
            Counter-Reformation
    1648–1789   Enlightenment
            (Age of Reason)

---

forming itself. During this *Counter-Reformation* the days of the high-living Popes were brought to an end, and steps were taken to make priests better educated.

Furthermore, the Church tried to increase control over the minds of Catholics. The Inquisition was given new power to root out and punish false believers. An *Index of Prohibited Books* was created— a list of works which Church members were forbidden to read on the grounds that they were a danger to faith and morals. During the four centuries of its existence, the *Index* included entire encyclopedias, novels like *The Three Musketeers*, and a great many important works of history, philosophy, and religion.

The growth of tolerance

Although Catholics and Protestants differed on many things during the Reformation and Counter-Reformation, there was one idea which they shared: intolerance. Each sect thought it had the one true religion and that no other kind of Christianity should be allowed. Luther, after having struggled to arrive at his personal faith, was cruel to those who wanted to seek their own religious beliefs. (In the same way, the Puritans, who came to America in 1620 to escape persecution, persecuted those who did not follow their teachings.) A few early Protestants did preach religious toleration, but they were hated by other Christians and were tortured and killed.

This left no room for compromise: Europe was split into armed camps, each inflamed with a mixture of religious passion and nationalistic pride. Horrible wars broke out—the worst came in 1618, when the Thirty Years' War began. In the next three decades a third of the German population was destroyed.

When this butchery finally ended in 1648, it was not because there had been a victory. Europe was simply too exhausted to continue fighting.

Yet if no side really won in these religious wars, the Pope and the Holy Roman Emperor clearly lost. The treaty which ended the Thirty Years' War stated that every ruler would decide for himself the religion his country would practice. This weakened the political power of the Pope and Emperor, and distributed it among the kings and princes of Europe.

As a result, many forms of Christianity were at last allowed to exist side by side. This was not the same as true toleration, for no prince was required to allow two versions of Christianity in the territory under his control, but it was a major step in the direction of religious freedom. Thinking people began to realize that there are many ways to think of God, no one of which can be proved absolutely right or wrong; they decided that it was immoral to kill others in the name of any one version of religious truth. Little by little, toleration of differing religious beliefs became part of the philosophy of Christian Europe.

Science and the "Age of Reason"

Another reason that Europeans became more tolerant of religious differences was that they had found a new kind of truth: science. Today we take science for granted, but until the seventeenth century, Christians as well as Jews believed that the only real source of truth was Scripture.

The REFORMATION in EUROPE
c. 1560

Roman Catholic

Protestant

Harold Faye

In Europe in 1560, countries or territories were either officially Catholic or officially Protestant; whether a country was Catholic or Protestant depended on the religion of the ruler. To simplify matters, this map considers Protestants as one group, but in fact there were several Protestant sects, of which the followers of Martin Luther (the Lutherans) were the most numerous. These Protestant sects disagreed about many things, but they were united in opposing the Catholic Church and the Pope. Shown on the outskirts of Europe are the Muslims and the Orthodox Christians. The Orthodox Christians refused to recognize the authority of the Pope (in this they were like the Protestants) and had split off from the Roman Catholic Church during the Middle Ages.

A beautiful wooden synagogue built at Wolpa, in Poland. During most of the Age of the Ghetto, Poland was the leading center of European Jewry.

In cases where they found a conflict between the use of reason and the teachings of religion, their question was whether *reason* might not be wrong. If a very serious conflict appeared, reason (and not religion) was discarded. For example, the scientist Galileo performed experiments proving that the sun is the center of the solar system; but this flatly opposed the Church teaching that the earth was the center of God's universe. The Inquisition brought Galileo to trial in 1633 and forced him to say that his own discoveries were false.

However, facts could not be held back for very long. One discovery followed another; throughout Europe, science was recognized as a key to knowledge, and people turned from thinking and arguing about religion to a fascination with logical reasoning. The new era became known as "The Age of Reason" or "The Enlightenment."

Equality—for some

Faith in science led to another major change. The powerful kings who took control of Europe after the Thirty Years' War thought God had picked them to rule by "divine right." A king like Louis XIV of France wanted to be treated almost like a god, and built huge palaces to his own glory. The nobles who served the king thought they shared his God-given right to rule the destinies of the "common people."

These arguments did not hold up under scientific investigation. Under a microscope, the blood of a king looked the same as that of a peasant. Slowly, Christian Europe moved toward the idea which Judaism had taught for thousands of years —that all people are equal. The classic statement of this Enlightenment belief was written in America by the scientist, philosopher, and politician Thomas Jefferson:

We hold these Truths to be self-evident, that all Men are created equal, that they are endowed by their Creator with certain unalienable Rights, that among these are Life, Liberty, and the Pursuit of Happiness.

These are the key words of the Declaration of Independence—the declaration of America's independence not just from England but also from the beliefs of the Middle Ages. No longer would kings be regarded as gods. No longer would "the Creator" have to be defined in terms of any single religion. No longer would earthly life be thought of as a place of suffering designed as a gateway to a Christian heaven. All people were to be equal, with an equal God-given right to earthly happiness.

The aristocrats of Europe did not, of course, accept these new beliefs, which attacked the roots of their privilege and power. England went to war to hold onto its New World colonies, and the rulers of Europe prepared to resist change in their own lands. The victory of the Americans encouraged liberals in France, however, and there, in 1789, the first European revolution broke out. With cries of *Liberté! Egalité! Fraternité!* ("Liberty! Equality! Brotherhood!") the French took up the struggle for national and personal independence which has been the keynote of the modern age.

Thus, in the course of the Enlightenment, Christian Europe came to know the principles of toleration and equality which had long been basic in Judaism. Surprisingly, the Jewish people played no direct part in this new age; nor, for the most part, did they gain from it. Just at the beginning of the Reformation period, the Jews of Europe were taken by their Christian rulers and locked away.

For the Jewish people, it was the Age of the Ghetto.

SUMMARY   *The division of Christendom during the Reformation and Counter-Reformation, the spectacle of useless bloodshed in religious wars, and the discoveries of science combined to bring about the Enlightenment.*
This was a time when the principles of the equality of man and toleration in religion became widespread.
Locked for the entire period within the walls of the ghetto, the Jews were largely isolated from these developments.

19

The Sixteenth
Century—In Isolation

A decree was sent to the Jews of Venice: Move all your possessions to certain buildings in the northern sector of the city.

From that day in 1516, Venetian Jews were allowed to live only within the walls of the area which had been assigned to them. Soon, their district was known by the Italian name for the nearby cannon factory—GHETTO.

The first official "ghetto" was born.

Origins of the ghetto

In a way, this event merely made legal what had been practiced for centuries. The Catholic Church had long been trying to keep Jews from mingling with Christians, especially since the Fourth Lateran Council of 1215. Jews, for their part, liked to live together, both from the natural desire to stay with one's own people and from the practical need to be within walking distance of the synagogue.

(The Ten Commandments order rest for animals as well as humans on the Sabbath, so Jews did not ride to services.) Some Jewish communities already lived behind walls they had built for their own protection.

Still, the ghetto system, as it was set up throughout Italy and Germany during the sixteenth century, did mark a major turning point in Jewish life. In the past there had been Christian homes in mostly Jewish areas, and vice versa. Now in community after community this was forbidden by law. Before the ghetto, there had been no easy way to control when Jews and Christians might meet. Now the ghetto gates were opened only during daylight hours—and not at all on Christian holidays. In the Gentile sector of the city, the laws requiring Jews to wear the Jewish badge were strictly enforced. And if a Jew was not back within the ghetto walls when the gates were shut at sundown, he was subject to a heavy fine.

What ghetto life was like

These anti-Jewish laws were often enforced in such a way as to make their effects even more serious than at first appeared. The places chosen for the ghettos were often in the most unhealthful sections of town. The assigned area soon became overcrowded—the population grew despite government laws limiting the number of Jewish marriages. Housing could only grow upward, and the "skyscrapers" of the ghetto were not always safe. Fire and disease were ever-present dangers.

Even in these terrible conditions the Jews could not feel secure. They were under pressure to convert and were often forced to hear Christian sermons urging them to be baptized. Heavy taxation was used to reduce them to poverty. Total expulsion was always a threat.

Nevertheless, the ghetto did have one good point: it gave the Jews some freedom from mob attack. Such violence did occur from time to time, but for the most part the Jewish people were locked away so well that the Gentile world left them alone. Even though in the same period Christians were being burned at the stake for minor disagreements over Church doctine, the Jews of Italy and Germany were permitted to preach their beliefs quite openly, as long as they stayed within their ghetto walls.

The Jews of Venice

The buildings of the Venice ghetto still stand, offering an exciting glimpse into the world of the past. Far from being gloomy, they give stirring proof of what Jews could do even under difficult conditions.

The streets of the ghetto are narrow; seen from outside, the buildings are not impressive. These outsides were kept simple to avoid attracting attention or jealousy from Christians who might pass within the ghetto walls. When you enter the buildings, however, you find another world, a world of taste and beauty. It is amazing to discover in this tiny community, only a few blocks in length, five lovely synagogues, each built and used by a group from a different area of Europe.

The cultural leader of the community was Leo da Modena, a preacher whose fame was so great that Gentiles came to hear his sermons. Writings of all kinds were encouraged, and within a few years the city became a center of Jewish publishing. A number of ghetto writers became famous, including several gifted female poets.

A seventeenth-century synagogue in Venice.

In the Age of the Ghetto

Jewish life in the ghetto period was a continuation of life as it had developed during the Middle Ages.

The more well-to-do Jews in Europe enjoyed a diet in which beef was prominent, but the poorer people, particularly in Eastern Europe, usually ate dairy foods and vegetables. Because of their poverty and the general shortage of kosher meat, they could only slaughter animals for the Sabbath or festivals. The usual Shabbat treat was a chicken, whose bones then yielded the prized chicken soup which is still a Jewish specialty.

The existence forced on our people was often gloomy, but our ancestors resisted despair. Jewish humor came to the fore. Ḥelm, a real town in Poland, became for no particular reason the object of good-natured teasing, and the "wise men of Ḥelm," who are convinced of their own genius but are really fools, became a favorite subject of Jewish folklore.

The general atmosphere of ghetto life was restrained, but special events were a time for joyful festivities. Weddings featured gay entertainment. When local laws prohibited music making, a rabbi ordered the wedding moved to another locale where a proper celebration could be held.

Virtually every holiday had its special toys and games. The dreydel was created to enliven Ḥanukkah. On the ninth of Av, children armed themselves with wooden swords and played "Fighting the Turks" for possession of the land of Israel. (This was the sixteenth-century equivalent of "Cowboys and Indians.") On Purim there were masquerades, stage shows, and street parades.

Popular Yiddish literature, which arose in the Middle Ages, began to grow and expand in the ghetto period. It included epic poems and dramas based on the Bible, stories and songs about contemporary events, and some original nonreligious works. Simple and sentimental Yiddish prayers, used for private devotion by women and perhaps written by women, were very much in demand.

Probably the most notable Yiddish work of the period was never intended for publication: the memoirs of Gluekel of Hameln. She was a Jewish woman who, over a span of twenty-eight years, wrote a historical record of her life to pass on to her descendants. In it she tells much of interest about life in Germany around 1700, and gives details about her own life—the fact that she married at the age of fourteen, a description of how she raised her dozen children, and the financial advice she gave her husband!

Directly above, a quiet moment in the Cracow ghetto. The other three scenes show ghetto children at their studies, either at home or in school. The inward-looking world of the ghettos of Eastern Europe was smashed forever by the Nazis during World War II.

When Christians attacked the Jews of Prague, "Jewish meat-cutters rushed out with their choppers and drove the attackers from the town."

Prague—a center of learning

One can also visit the site of the Prague ghetto, though since the Nazis came little but the synagogue and cemetery are left of what was once the most celebrated Jewish community in Europe. Prague is now the capital of Czechoslovakia, but until modern times it was part of the Holy Roman Empire—the chief city of its large eastern province, Bohemia.

The origins of its ghetto date back six centuries before that of Venice. By about 900 C.E. there were so many Jews in Prague that they were granted a large site on which to build their own community. They slowly became known for outstanding scholarship—and for their seemingly secure life. When the plague reached Bohemia in 1349, for example, the Jews were protected from mob violence by the Holy Roman Emperor.

At the end of the sixteenth century, Prague gained new fame because of its chief rabbi, Judah Loew. Rabbi Judah was known in his own time for his piety and scholarship—he wrote many books of commentary, ethics, and law—but in later years he became even more famous as the hero of legends. Of these the best known was that of the GOLEM (גֹּלֶם), a robot-like creature which, it was said, the rabbi could bring to life by placing in its mouth a paper with the name of God written on it. The golem was able to do all sorts of tasks for its master and the community —though of course it only worked on weekdays, and rested on the Sabbath!

In the eighteenth century, Jews were allowed to serve as teachers and professors at the University of Prague. This school was one of the first European universities to admit Jewish students.

Yet even this highly favored community knew its share of horrors. As early as 1150 it was attacked by a Christian sect which had just been exiled from Bohemia. The Jews resisted successfully: "The Jewish meat-cutters rushed out with their choppers and drove the attackers from the town." After that, defenses were built which gave the settlement the appearance of a fortified ghetto. Nevertheless, 4000 Jewish men, women, and children were massacred in 1389. Several times, the Jews of Prague suffered terrible fires, heavy taxes, anti-Jewish laws, and even expulsion.

The Jews of Rome

If such events were unusual in Bohemia, they were commonplace in other ghettos of Europe. In Rome, for example, the Jews were herded into a tiny area which was regularly flooded by the River Tiber. The Popes who ruled the city imposed high taxes and oppressive laws. Jewish people were allowed to deal only in used goods,

The Old Jewish Cemetery of Prague is a silent memorial to the era when Prague was a center of Jewish life and learning. Among those buried here are Rabbi Judah Loew, famous as a scholar and as a subject of legend.

Legend says that Judah Loew had power over the golem, a robotlike creature who helped the Jews on weekdays but rested on the Sabbath.

making every Jew a ragpicker. The entire community was finally made bankrupt.

At the same time, the Roman Jews were under all sorts of mental pressures. Every year until 1850, they were forced to undergo a humiliating ceremony in which they had to beg for permission to live in their crowded and unhealthful homes. (In reality, of course, they had no way to escape to any better place and had to pay a heavy tax for staying put.) When walking out of the ghetto, the Jew, known by his badge, risked attack and abuse. In fact, he had only to step past the gate to be insulted with a quotation drawn from the book of Isaiah (65:2). It was carved in Hebrew and Latin on a church which stands to this day near Rome's modern synagogue, facing what was once the ghetto:

I have spread out My hands all the day to a rebellious people that walks in a way which is not good, after their own thoughts.

Ethics in the ghetto

Despite the terrible mental and physical pressures of ghetto life, Jewish society kept its high moral level.

The constant lack of housing, for example, meant that Jews might have begun bidding against each other for the available space. To meet this danger, the rabbis, adapting Talmudic law, ruled that no Jew could offer to pay a higher rent for a home than the person living there was already paying.

In ways such as this, Jewish ethics were an important part of daily life. Indeed, Jewish religion filled the life of the ghetto. On it, the Jews based their communal organization and their calendar. They learned their public and private duties, even on such questions as how to dress or the amount that could be spent to celebrate a wedding. Most of all, Judaism gave them a sense of holiness and of closeness to God. They held fast to their belief that all they had lived through was part of a divine plan. They were sure that poverty and persecution would one day be ended by the coming of the Messiah.

Since their religious heritage was the very key to community survival, Jews treated it with the greatest care and respect. There was no desire to change practices which were blessed by tradition. This feeling was made stronger by the work of a Jew who spent most of his life in freedom. He and his family were expelled from Spain in 1492, when he was only four, but after six years of wandering they were able to settle in Turkey under a tolerant government.

The boy's name was Joseph Karo.

Joseph Karo and the "Shulchan Aruch"

Karo must have grown to manhood hearing stories of the cruel exile from Spain, and perhaps this made him dream of the day when the Messiah would bring an end to suffering and injustice. In his thirties he became a follower of Solomon Molcho, a Portuguese Marrano who in 1525 publicly rejected Christianity and announced that the days of the Messiah were at hand. Molcho had so much charm and strength of character that he attracted many Jews and Christians—he even gained an audience with the Pope! In the end, however, he was arrested and burned at the stake, proudly proclaiming his Jewish identity and rejoicing that he could offer his body as a sacrifice to God.

This execution deeply moved Karo, who considered following Molcho's example by seeking a martyr's death. He soon realized, however, that he had already found a more important and positive way to give his life to Judaism. Ten years before, noting the many ways in which Jews practiced their religion, he had made it his task to unify the Jewish people by showing how Jewish ceremonies and laws *should* be observed.

He spent a lifetime on this task, working first in Turkey and then moving to Palestine to be among the Kabbalists at Safed. He read widely in the opinions of earlier sages and developed a range and depth of knowledge that made him the greatest authority of the era. His teachings were gathered in the *Shulchan Aruch*, שֻׁלְחָן עָרוּךְ ("Prepared Table"). In this work he set out detailed instructions on every part of Jewish life.

Ashkenazic Jews objected that Karo used too many Sephardic traditions in preparing his work. For this reason, a Polish rabbi, Moses Isserles, wrote an addition to the "Prepared Table," which he called the *Mapah*, מַפָּה ("Tablecloth"), giving the practices current among Ashkenazim. In this larger form, *Shulchan Aruch* became authoritative for the vast majority of Jews, and today it still remains the basis for Orthodox practice.

Growth of Yiddish

The isolation and traditionalism of Jewish scholarship was both reflected and increased by the fact that the Ashkenazim spoke their own language, Yiddish. This language had grown from an old German dialect which many of our people took with them when, about 1250, they fled from German oppression and settled in Poland. There it took on words and grammatical forms of the Slavic tongues, as well

The Wise Men of Ḥelm

The Jews of Europe would not let their spirits be broken by the suffering they experienced during the Age of the Ghetto. In their own rich language—Yiddish—they joked about their problems, and so made them easier to bear. These "Ḥelm stories," some of them hundreds of years old, show how our ancestors were able to develop a kind of "Jewish humor" that can still amuse us.

PAID TO WORRY

The people of Ḥelm were great worriers. If it rained—they worried there might be a flood. If it was sunny—they worried there might be a drought. They worried so much that they even worried about how much time they spent worrying. So they called a town meeting to deal with the problem of worry. After much discussion, someone suggested that the town appoint one person to do all the worrying. Yossel, the cobbler, would be hired by the entire community to do all its worrying, and he would be paid one ruble a week.

But just as the idea was about to be put to the vote, one wise man objected: "If Yossel is paid a ruble a week, what will *he* have to worry about?"

TOO FAST FOR A HORSE

A wise man of Ḥelm went to the marketplace to buy a horse.

"What a wonderful horse I have here—you won't go wrong," said the horse dealer. "A noble steed. Like the wind he gallops. If you leave Ḥelm at three in the morning, this horse will carry you to Lublin by six."

The wise man thought hard for a minute.

"No," he said at last. "This horse is no good. What in the world will I do in Lublin so early in the morning?"

THE COMING OF THE MESSIAH

Word reached Ḥelm that the Messiah was coming—in fact, he was only three hours away. Most people were overjoyed, but not Itzik, Ḥelm's leading landowner.

"What will I do now?" he asked his wife. "The house is still new, I just spent all our money to buy cattle, and the crops have just been planted!"

"Don't worry," she reassured him. "Think of everything we Jews have suffered—bondage in Egypt, the wickedness of Haman, all the persecutions year after year. All this the good Lord has helped us to overcome, and with just a little more help from Him, we will overcome the Messiah, too."

as many elements of Hebrew. This uniquely Jewish speech spread both east and west, until it became the language of Northern European Jewry from Holland to Russia.

Yiddish was written in Hebrew characters, which meant that the education children received in synagogue Hebrew schools made it possible for them to read and write their own Jewish dialect. It also meant, on the other hand, that not just the words they spoke but even the alphabet they wrote divided them from the Gentile world.

The ghetto wall had more than done its job. In isolating the Jews both physically and mentally, it had led to traditionalism and resistance to change. This way of life gave our people remarkable strength and endurance in the face of pressures from the Christian community—but Jewish intellectual life grew weaker.

SUMMARY   *The development of the ghetto system was the result of the Church's attempt to separate the Jew from Christian society. While it offered the Jews a certain degree of security, for most Jews the ghetto meant terrible overcrowding in unhealthful and dangerous conditions, and continuing intellectual and monetary pressures of all kinds. These circumstances led to dependence on tradition as the key to survival, a dependence reinforced by the work of Joseph Karo. Isolated from the non-Jewish world by walls, custom, laws, and even language, Jewish intellectual life declined.*

20
Lands of Hope

The Ottoman Empire was a huge collection of lands, conquered by warriors and ruled by a sultan in Constantinople. The Netherlands was (and is) a tiny European state, built by a sturdy middle class on a small bit of territory rescued from the North Sea. Yet they had one thing in common: they were the only countries which, during the dark days of the ghetto age, offered religious freedom to the Jewish people.

The Ottoman Empire

Perhaps you have never even heard of the Ottoman Empire, but it was a truly great power, one which controlled large sections of Europe and the Near East for centuries, and which played a key role in Jewish history. Moreover, it survived until 1922, when, reduced in size, it became the state of Turkey.

The Ottoman Turks gave homes to the majority of the exiles from Spain and Portugal. A large number of the refugees went to North Africa, which had not yet been conquered by the Ottomans, but far and away the largest group—some 100,000 Jews and Marranos—settled in Turkey itself. The city of Constantinople, which as capital of the Byzantine Empire had seen a thousand years of Jewish suffering, became under the Muslims a place of safety.*

The welcome which the Jews received was not only a matter of generosity. The Ottomans were an agricultural people who had become expert warriors, but they had little experience in commerce—an area in which the Jewish people were traditionally excellent. The sultan is said to have scoffed at the Spanish for exiling the Jews: "You call Ferdinand a wise king, he who makes his land poor and ours rich!"

Within decades of their arrival, Jews had

---

* The Byzantine Empire was the descendant of the Eastern Roman Empire. It survived until 1453 when its capital, Constantinople, was conquered by the Turks.

gained a large measure of control over the rich international trade in the eastern Mediterranean. By the middle of the sixteenth century, the Jews of Turkey had entered a "Golden Age" of their own, and many individuals rose to stations of importance and influence as physicians, financiers, and statesmen.

In the Holy Land

By 1517 the Turks had conquered Palestine, and this too brought great gains to our people. When the Ottomans took over the country, they found barely a thousand households and an economy on the brink of ruin. In a short time, immigrants revived the country and brought new riches to Jerusalem, Gaza, Acre, and Tiberias.

The largest and most important Jewish community was perched on the hills of Galilee in the ancient town of Safed. It thrived as a marketing center and as the home of a cloth and dyeing industry, but its greatest fame was as a city of learning. Many celebrated rabbis from Europe found refuge in Safed. Here was the great center of Kabbalah in which Joseph Karo wrote the *Shulchan Aruch*, and in which the popular Sabbath hymn "L'chah Dodi" was written.

Here also was the home of the awe-inspiring mystic, Rabbi Isaac Luria, who became known as ARI, אֲרִ"י ("The Lion"). He was quite young—he was only in his thirties when he died—but his followers thought of him as a saint, with more than human powers. His message that the days of the Messiah were not far off spread through world Jewry and had, as we shall see in the next chapter, explosive results.

Gracia Mendes

Within Turkey itself the Jewish community was led by two talented people: Gracia Mendes and her nephew Joseph Nasi.

Gracia Mendes was born in Portugal to a family of wealthy Marranos. Her husband and her brother-in-law were important bankers who died shortly after building a large financial firm. As a result, she found herself managing a family fortune of enormous size.

She used her wealth and power to help other Marranos escape from the Inquisition—Gracia Mendes became known as "The Angel of the Marranos"—but she too was forced to flee. In Italy her Jewish identity became known, and she was given a prison term which lasted for two years.

A portrait of a seventeenth-century Jewish woman in Turkish dress.

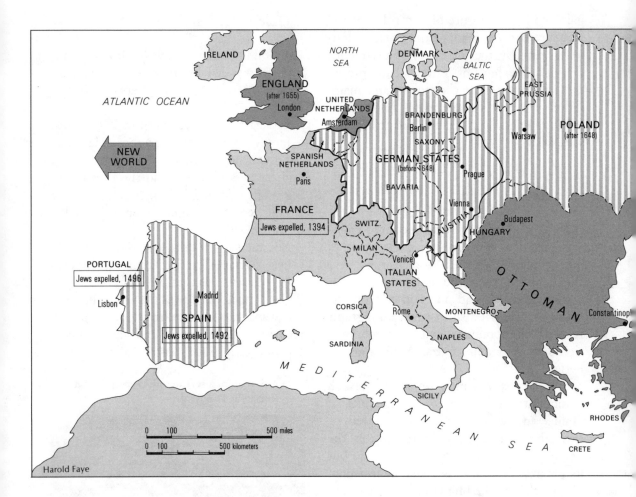

Harold Faye

Fortunately, at this time the physician of the Turkish sultan was a Jew, and he used his influence with his master to have her set free. In time, she settled in Constantinople and lived in great splendor, while continuing to build synagogues and schools, supporting charities, and resettling exiles.

She also took the lead in a unique effort at Jewish self-defense. When the Church sent some two dozen Marranos to the stake in the Italian port of Ancona, Gracia Mendes urged the Jews to fight back. She organized a boycott of that port by Jewish merchants and shipowners in an effort to ruin the city financially. This project failed, partly because many feared it would lead the Pope to seek revenge against other Jews, but it was the first attempt to use Jewish economic power as a weapon against persecution. It is also evidence of the power that a Jewish woman could have in the local and international life of the age.

Joseph Nasi

Joseph Nasi spent many of his early years traveling with Gracia Mendes and

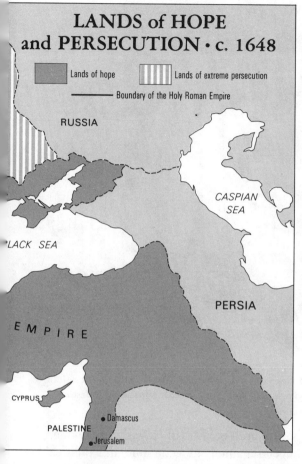

LANDS of HOPE and PERSECUTION · c. 1648

Lands of hope

Lands of extreme persecution

—— Boundary of the Holy Roman Empire

RUSSIA

CASPIAN SEA

BLACK SEA

PERSIA

EMPIRE

CYPRUS

• Damascus

PALESTINE

• Jerusalem

This map shows the main political divisions of Europe and the Middle East in 1648, the year the Thirty Years' War ended. You may want to compare this map to the one on pages 128–129. What empire has entirely disappeared since the time of the earlier map? What new empire has made its appearance? Does the Holy Roman Empire seem larger or smaller than before? You may have noticed that in 1648 there were *two* Netherlands: the United Netherlands was free and tolerant, while the Spanish Netherlands remained under the control of Catholic Spain. It is important to realize that the terms "lands of hope" and "lands of extreme persecution" can give no more than a general idea of where Jews were best and worst off. For example, Poland might have been considered a "land of hope" before 1648, and some German states in the eighteenth century were "lands of hope" for at least some of our people. The map also shows several countries which had expelled their Jewish citizens and where, for that reason, few or no Jews were living in 1648. Can you name any countries *not* shown on the map where Jews were living at this time?

taking part in her adventures, but after he joined her in Constantinople he rose to fame in his own right as adviser to the sultan. He served his ruler brilliantly through his worldwide diplomatic and commercial contacts, soon becoming one of the most important men in the empire. Ambassadors who wished to make treaties with the Turks had to visit Nasi and make their requests of him.

He was rewarded for his achievements with the gift of a group of islands in the Aegean Sea and the rank of "Duke of Naxos." In addition, he was granted control of Tiberias, a district in Palestine on the Sea of Galilee, to use as a home for Jewish refugees. He had the walls of the city rebuilt, imported silkworms and mulberry trees in order to start a silk industry, and called for immigrants. Unfortunately, the first shipload of Jewish settlers was captured by pirates and sold into slavery. After that, Joseph Nasi was too occupied with duties in Turkey to give the project the attention it needed, and it failed. Nevertheless, this must be counted as the first practical plan for the resettlement of Jews in their homeland, and a forerunner of the programs of modern Zionists.

Joseph Nasi and Gracia Mendes visit the Turkish sultan. The sultan helped Joseph with a plan to resettle Jewish refugees in Palestine.

Ottoman Jewry in perspective

The following centuries of Ottoman rule were not without periods of oppression, but for the most part the Jews of Turkey continued to enjoy toleration, as they do today. On the other hand, they never fully joined in Turkish life. Unlike the Jews of the Golden Age, who adopted the Arabic language of their Muslim rulers, the Jewish community in Turkey spoke their own mixture of Spanish and Hebrew, LADINO. (This, like Yiddish, is written in Hebrew characters.) Furthermore, although the Ottoman Empire survived until the twentieth century, it had entered a long period of decline by the late 1600's. This could be seen in the health and quality of Jewish life, which never regained the economic and political heights it had enjoyed in the sixteenth century.

None of this, however, is meant to downplay the accomplishments of the Ottoman Turks. Theirs was a nation great in achievements, and great in its kindness to the Jewish people at a time when we were oppressed throughout the rest of the world.

The Netherlands

The Netherlands, the second "land of hope," did not exist as an independent country during the great expulsion of 1492.

At that time, it was part of the kingdom of the Catholic Spaniards. During the Reformation, however, the people converted to Protestantism and revolted against their foreign lords, gaining full independence in 1579. (This country was known at the time as the United Netherlands, to distinguish it from the areas—now Belgium and Luxembourg—still held by Spain.)

Almost immediately, Marranos began escaping from Spain and Portugal to find safety in the new country. The first immigrants to Amsterdam were arrested while praying on the Day of Atonement—not because they were Jewish but because it was thought they were Portuguese Catholics in disguise! The error was soon explained, and the Jews were given the right to worship as they chose. In 1598 they were allowed to build a synagogue. News of this favorable treatment encouraged others to settle in Holland, and soon Amsterdam boasted a lively Jewish community of 400 families and a Hebrew press.

Yet the community had problems. The ex-Marranos had risked their lives for Judaism, but they knew very little about it, so they imported rabbis from Germany and Italy to teach them their religion. These men, faced with the task of rebuilding the Jewish faith for the Spanish and Portuguese exiles, imposed strict religious discipline. And it was just at this time that the Jews of Holland were faced with their most brilliant—but most independent—philosopher, Baruch Spinoza.

Baruch Spinoza

Spinoza rejected the Bible as a source of truth and built his beliefs on mathematical logic. He even said that God had not given His Law to Israel. This was an open break with the teachings of both Judaism and Christianity. The Jewish community was deeply troubled, not only because his philosophy might influence their own people but also because it could easily insult the beliefs of Dutch Protestants. The Jews were not yet citizens of Holland, and as a group living on toleration they could not afford to be thought of as revolutionaries.

The Jewish leaders tried to reach a compromise with him. They would not argue with his ideas if he would observe traditional practices and avoid teaching his views to young people. Spinoza refused.

Once a promising rabbinical student, Baruch Spinoza came to reject the teachings of both Judaism and Christianity.

He could accept no conditions which would keep him from thinking and speaking freely.

Discussions broke off, and Spinoza was excommunicated from the Jewish community at the age of twenty-four. From our point of view it seems sad that this happened to a man who was saintly in character and who was and is a major figure in world philosophy; but, in those times, it may well have been necessary. The result of the strong religious discipline was that the major outpost of Jewish life in Western Europe remained united and secure, free to take an active part in the life of one of the most forward-looking countries in Europe.

Toleration—a Dutch tradition

As usual, the Jews were good for the country which gave them good treatment.

In fact, Jewish merchants were so successful at building up the Dutch sea trade that other European monarchs invited Jewish settlers to work in their lands too.

Over the years, decent treatment for Jews became a proud Dutch tradition. Holland is the only European country with a fairly large Jewish population which has never persecuted its Jewish citizens. In fact, Dutch Christians risked their lives to protect their Jewish neighbors during the Nazi era, and continued to speak out on behalf of Israel during the Arab oil blockade of 1973–74.

England

The Dutch—Christians and Jews—were also responsible for two important new Jewish settlements: England and America.

In 1655 there had been no Jewish community in England for 365 years, but the

Spinoza tried to defend himself,
but the rabbis were not convinced.

time was ripe for a change. The English had executed their king and selected as their "Lord Protector" a Puritan, Oliver Cromwell. The Puritans believed strongly in the importance of our Bible (what Christians call the Old Testament), and it seemed likely that their leader would be helpful to the people who had brought the Hebrew scriptures to the world.

The movement for allowing Jews to return to England was headed by the leader of Dutch Jewry, Rabbi Menasseh ben Israel. He based his appeal on two totally different points. First, it was morally right that the Jews be allowed to live and worship in Britain. Second, according to an interpretation of a verse in the Torah (Deuteronomy 28:64), the Messiah would not come until the Jews were scattered to the corners of the world—which would have to include England.

Cromwell was favorably impressed. We do not know which idea was most important to him—messianic dreams, common decency, or the hope of profiting economically from Jewish skills—but he worked to bring his government to admit Jewish immigrants. Before long, Jews were allowed to live in England and to open a house of worship in the upper floor of a London house. By 1701 they had built a beautiful new synagogue. It still stands, a proud monument of the United Kingdom, which is now home for more than 400,000 of our people.

The New World

Finally, it was through the Dutch that Jews were permitted to settle in America.

Columbus discovered the New World just two months after the expulsion from

Rembrandt's portrait of Rabbi Menasseh ben Israel, the leader of Dutch Jewry.

Spain, but since Spain and Portugal took possession of the western hemisphere, it offered no refuge for Jews. Those Marranos who crossed the Atlantic were pursued by the Inquisition, which continued its brutal persecution in Mexico, Colombia, and Peru.

Thus, Jewish colonization could only follow the flag of the Netherlands. When the Dutch settled Brazil, the Jews gained a brief foothold in South America, but when Holland lost control of Brazil to Portugal, the Jews again had to flee.

Twenty-three headed for North America, but on the way they were captured by pirates who took them to sell as slaves. When it seemed only a miracle could save them, a storm drove the pirate ship onto a deserted island. There the Jews were stranded until, by chance, they were discovered and picked up by a French ship. Finally, in September 1654, the weary and impoverished refugees completed their fantastic voyage to the little community of New Amsterdam.

Though citizens of the colony gave them temporary shelter, the governor, Peter Stuyvesant, wrote to Holland asking that "the deceitful race—such hateful enemies and blasphemers of Christ—be not allowed to infect and trouble this colony." A bold petition from the Jews in Amsterdam and help from Jewish stockholders of the Dutch West India Company resulted in the denial of this cruel request. Ten years later, when the English took control of the colony and renamed it New York, the Jews had gained most of the rights of citizenship.

The group was a tiny one. Even by 1812 there were no more than 400. Nevertheless, thanks to the Dutch, they had founded what would one day be the largest Jewish community in the world.

SUMMARY   *When Spain and Portugal expelled their Jewish citizens, and most of the other communities of Europe persecuted them or locked them in ghettos, the Ottoman Empire provided sanctuaries in Turkey, Palestine, and North Africa. Later, the Netherlands became the first outpost of Jewish freedom in Western Europe and was important in obtaining new homes for Jews in both England and North America.*

21

The Seventeenth Century—Major Centers and Major Upheavals

The vast majority of the Jews who settled in Turkish and Dutch lands were Sephardim who had been exiled from Spain and Portugal. Most of the Ashkenazim, through choice or through need, remained in the lands of Central and Eastern Europe where they had been living for centuries. By far the largest group among them—the largest single Jewish community in Europe—was that of Poland, which in 1640 numbered 500,000.*

The Jews of Poland

Before 1240, there were few of our people in Poland, but in that year the country was largely ruined by invasions, and its king invited German merchants to go there

and rebuild the economy. Jews were among those who came, and they soon were succeeding in every branch of wholesale and retail trade, as well as in money-lending and industry. As persecution in Western Europe grew worse, more and more of our people fled east, until the Jewish community became a large and essential part of Polish economic life. At the same time, the nation also grew larger. At the end of the fourteenth century, Poland and Lithuania formed a federation which was as big as the Holy Roman Empire and was the greatest power in Eastern Europe.

The Jews who settled in Poland brought with them their love for knowledge, and Polish Jewry became famous for its high educational standards. Every child was taught to read and write, and any boy who showed talent was given almost unlimited chances to continue his Jewish studies.

* By comparison, even a century later there were only 300,000 Jews in Germany and 100,000 in all the other European communities combined.

Communities prided themselves on the number of students their rabbis could attract, and supported young scholars who could not otherwise afford higher education.

A brilliant student would be widely admired. Even if he were from a poor background, his learning might make him a likely husband for a rich man's daughter. Because of this respect for scholarship, Poland's teachers became the intellectual leaders of the entire European Jewish community.

Yet life in the East was not without its dark side. If the Jew brought from Germany his love for the scholarly and religious life, the German Christian brought his religious intolerance and his custom of political oppression. As early as 1264, the Polish king Boleslav the Pious had to issue a charter to protect the Jews from attack by their Gentile neighbors.

The Catholic Church worked hard to keep the Jews apart from the Christian population. While the Jew was not locked in a physical ghetto,* he was put into a spiritual one. The nobility used him only when profitable, and the general Christian community hated and feared him.

Separated in this way, the Jews concentrated on their own culture. They used the Polish language only for business with Gentiles, speaking Yiddish among themselves.

The absence of contact with the general culture caused a decline in the quality, though not the quantity, of Jewish studies, much as in the ghetto. Talmudists practiced PILPUL, פִּלְפּוּל (which means pepper), searching out problems in order to

solve them in clever ways. It was a nice mental exercise, but offered little real wisdom or inspiration.

Democratic institutions

In the middle of the sixteenth century, the Jewish population was forced to organize for collecting and paying taxes from their widely scattered communities. The Jews did this by setting up a structure which served not only as an agency of tax collection but also for Jewish self-government.

Each Jewish community, or KEHILLAH (קְהִילָה), voted for a governing committee to look after local affairs. It sent representatives to a provincial council which, in turn, was represented in a body called the "Council of the Four Lands" (וַעַד אַרְבַּע אֲרָצוֹת)—the one supreme governing body for the Jews of Eastern Europe.** In practice, only rabbis and members of the leading families were chosen to sit on these committees, yet the basic structure of the system was a remarkable expression of the democratic spirit of the Jewish people.

The Council had the power to make rulings and laws that were binding on all member communities. It also represented the Jewish people in dealings with the Polish government. The elected representatives were not paid, and so might have been corrupted by their connections with public officials. Instead, the Jewish leaders were known for their loyalty, piety, and scholarship. Thus, they deserved the confidence of their people and, for more than a cen-

---

* The famous Warsaw Ghetto was built much later, by the Nazis in 1940.

** The four "lands" were two divisions of Poland, one of Russia, and Lithuania.

tury, brought order and renown to the life of Polish Jewry.

Agents of hate

The situation in Germany was far worse. Anti-Jewish feelings were on the rise, especially among Protestants. In this they were led by Luther himself, who was angered when he found that Jews would not accept his version of Christianity any more than the teachings of the Catholics. In a vicious pamphlet, entitled "Of the Jews and their Lies," Luther urged that synagogues be set on fire and then buried forever, that Jewish homes also be de-stroyed, and that Jewish education be forbidden. His teachings led to the expulsion of the Jews from Saxony and to this day have provided fuel for anti-Semites, most notably the Nazis.

But suddenly, in 1648, the conditions of the two great Ashkenazic communities were reversed. In Germany, the Thirty Years' War ended and the Enlightenment began. In Poland, however, disaster arrived at the hands of the Cossacks.

The Cossacks were a people of southern Russia whose territory had been conquered by Poland. Under the leadership of the barbaric Bogdan Chmielnitski, they exploded in a revolt of terrible violence in which their anger against the Polish lords

---

Luther and the Jews

"Of the Jews and Their Lies," a pamphlet by Luther.

Martin Luther started out as a defender of the Jewish people. Luther's defense stemmed from his attack on the Roman Catholic Church and the Popes who led it. Since the Church had persecuted the Jews, Luther was against that, too. The Church had treated the Jews like dogs, he said—no wonder the Jewish people had turned their backs on Christianity. Some Jewish leaders actually thanked the Protestant reformer for what they thought was his defense of Judaism.

You may recall another religious reformer who started out as a friend of the Jews. That man was Muhammad. He felt sure at first that the Jews would flock to Islam and convert. He was furious when they did not, and soon became a bitter enemy. In the same way, Luther believed that our people would respond to his "kindness" by abandoning Judaism. In fact, Luther was as insistent on converting our people to Christianity as the Popes were. Only he thought his soft words would succeed where the Church's harsh measures had failed. When the Jews held firm to their faith, Luther became more and more bitter, finally outdoing the Popes in his denunciations of Judaism and the Jews.

Led by the bloodthirsty Bogdan Chmielnitski (center), the Cossacks went on a rampage through Poland, murdering thousands of Jews.

also turned against Jewish "infidels," some of whom had been used by the Poles as tax collectors. Hundreds of Jewish communities were burned to the ground, their men slaughtered, their women raped, their civilization destroyed. In the town of Nemirov alone, 6000 Jews were massacred in a single day.

This was only the beginning of the destruction which spread over Eastern Europe. No sooner were the Cossacks put down than the Russians invaded Lithuania from the east and the Swedish forces invaded Poland from the west. Even the Polish militia, once it had reconquered the territories taken by the Swedes, fell on the Jews with brutal fury.

In the ten years between 1648 and 1658 no fewer than 100,000 Jews were killed.

Others were forced to convert or sold as slaves. Only a fortunate few could escape as refugees to Hungary, Turkey, Holland, and Germany from the homes their families had known for four centuries and more.

Messianic hopes

In the face of these new horrors, the Jewish people seemed to have only one remaining hope: the Messiah.

The belief in the Messiah, the King who would bring the people of Israel back to their land and rule the world in peace and righteousness, had been part of Jewish thought for more than 1500 years.

Throughout the ages, even the most favored Jewish communities longed for the savior who would lead them back to Zion. Small wonder, then, that in the dark period which began with the expulsion from Spain, the dream of a miracle spread through the Jewish world.

By 1648, Jews were ready for a major event. Kabbalists had calculated that year as the date of the "birthpangs of the Messiah": horrible disasters would come before the Anointed King appeared. This prophecy seemed to be true when the Polish communities were destroyed. Some of those who were murdered in Poland died with a strange joy, convinced that their deaths would bring the Kingdom of God more quickly.

Shabbetai Zevi

And in that same year an odd young Jew, Shabbetai Zevi, entered the synagogue in his native town of Smyrna, Turkey. There he spoke out loud the Sacred Name of God—the first step in announcing that he was the long-awaited Redeemer of Israel.

Waiting for the Messiah

Can you imagine believing in someone so much that you would sell your home, pack up your belongings, and get ready to follow him down the road? Hundreds of thousands of Jews were ready to do just that for Shabbetai Zevi, the false Messiah. In her diary, Gluekel of Hameln recalls the excitement . . . and the disappointment.

About this time people began to talk of Shabbetai Zevi. . . . Many sold their houses and lands and all their possessions, for any day they hoped to be redeemed. My good father-in-law left his home in Hameln, abandoned his house and lands, and all his goodly furniture, and moved to Hildesheim. He sent on to us in Hamburg two enormous casks packed with linens and with peas, beans, dried meats, shredded prunes and like stuff, every manner of food that would keep. For the old man expected to sail any moment from Hamburg to the Holy Land.

More than a year the casks lay in my house. At length the old folks feared the meat and other edibles would rot; and they wrote us, we should open the casks and remove the foodstuffs, to save the linens from ruin. For three years the casks stood ready, and all this while my father-in-law awaited the signal to depart. But the Most High pleased otherwise.

Hundreds of Jews visited Shabbetai Zevi in prison, hoping he was the Messiah. How could anyone have imagined he would convert to Islam?

Shabbetai was accused of blasphemy and excommunicated, and so he left his homeland; but as he traveled through the Near East he gained more and more followers. A strange and beautiful woman who had escaped from the Polish massacres announced that she was meant to be the bride of the Messiah. Shabbetai sent for her, and they were married. News of the supposed Messiah traveled through Europe, creating a frenzy of excitement.

At last the year 1666 approached—the date which Jewish and Christian mystics believed was the beginning of the messianic era. Shabbetai set out for Constantinople, where the first event of his reign, the overthrow of the Ottoman sultan, was supposed to take place. The false Messiah was promptly arrested, but the Turks, eager to avoid violence, treated him with mercy. His followers were permitted to

visit him and serve him—all of which was seen by his disciples as further proof that he was truly the Chosen of God. Hundreds flocked to be near his jail, while hundreds of thousands all over Europe began to pack their belongings, waiting for the signal which would start them on their sacred journey to the Holy Land.

Finally, the sultan, urged by a Polish Kabbalist who accused Shabbetai of being a fake, decided to end the whole affair. He offered the would-be Messiah the choice of conversion to Islam or immediate death. With shameful speed, the self-proclaimed king of the Jews became a Muslim.

Many of his followers refused to believe that this was an act of cowardice. They explained it by talking of certain Kabbalistic mysteries and eagerly awaited Shabbetai's return in full glory as the true

Messiah. In Europe an "underground" movement developed, made up of Jews who still believed in Shabbetai. Despite the efforts of Jewish authorities to bring an end to this sad incident in our history, the "believers" did not completely disappear until the nineteenth century. In Turkey, others even followed Shabbetai by formally converting to Islam while secretly remaining Jewish. Some groups of these Shabbatean pseudo-Muslims still exist today.

Most of the Jewish world, however, reacted to Shabbetai's betrayal with shock, horror, and despair. The Jewish heart, stirred almost to the breaking point, returned to a cautious, quiet sanity in which the reign of the Messiah was seen as a distant goal. The ghetto closed in on itself in a kind of self-protection, seeking safety in rabbinic law.

This did not mean the end of messianic ideals in Judaism. In fact, they were reborn. The Jewish people, freed from the belief that a single man would soon remake the world miraculously, dedicated themselves to improving the world through their own actions. It was still hoped that one day the Messiah would come—Orthodox Jews continue to pray for a Messiah —but this hope no longer seems more important than the events of daily life.

As individuals, and in modern group efforts such as Reform Judaism, Jewish socialist movements, and Zionism, Jews have committed themselves to making life on earth more like the messianic age envisioned by the prophet Micah (4:4):

וְיָשְׁבוּ אִישׁ תַּחַת גַּפְנוֹ
וְתַחַת תְּאֵנָתוֹ וְאֵין מַחֲרִיד

They shall sit every man under his vine and under his fig tree, And none shall make them afraid.

SUMMARY *The largest Jewish community during the Reformation and Enlightenment was in Poland. The Polish community was not locked up in a ghetto, though religious and social conditions served to isolate the Jews from the Gentile community. Well-to-do, highly educated, and democratically governed, the Jews of Poland lived under comparatively good conditions—far better than those of the second largest community, in Germany—until 1648, when bloody massacres swept through Polish Jewry. The belief that these agonies were "the birthpangs of the Messiah" added to the messianic fervor of the age, which lasted until Shabbetai Zevi, the most famous of the false Messiahs, converted to Islam. After that, the messianic beliefs of Judaism became again a distant but noble goal.*

22

The Eighteenth Century — Mystics and Moderns

The beginning of the eighteenth century was the darkest period the Jews of Poland had ever known. Political and economic pressures were unbearable. Jewish lives were in constant danger of mob attack. Jewish souls were almost hopeless after the betrayal by Shabbetai Zevi.

Yet once again, Judaism adapted to the needs of an age. From the dreadful conditions of Eastern Europe, a new and vigorous religious movement emerged. That movement was called Hasidism (חֲסִידוּת), the "Religion of the Pious."

Ḥasidism

Polish Jewry had become divided into upper and lower classes, with all power in the hands of the wealthy and educated. The needs and interests of the poor and unlearned were often neglected or forgotten. Their religious beliefs were mixed with superstition, and at times they looked for leadership to wandering men who claimed to perform miracles by using the sacred name of God. Such a person was known as a Baal Shem, בַּעַל שֵׁם ("Master of the Name"), and his seemingly magical powers filled simple Jews with a mixture of awe and fear.

In the 1730's, however, a new sort of Baal Shem appeared. He was a teacher of extraordinary charm, a man of warmth and kindness and deep religious feeling. His real name was Israel ben Eliezer, but he was called the "Good Baal Shem." We know him by the name Baal Shem Tov, בַּעַל־שֵׁם־טוֹב . His followers also called him Besht (בֶּעְשְׁ"ט) for short.

The Baal Shem Tov

Though the Baal Shem Tov had studied Talmud, he found his true religious feelings in the marvels of the natural world. He felt that the Lord was to be found in the beauty of creation more than in the pages of a book, and could be reached through the heart more easily than with the mind. He urged his followers to speak to God through prayer—not merely the set prayers, offered in a set manner at set times, but in living prayer, filled with joy and excitement, with songs and dances.

Hasidism was not a system of belief but a way of thinking about God and religion —and it was a path which common people could easily follow. Feelings were seen as the key to reaching God, and lack of education was no longer viewed as an obstacle to Jewish involvement. In fact it could even be a help. In one of their many appealing stories, the Hasidim told of a simple man who did not know how to read the prayer book and so, in the synagogue, only recited the alphabet. Yet he did this with such deep feeling, and with such true desire to speak to the Lord, that of all the prayers offered by the congregation, his was the dearest to God.

Against Hasidism: the Vilna Gaon

In the generation which followed the death of the Baal Shem Tov in 1760,

Music, dancing, singing—the Baal Shem Tov and his followers, the Hasidim, found an ever-present joy in Judaism. They felt the way to reach God was not through scholarship but through feelings.

Ḥasidism gained hundreds of thousands of followers. It was adopted by a great many Jews in Eastern Europe—but there were many who fought long and hard against it. In Poland the new movement was banned by the Council of the Four Lands, though this did not stop its growth. In Lithuania it was met by a more powerful weapon— the opposition of one remarkable man.

This man was only a private citizen in the Lithuanian capital, Vilna. However, he had more power than either the city's official rabbinate or its famous Talmudic academies. His authority came from his great scholarship. He was a master of all standard Jewish texts; but unlike most Jews of his time, he also studied the sciences and was interested in such almost forgotten subjects as Hebrew grammar and the Palestinian Talmud. His name was Elijah ben Solomon, but he was given the title of Gaon and was known far and wide as the Vilna Gaon.*

Despite his fame, he was a very modest man who tried to stay out of the public eye. Instead of teaching in a school, for example, he worked privately with a few students. He avoided the debate over Ḥasidism for as long as he felt he could. Not until he felt the movement had become dangerous did he speak out; but when he did, his attack on Ḥasidism was strong and clear.

Ḥasidism was wrong, he said, not only because it changed ritual but because it attacked one of Judaism's most valuable tools—scholarship. Furthermore, it glorified feelings, while Jewish tradition, as well as modern science, proved the importance of reason.

* In this case, Gaon was an honorary title. The original Gaonate in Babylonia had passed out of existence many centuries before. (See pages 95–96.)

For a time, Eastern Europe was divided into two camps, the disciples of the Baal Shem Tov versus the followers of the Vilna Gaon (who were called MITNAGDIM, מִתְנַגְּדִים , which means "Opponents"). In time, each side became more tolerant: the Ḥasidim saw the importance of the traditional order, while the Mitnagdim began to understand the warmth and energy of the new forms.

But by then, the Ḥasidic movement was already in decline.

Strengths and weaknesses of the Ḥasidic movement

In the days of the Baal Shem Tov, the Ḥasidim had brought about revolutionary changes. Fifty years later, they had become very strict about their own traditions. Every detail of their brief past had been given a special meaning, and any change was regarded as a threat. Clothing style was fixed, so that, even today, whether in the cold regions of North America or in the hot climate of Israel, Ḥasidim wear the heavy garments and fur hats which were stylish—and practical— in eighteenth-century Poland.

Moreover, the movement had a continuing problem of leadership. Those who came after the Besht were known as ZADDIKIM, צַדִּיקִים ("Holy Men"). Every Zaddik had absolute control over his followers, who obeyed his commands without question. Each group of Ḥasidim was sure that its Zaddik had direct contact with God and was able to perform miracles. His words, his personality, his habits—all became the object of adoration. Some of the great Zaddikim were true examples of personal strength in faith and deed, but others turned their "courts" to their own advantage.

Nevertheless, the Ḥasidic movement has had very real achievements. It answered a deeply felt need in Jewish religious life and brought the oppressed masses back into living contact with Jewish values. Its spirit of creative religious feeling and ethical idealism has become a living part of modern Jewish thought, especially through the work of the philosopher Martin Buber, and its tales have inspired artists of all kinds. Furthermore, ḤABAD (חַבַּ״ד), a branch of Ḥasidism that grew up in eighteenth-century Lithuania, has operated on a more scholarly and intellectual level than the movement in Poland. Today, in the United States and elsewhere, this group runs an active educational program. It has also worked to reintroduce other Jews to Jewish traditions.

The Court Jew in Western Europe

Long before Ḥasidism swept over Eastern Europe, a slower but all-important change had begun in the West. As early as the Reformation, some German rulers began to feel that, even if the Jews were to be despised as a group, Jews as individuals could be extremely valuable. Once again, the states of the Holy Roman Empire needed men with financial skills, and these skills could often be found among the Jewish people.

And so the princes created a new rank—that of "privileged" or "Court" Jew. This was a man who, like the medieval money-lender, was expected to keep his master supplied with funds; but his duties went far beyond this. He was in charge of supplies for the prince's army. He was used as a messenger in diplomatic and military missions. He might even serve as one of the prince's leading political advisers.

Performing these varied duties was a demanding task; yet the challenge was met so well that, by the middle of the seventeenth century, almost every one of Germany's 300 principalities—even those with no Jewish people in the general population—was served by a Court Jew.

The Court Jew, for his part, gained privilege and wealth. He was free from oppressive laws—which ranged from vital matters, such as limits on the number of allowable Jewish marriages, to seemingly silly requirements that Jews buy specified amounts from a royal porcelain factory. He could live where he liked and, in many cases, he was allowed to enter the ranks of the nobility.

Still, his position was a lonely one. He was never truly accepted by the nobles among whom he lived; and although he might urge the cause of his fellow Jews and help relieve their suffering, he remained remote from the ghetto society of the Jewish masses.

Furthermore, he succeeded only as long as he could please his lord and as long as his lord was able to protect him. The dangers which a Court Jew faced can be seen in the career of Joseph Suess Oppenheimer, a man whose personal charm and financial connections brought him to power and wealth. For four years he served as the state counselor to the Duke of Wuerttemberg, yet the very day the Duke died, Oppenheimer was arrested and charged with treason. After an unfair trial, he was hanged, and his body was publicly displayed in an iron cage—an example to any Jew of the risks of entering public life.

Moses Mendelssohn

Moses Mendelssohn overcame many handicaps to
win the admiration of Jews as well as Gentiles.

Moses Mendelssohn

But the Jewish world was not easily
scared by acts of violence. Those who
saw opportunities for self-improvement
were prepared to follow the promising,
if dangerous, road from the ghetto which
the Court Jews had paved. Of these courageous men, the most outstanding was born
to the family of a poor Hebrew teacher
and Torah scribe named Mendel. The
child was called Moses, the son of Mendel
—or, as he became known to the world,
Moses Mendelssohn.

When he was only fourteen, Mendelssohn left his home in Dessau to follow his
teacher to Berlin. The boy was a pitiful
little figure—poor, frail, and hunchbacked
—but he had a brilliant mind which he
turned to both Jewish and secular subjects.

For seven years he studied in dreadful
poverty. At one time he even had to cut
notches in any loaf of bread he bought
to show himself how much he could eat
and still have enough left over for the
next day! At last he was able to find a
job in the home of a silk manufacturer,
and by working his way up in the business
he was able to earn a good living.

Meanwhile, his intellectual genius and
personal kindness had earned him a growing circle of friends. Of these, the most important was Gotthold Ephraim Lessing, a
writer who, before the two met, had
created a sensation with his play *The Jews*.
This was the first work by a Christian in
modern times to show our people in sympathetic terms. Lessing remained a spokesman for religious freedom all his life. His
later play *Nathan the Wise* was an appeal for toleration; the title character was
modeled on Moses Mendelssohn.

Lessing encouraged and guided his
friend's literary work, and gradually the
fame of the Jewish scholar spread. One of
his greatest honors was winning an essay
contest sponsored by the Berlin Academy
in which the runner-up was Immanuel
Kant, a man who became the most prominent German philosopher of the age. Before long, Mendelssohn, a physically un-
attractive member of a despised group, had
become a popular figure in the finest social
circles of Germany.

Jews and German culture

While moving from one triumph to
another among the Gentiles, Mendelssohn
kept a deep personal commitment to his
religion and his people. At that time, most
Jews spoke only Yiddish. Mendelssohn felt

that if they learned the German language, they could overcome the harmful effects of ghetto education. Then, as participants in European culture, they would inevitably be granted full legal equality.

This thought led him to his most important project, the translation of the Torah into German. The work was printed in Hebrew characters, so that readers could learn the correct pronunciation of German words while finding their meaning by setting them alongside the Hebrew text. His version of the Five Books of Moses was for many Jews their first taste of the language of the outside world. Using this as a starting point, a number of our people

---

Hasidism, Enlightenment, and the Modern World

The Enlightenment and Hasidism both grew out of the world of the 1700's. In many ways they were completely different. The Enlightenment in Germany (and later in Russia) called for the use of reason and science, while Hasidism in Eastern Europe thought more of feelings and beliefs. "Enlightened" Jews hoped that the non-Jewish world would accept the Jews as equals; Hasidic Jews turned their backs on the non-Jewish world and based their lives on Jewish attitudes and traditions.

The two movements also differed sharply in their choice of heroes. The Baal Shem Tov, the founder of Hasidism, was a man of great piety, a true nature lover, a wonderful story teller, but no scholar. Moses Mendelssohn, the leading figure of the Jewish Enlightenment, was also a pious man, but in addition he was one of the most brilliant scholars of his time.

How did two such different movements arise in the same era? The answer lies in the places where each began. Hasidism came out of Poland, where Jews had suffered terrible hardships: first the Chmielnitski massacres, then the tragedy of Shabbetai Zevi, and finally an invasion of armies from Russia. The Polish state was weak and its people were mostly backward. On the other hand, Germany was growing ever stronger and was open to all the newest ideas. Germany also had a rising merchant class, and many of these merchants were Jews.

Polish Jews had so few chances for success and happiness that they needed to find joy in the simple things of life—joy which Hasidism gave them. German Jews glimpsed a new world of opportunity which they could enter only if they mastered the tools of modern learning.

Street scene and synagogue
in Frankfurt—an artist's
view in 1711.

did master the language and culture of Germany, touching off a quiet revolution in Jewish intellectual life.

Mendelssohn died in 1786, three years before the French Revolution. To him, the future looked simple and bright: Jews would become better adjusted to European society, and Europeans would be more and more willing to accept them as equals. Unfortunately, the German language did not provide Jews with an entry into Gentile society, and the centuries that followed have not been as happy and enlightened as the philosopher believed they would be.

Nevertheless, he was right in seeing that the Jews would have to change rapidly if they were to become part of the modern world. This was to be the main theme of Jewish life in the centuries after Mendelssohn's death; and he, by introducing Jews to the speech of secular Europe, had given them the basic tool with which to face the challenges of the modern era.

SUMMARY *Two men were the outstanding leaders of Eastern European Jewry during the gloomy century which followed the catastrophe of Shabbetai Zevi. Israel ben Eliezer, the Baal Shem Tov, created a movement based on personal piety and emotional contact with God. His followers were called Ḥasidim. The Vilna Gaon, leading the Mitnagdim, stood for traditional Judaism and scholarship. But it was in Germany that the wave of the future—bringing the Jews into modern society— truly began. The first of our people to be accepted by German society were the Court Jews. The most prominent Jewish scholar, and the one who tried to prepare the Jews of the ghetto for secular society, was Moses Mendelssohn.*

PART SIX

A Glance at the Modern Era

The Age of Uncertain Freedom

As I stated in my first note to you, this book is intended to deal primarily with the period before the American Revolution. But I do not wish to break off our story before giving you an idea of how the world of the ghetto changed into the world we know today.

The modern period is, of course, the one in which I have played some part in the history of our people, and particularly in the history of the State of Israel. I was associated with Chaim Weizmann in his final days as political leader of Israel, when he secured President Truman's pledge to grant diplomatic recognition to the Jewish state. I was Ambassador to the United Nations (1949–59) when it was my job to win Israel's admission to the international community. As Ambassador to Washington (1950–59), I was close to the early development of the partnership between Israel and the United States. As Minister of Education and Culture (1960–63), I gained a very intimate view of our spiritual and intellectual problems. Later, as Foreign Minister of Israel, I

Israel and the Diaspora

In Israel and Egypt, Russia and America,
Australia and Ethiopia, Poland and Belgium.
Black faces, white faces . . . all shades between.
Old and young. At play and at prayer.
Of different continents and divergent customs.
What do all these people have in common?
They are all Jews, and sometimes, against
tremendous odds, have struggled to remain so.
They are—we are—one people.

---

had central responsibilities, especially during the Six-Day War (1967)
and the Yom Kippur War (1973).

It is possible that my judgments of recent events are colored by my
own likes and dislikes and by my own experiences. On the other
hand, most historians now admit that there is great value in histories
written by the people who actually helped make history. The man
who was there does not have to ask, speculatively, "Why do we
suppose these decisions were taken?" Instead he can say, "These,
to my certain knowledge, were the reasons and motives for our
actions."

ABBA EBAN

In the State of Israel, dancing the hora in the fields.

Because Jews from all over the world have flocked to the Jewish homeland, the State of Israel is nearly as diverse as the Diaspora itself. Above, an Orthodox Israeli praying; below, a Yemenite wedding in Jerusalem; opposite page, the Western Wall, the last physical link between the Jerusalem of today and the ancient Temple.

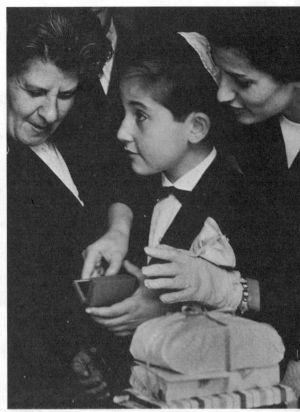

Opposite page: top left, a
shul in Antwerp, Belgium,
gets ready for Sukkoth; top
right, a German Bar Mitzvah
boy; bottom left, lighting
Shabbat candles in Germany;
bottom right, soccer-playing
Jewish schoolboys in Australia.
This page: above, a rabbi
from Cardiff, Wales; upper
right, elderly Jews in Russia;
lower right, a Jewish children's home near Warsaw.

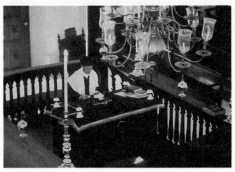

Ten thousand miles separate the two
synagogues shown above. The top
one is in Hong Kong; the one below
it is the famous Mikvé Israel on
the Caribbean island of Curaçao,
the oldest synagogue in the
New World.

Four Jewish communities in Africa, each with its own remarkable story. The Jews of Djerba (opposite page) first settled 2000 years ago on this island off the Tunisian coast. The oldest synagogue in Cairo (upper left) is still beautiful, but Egypt's Jews have fallen on hard times. No one quite knows how the Falashas of Ethiopia (lower left) came to be Jewish more than 2000 years ago. And the Jews of South Africa (shown above, celebrating Israel's twenty-fifth birthday) have long prospered but are now caught in the middle of an explosive racial conflict.

The largest, wealthiest, most influential Diaspora community is that of the United States, which throughout its history as a free nation has let our people live and worship wherever they chose. Above, the interior of a splendid modern temple, Congregation Beth Jacob of Columbus, Ohio; right, a quiet moment at Hanukkah.

INTRODUCTION TO PART SIX

The Modern Era

Late on the morning of April 19, 1775, British soldiers marched into the small town of Concord, Massachusetts, in search of weapons stored by the New England colonials. Suddenly rifles were shooting and the "Redcoats" were in retreat. The American Revolution had begun.

The first bullet fired in this battle may be said to have opened the modern period. It has been called "the shot heard round the world," because it began a war which led others to overthrow hated monarchs. France sent its king to the guillotine and established a republic. South America expelled the armies of Spain and Portugal. Italy and Germany freed themselves from foreign powers and became unified and independent.

But the modern age is full of problems. Though it was born from a burning desire for freedom, it has given rise to the worst dictatorships ever known. While it has developed tools which could create tremendous prosperity, it has invented weapons which can destroy civilization.

In this section we will try to give an account of this confusing era in which we live; or, rather, we will give a brief outline of it. Although we have already described the events of forty centuries in this book, it will take another volume just as large to deal properly with the last 200 years. We will need that much space because we know so much about the modern era—and, strange to say, because we know so little.

Understanding the present

We know "so much" because of our ability to record recent facts. A single daily newspaper contains more data than we have about entire decades, or even centuries, of earlier periods. And still we know "so little" because we cannot tell the end

Jews helped fight and finance the Revolutionary War. Haym Salomon,
a wealthy patriot, was once even called from prayer on Yom Kippur to
read an urgent plea from General Washington for funds for his army.

of our story. We know what happened to
Ancient Rome, we understand the signi-
ficance of the Middle Ages, but we can
only guess the future of our own world.

So in writing modern history we have
to tell all the things we feel *might* turn out
to be important; but even there we are
uncertain. It is interesting to realize that
many of the turning points in the story of
humanity—Abraham's journey to the
Promised Land, the Exodus from Egypt,
the establishment of Ben Zakkai's school
at Yavneh, the crucifixion of Jesus, and
Muhammad's flight from Mecca to Medina
—went almost unnoticed in their own
time. If newspapers had existed in the ancient world, they might not even have
mentioned these events.

Still, it is important that we try to bring
this book up to our own day, for the most
important fact about Jewish history is that
it *does* continue to the present. It does not
stop with the destruction of the Temple,
or with the expulsion from Spain, or with
the gas chambers of Hitler. The great fact
of Jewish existence is that we Jews have
survived every threat the world has offered. Today, stronger than ever, we play
a leading part in the cultural and spiritual
life of humanity.

Freedom and exploitation

The modern era has been one of extraordinary change for Jews and Gentiles

alike, largely because of the discoveries of science. While the civilization George Washington knew was in many ways like that of King Solomon—manufacturing was done by hand, the best transportation was provided by horses—the 1800's saw life totally changed. Machines began to produce more and more goods, which were moved from place to place on a vast international network of railroads.

This development of mechanical power is known as the Industrial Revolution. It created a wealth of new comforts and luxuries—benefits which were not, however, equally shared. Those who worked in factories and mines were forced to risk life and health to earn a few pennies a day, until laborers in North America and Western Europe organized unions to protect their rights. This was one of the ways the "common people" became more and more powerful; and through their progress, democracy increased.

In Eastern Europe, the home of most of the world's Jewish population, the situation was quite different. Despite a wave of revolutions, which reached flood tide in 1848, the old aristocracy kept control and crushed all liberal movements. Not until World War I were any real steps taken toward democracy, and these were soon wiped out by Fascist and Communist dictatorships.

While the struggle for freedom was a major force within many of the nations of Europe, their policy in Africa and Asia was one of colonization. This was spoken of as an attempt to modernize "primitive" areas, but it was really an effort to control the materials and markets needed to make Western merchants wealthy. In effect, Europe became the largest empire in history. England boasted that its terri-

tories were so widely spread about the globe that "the sun never sets on the British empire," and other nations could say the same.

Today we are living with the aftereffects of colonization and exploitation. Throughout much of the world we see oppressive governments and dictatorships, anti-Western attitudes, Communist-led revolutions, and the possibility of mass starvation. Nevertheless, it must be said that during the nineteenth century the world was remarkably peaceful. After 1815, when the French emperor Napoleon was defeated in his attempt to conquer Europe, ninety-nine years passed in which there were few major wars.

Then came the twentieth century, and society exploded.

The American trade union movement also found Jews in the forefront. Notice the Yiddish signs held by these striking clothiers in 1909.

Three
Revolutionary
Thinkers

These three European men of Jewish birth
changed the way we think about nature,
society, and ourselves. Above, Albert Einstein
(1879–1955): a great physicist, he also helped
many Zionist causes. Karl Marx (1818–83),
at upper right, was the father of the modern
socialist and Communist movements. The third
revolutionary, Sigmund Freud (1856–1939; at
right), founded psychoanalysis, a new way of
thinking about why we behave as we do.

The two world wars

World War I broke out in 1914 and lasted four terrible years. When peace returned to Europe in 1918, not only lives and property but also social structures that had lasted for centuries were destroyed. The empires of Eastern Europe, including the Ottoman Empire, were carved up. The czars were overthrown in Russia, where the Communists seized control.

The League of Nations was created in the hope of preventing another such catastrophe. It was a congress of many states, much like the United Nations in its ideals —and it too could not stop great powers from breaking international law. It suffered from the additional drawback that the United States refused to be a member. When real crisis came, the League was helpless.

In the 1930's, the world was plunged into a great economic depression. Germany, still feeling disgraced by its defeat in World War I and suffering from financial chaos, found new hope in a leader who promised to rebuild the nation.

His name was Adolf Hitler.

Hitler broke international treaties, rearmed his country, and occupied the territory of other states, saying that he was "liberating" their German citizens. At the same time, he withdrew all rights of citizenship from the German Jews. The rest of the world, fearful that resisting him would lead to another war, gave in to him in the continuing hope that he would be satisfied with "just a little more." Not until Hitler's armies invaded Poland in 1939 did the democracies of Europe see that he intended to conquer the globe. They fought back, and World War II began.

On December 7, 1941, the Japanese launched a surprise attack on the American naval base at Pearl Harbor, Hawaii. Now the United States joined the fighting, and World War II truly involved the whole world. It raged in both Europe and the Pacific until 1945, and did not end until two Japanese cities, Hiroshima and Nagasaki, were destroyed by atomic bombs.

The postwar era

In the postwar period, the Soviet Union and the United States became the most powerful nations on earth. Though the world leadership of Western Europe came to an end, the ideas of political freedom which had developed there took on new life. One after another of the European colonies in Africa and Asia demanded and received independence.

The results of this newfound freedom have not always been happy. Many of the countries that threw off foreign rule have come under the control of cruel dictatorships. The totalitarian government of China, like that of the Soviet Union, ignores the rights of the individual whenever they come into conflict with the interests of the state. And while these two nations have at least improved the living standards of their citizens, other dictatorships have done little to help their people either politically or economically.

In the 1970's, nations of Africa and Asia (and, in some cases, South America) identified themselves as the "Third World." This was a name for a group whose members, neither Western nor Communist, were linked by the belief that they had been exploited by the great powers. Led by the oil-producing states,

Science has shaped the modern world, and Israel has been in the forefront of scientific research during this century. Here an Israeli scientist seeks new ways to harness energy from the sun.

the Third World began to put economic pressure on the industrialized West. What the results of this new development would be, no one could say.

For the Jews, who had been trapped in the ghetto for nearly three centuries, the rapid changes of the modern era were dazzling; yet our people adjusted to the unfamiliar conditions with incredible speed. They played important parts in major social and political movements: for trade unions, democracy, civil rights, national independence, and socialism. They were outstanding in art, business, and science. They became moving forces in world events—sometimes as leaders, sometimes when others plotted to destroy them.

These amazing—but at times horrifying—events will be summarized in the next two chapters.

SUMMARY *The modern era has been filled with problems. Science has brought many benefits to daily life, but has also created the destructive power which was unleashed by two world wars. The Jewish people emerged from the ghetto to be involved, though not always by choice, in nearly every type of change which the world has gone through in modern times.*

24

The Jews in
Modern Europe

The French Revolution overthrew the monarchy, but the revolutionary government soon became as oppressive as the old. Within four years it produced the bloody "Reign of Terror" during which many innocent people were sent to the guillotine. Order did not return until 1799, when control of the country was seized by one of the greatest soldiers the world has ever known, Napoleon Bonaparte.

The new ruler said he would "take every means to ensure that the rights which were restored to the Jewish people [under the Republic] be not illusory . . . to find for them a Jerusalem in France." In fact, he never granted full equality to French Jewry, but he did make a tremendous difference to the Jews of other countries. He sent troops all across the continent as part of his plan to become emperor of Europe, and wherever his forces conquered they freed Jews from the ghettos.

Freedom—at any price?

Napoleon's empire collapsed after his unsuccessful campaign against Russia—he was finally defeated at the battle of Waterloo in 1815—and the hopes that he had given the Jews fell with him. As soon as the German and Italian states forced out the French army, they restored their old anti-Jewish laws.

Many of our people felt that the freedom they had tasted so briefly had to be regained—at any price. Merely by becoming Christians, they thought, they could escape the miseries of oppression. A very high number of German Jews gave in to this temptation, particularly those who were wealthy, educated, and ready to advance in society. Fully one-tenth of the Jewish population in the German states converted between 1800 and 1810. It has been estimated that half the Jews of Berlin were baptized. Even four of the children of Moses Mendelssohn became Christians.

Leopold Zunz and the Science of Judaism

More important than these deserters were those who learned from and became part of European culture without losing their Jewish identities.

One such man, Leopold Zunz, set out almost single-handedly to make Jewish studies an important area of human knowledge. He had been the first practicing Jew to graduate from a German university. Then he applied his knowledge of modern historical techniques to create what he called the "Science of Judaism," the scholarly study of the Jewish past. He tried out his new approach by research into the commentaries of Rashi, from which he was able to get a picture of the man, his society, his family—even the books in his library! This was the first big breakthrough in the field of Jewish biography, an area unknown to earlier writers.

Zunz's work gained followers, and the Science of Judaism became an active movement. Soon German scholars were preparing booklists and reference works, republishing long-forgotten works of Jewish literature, and using the latest scholarship on the study of Jewish writings, music, and art. Outstanding books of Jewish history were written, most notably the eleven-volume *History of the Jews*, by Heinrich Graetz, a professor of history in Breslau.

Although freedom meant for some German Jews the chance to abandon their faith, many (like the maker of this beautiful ḥallah cover) were able to maintain their Jewish identity and traditions.

Abraham Geiger and the Reform movement

Meanwhile, members of some traditional synagogues began to modernize Jewish worship. They gave up certain old practices and introduced new ones, such as using an organ and reciting some prayers in German, in an effort to make their services more pleasant and understandable.

About 1840, Abraham Geiger and certain other rabbis who had been trained in the Science of Judaism went beyond these changes to break with tradition on a central issue. For centuries, Jews had taught that the Torah is the actual and unchanging word of God, given to Moses at Sinai. The new leaders said that the Torah is the work of people, many people, written over a period of more than a thousand years and showing a wide range of thoughts and feelings about the world and God.

This idea had been worked out by Gentile scholars, some of whom wanted to attack Jewish traditions. For Geiger and his group, however, the knowledge that our religion had been growing and changing since ancient times was a source of enormous strength. It explained in a realistic way why some Biblical laws appeared to be outdated. For example, the Torah had been revolutionary in its day in saying that slaves should be given kind treatment, but now it was understood that slavery itself was wrong. As long as the Torah had to be viewed as the one true source of ethics, this change was hard to accept. But to the reformers it simply proved that Jews were gaining greater understanding of God's will in every generation.

And since change was never complete, modern Jews had the right and duty to be a part of it, said Geiger. Our beliefs needed constant rethinking. New ways had to be found to express lasting Jewish values, even if this meant giving up rituals which no longer seemed meaningful.

A large and enthusiastic group responded to this challenge. Their movement, which became known as REFORM JUDAISM, immediately halted the mass trend toward baptism and conversion. Jewish life revived: good Jewish books were made available and were widely read, fine synagogues were built and attracted large groups of worshipers. Seminaries for the instruction of rabbis were started, and modern religious schools with specially trained teachers appeared.

Samson Raphael Hirsch and Neo-Orthodoxy

The success of Reform Judaism led the Orthodox to rethink their position. Some Jews were opposed to changes of any kind; but the leading spokesman of the traditionalists, Samson Raphael Hirsch, was no blind follower of ancient practices. Understanding the need for change in Jewish life, he introduced a choir into the services of his congregation and gave sermons in German. Moreover, he accepted the value of secular culture—he himself studied at the University of Bonn.

On the basic principles of Orthodoxy, however, he was steadfast. In order for the Jews to succeed in bringing people closer to God, said Hirsch, they must keep their unique identity. They can do this only by observing the laws of Judaism as taught in the Torah and interpreted in the Talmud.

Hirsch dedicated his life to spreading his ideas by starting schools, editing periodicals, and serving as a rabbi. The movement he created is usually known as NEO-OR-THODOXY (New Orthodoxy). Through it, traditionalism became intellectually more "up-to-date."

Conservatism and Reconstructionism

At first, the debate between Reform and Neo-Orthodoxy was bitter and impassioned; but after the unsuccessful revolutions of 1848, tempers cooled. Reform Judaism, like all liberal movements, lost much of its energy in the face of government suppression, and the German congregations learned to live in peace with each other. Differences in synagogue practices grew smaller as time went on.

Many Jews looked for greater freedom in the United States, and it is here that the Reform movement has had its greatest growth and influence. Here Orthodoxy also grew, and two new philosophies developed. CONSERVATIVE JUDAISM offered a home for those who accepted the idea of religious change while remaining rather traditional in practice. RECONSTRUCTIONISM, founded in the 1930's by Rabbi Mordecai Kaplan, is concerned with the whole Jewish way of life. It has helped build Jewish Centers throughout the country for the physical as well as mental education of Jews.

The different branches of Judaism allow room for Jews of every shade of belief, giving the American Jewish community its many-sided growth. The groups, despite their differences, have been able to remain strong and united in their dedication to the ethical principles of Judaism and to the welfare of the Jewish people.

The growth of anti-Semitism

Those Jews who remained in Europe suffered new outbreaks of prejudice. The Blood Libel was brought up again in Rumania, Poland, Russia, Italy, and Germany. More dangerous than these expressions of old religious hatred were the efforts by "scholars" to turn traditional anti-Jewish feelings into the principles of modern anti-Semitism. Shocking as it may seem, respected scientists of the nineteenth century misused their knowledge to claim that the Jews were an "inferior race," with short bodies and dark coloring, unlike the "superior" tall, blond, blue-eyed "Aryan." This nonsense convinced an enormous number of people, sinking deeply into German thought long before it became the philosophy of the short, dark Fuehrer, Adolf Hitler.

The Dreyfus case

The first international effects of modern anti-Semitism were not seen in Germany, however, but in France. A French artillery officer, Captain Alfred Dreyfus, was charged with selling secret documents to the Germans. He was not guilty—the real traitor was a nobleman who had gone into debt through high living—but he was a Jew, though not a deeply religious one. In 1894 he was brought to trial, convicted with forged evidence, and sentenced to life imprisonment on Devil's Island, in the Caribbean Sea.

His defenders, both Jewish and Gentile, angrily protested this injustice until, after twelve years, Dreyfus was proved innocent and set free. Yet his case brought

Falsely accused of selling secret documents to the Germans, Dreyfus (left) was stripped of his military rank and imprisoned as a traitor.

to the surface the anti-Jewish hatred of the French masses, and this hatred dramatically affected a young journalist from Vienna, Theodor Herzl.

Theodor Herzl and the Zionist movement

Herzl had grown up with little interest in his Jewish heritage. But the Dreyfus case and the anti-Semitism of the French completely overwhelmed him. As he wrote in his diaries:

The Dreyfus case contains more than a miscarriage of justice: it contains the wish of the vast majority in France to damn one Jew and through him all Jews. "Death to the Jews!" the crowd yelled when they ripped the Captain's stripes from his uniform. And since that time, "Down with the Jews" has become a battle cry. Where? In France. In Republican, modern, civilized France. . . .

Up to that time, most of us had believed that the solution of the Jewish question was to be expected from the gradual progress of mankind toward tolerance. But if an otherwise progressive, surely highly

Theodor Herzl addresses the First Zionist Congress, in 1897.

civilized people could come to such a pass, what was there to be expected from other people?

Herzl dedicated the rest of his life to the creation of a homeland for the Jews. There were just ten years remaining to him—he died when he was only forty-four—but in that short time he changed the Jewish people forever.

His first step was publishing his ideas in a messianic document called *The Jewish State*. In it he argued that the Jews needed a land where they could rule themselves and be free of oppression. The notion was not completely new, but Herzl expressed it in a way which demanded attention.

He immediately put his dreams into practice. He called for the First Zionist Congress, which assembled in Basel, Switzerland, on August 29, 1897. It was the first official and worldwide gathering of the Jews since their dispersion—and it was the work of one man. The Congress committed itself to a program stating that "the aim of Zionism is to create for the Jewish

people a home in Palestine secured by public law."

The Zionist movement grew. So did anti-Zionism. Many feared that, if an independent state were created, Christians would doubt the loyalty of Jews to their European or American homes. Others, clinging to extreme Orthodox views, felt that the return to the Promised Land could, and should, only be brought about by the Messiah—by a miracle rather than by politics.

Herzl kept on. Driving himself to the limits of his strength, he followed an exhausting schedule which included meetings with world leaders, Zionist congresses, a visit to Jerusalem, and writings of all kinds. At his death, many thought the future of his dream was in doubt, but in 1897 he had written: "At Basel I created the Jewish State. In five years, perhaps, and certainly in fifty, everyone will see it."

It was actually fifty-*one* years later that the State of Israel proclaimed its independence.

The rise of Hitler

Most of the Jews of Germany did not believe they would ever need another home, for they had begun to play leading roles in nearly every important field in their own country. Yet no achievement, no service to Germany, could overcome the deep-rooted German hatred of the Jews. Hitler played on these prejudices to gain support, and as soon as he became chancellor he made our people the victims of worse and worse oppression. Nazi guards were posted at Jewish businesses and offices to keep "Aryans" out, robbing Jews of their livelihood, though not protecting their stores from vandalism. Jews were banned from parks and theaters, from universities and scientific institutions, and were finally stripped of all rights of citizenship by the Nuremberg laws of 1935.

The world remained largely silent before these outrages, so Hitler went on with his brutal schemes. On the evening of November 9–10, 1938, he unleashed riots in which almost every German synagogue was destroyed, Jewish shops were demolished, and at least 30,000 Jews were arrested. This event, which became known as *Kristallnacht* ("The Night of Broken Glass"), marked the end of organized Jewish life in Germany. After it came increasing persecution, the concentration camps, and death.

Anti-Semitism and the Holocaust

The Holocaust did not just happen. Before the terrible reality of Hitler's war against the Jews there was a vicious idea called anti-Semitism.

Anti-Semitism was a new kind of Jew-hatred which arose in the nineteenth century when certain "scientists" taught that the most important characteristic of any group was the race to which it belonged. (The Jewish people came from the Semitic race, hence the term anti-Semitism.) These "scientists" taught that you might change your habits or beliefs— but you could no more change your race than you could change your skin color or who your parents or grandparents were. It did not take long before some people decided that a few races were "better" than the others.

Earlier persecutions of the Jews were for religious or economic reasons; the Catholic Church never condemned the Jews as an entire people. But that is exactly what the Nazis did. Every person with "Jewish blood"—even those who had abandoned Judaism—was branded by the Nazis as part of an "inferior race." When Hitler declared that "superior" races had the right and duty to exterminate "inferior" ones, the Holocaust was the inevitable outcome.

Six million—that number tells us less about the horror of the Holocaust than do the terrified faces of these Jewish men, women, and children held at gunpoint by Nazis in the Warsaw Ghetto.

The Holocaust

By January 1942, Hitler had reached the height of his power. The Nazis had taken over most of the European mainland and North Africa, and were only a few miles from the key Russian cities of Moscow, Leningrad, and Stalingrad. At this point, the Fuehrer began the "Final Solution" —his plan for the total extermination of the Jewish people.

The period which followed has been called the HOLOCAUST. The word means widespread destruction, especially by fire, and the name makes sense; but neither it, nor any word or picture, can give us a true understanding of the German crime against our people. No one can really imagine the horror and suffering contained in the statement that Hitler and his henchmen butchered 6 million Jews. Perhaps we can begin to understand at least the size of the slaughter with this fact: during World War II there were about 3 million minutes. This means that for six years, on the average of once every thirty seconds of every hour of every day and every night, the German war machine murdered a Jewish human being.

Almost as horrifying as the inhumanity of the Nazis was the indifference to it shown by the rest of the world. No effort was made to stop the German persecution in its early stages, and as Nazi brutality increased and the number of homeless Jews grew, the nations of the West closed their doors. America refused to admit more than a small number of those who begged for admission. The British stopped immigration to Palestine, despite their promise to make the country into a Jewish homeland. Just before the war broke out, one ship with 900 Jewish refugees sailed along the U.S. coast for three weeks until it was forced to return to Europe because no American port would accept its human cargo.

Two countries defended their Jewish citizens. In Holland, Dutch Christians risked their lives to protect their threatened countrymen. Even more remarkable, perhaps, was the fantastic story of how the brave people of Denmark helped bring the entire Danish Jewish community—over 7000 people—to safety in Sweden, which was never occupied by the Nazis.

Yet these two exceptions make the behavior of the rest of Europe all the more horrible. Poland, the Ukraine, and France must carry special shame for the willing and sometimes enthusiastic help they gave the Nazis in rounding up and killing Jews on their soil.

Even after the war, the Jewish survivors were faced with vicious anti-Semitism, violence, and riots. Still the nations of the world closed their doors. Some 300,-000 of our people became a "huddled, homeless humanity," most of them grouped in displaced persons' camps with no real place to go. A Jewish state in which they could settle, formerly an inspiring hope, now became an overwhelming, practical necessity.

And so, strangely enough, Hitler's nightmare was crucial in bringing about Herzl's dream: the creation of a Jewish homeland. This is perhaps the best proof of the failure of the "Final Solution," but even in Europe that horrifying plan did not succeed. Today there are Jewish congregations in many countries and cities on the continent, including the former Nazi capital, Berlin.

Yet the Fuehrer's insane schemes took a terrible toll. He killed so many people that even thirty years after the war, the world Jewish population was 2½ million less than it was in 1939. Moreover, he turned Eastern Europe, the former heartland of Jewish life, into a graveyard, bringing the thousand-year period in which Europe was the center of the Jewish world to a sudden and terrible end.

SUMMARY *Modern Europe has brought the Jews great joys and great horrors. When liberated from the ghettos and anti-Jewish laws, the Jewish people excelled in a wide variety of secular and religious fields. The "Science of Judaism" produced outstanding scholarship. New religious developments—Reform and Neo-Orthodoxy (and later, in America, Conservative Judaism and Reconstructionism)— gave Judaism new meaning in the contemporary world. Yet anti-Jewish feelings, given new and false support by certain scientists, continued to plague our people. Anti-Semitism erupted in France in the Dreyfus affair, which led Theodor Herzl to launch the Zionist movement. In Germany, anti-Semitism led to the Nazi massacre of European Jewry which, unintentionally, played a part in the creation of the State of Israel.*

25

Today's Major Centers

Today's two largest Jewish communities are in North America and Asia. These are the United States (5,840,000 Jews) and the State of Israel (2,953,000). The only other country with a Jewish population of more than a million is also largely in Asia. This is the Soviet Union (2,680,000).

Russian Jewry

Although the Soviet Union is the oldest of these major centers, its history is in some ways the simplest. At the end of the fifteenth century, the principality of Moscow began to gain land. The new territories were added by various means, peaceful and otherwise, but the goal was always continual growth. This policy was pursued successfully by the czars, as it has been by the Communists who replaced them, until today the U.S.S.R. is by far the largest country in the world.

Almost as constant as its policy of ter-ritorial growth has been its practice of anti-Semitism. From the beginning of Moscow's growth into modern Russia, Jews were forbidden to enter the country, even for temporary purposes, until finally the principles of national growth and Jewish exclusion collided. In 1772 the czars took over Lithuania and large sections of Poland, and suddenly they found themselves ruling the world's largest Jewish community.

The first reaction of the Russians was to keep the Jews in those areas where they had been living—territory which became known as the "Pale of Settlement." This might have worked well enough if the Jewish people had been left in peace. Instead, they were subjected to unending and merciless persecution.

A particularly cruel example of this was the drafting of Jewish boys into military service at age twelve (or younger) and stationing them in distant areas, such as Siberia. There, violence and starvation were used to force the children to convert to Christianity. These "Cantonists," as they were called, were kept in the army for thirty years or more, and needless to say, most of them gave in to the unending pressures and disappeared among the Russian Christians. More remarkable is the fact that a number held to the religion they barely remembered from their childhood. Some even managed to return to the Jewish people when they finished their term of military service.

From "enlightenment" to persecution

In 1855, Alexander II became czar and startled the Jews with acts of kindness. He reduced restrictions on their lives and livelihood, and urged them to be educated in Russian culture. Jewish liberals, who had adopted Mendelssohn's goal of becoming involved in modern life, were encouraged, and their movement, known as HASKALAH, הַשְׂכָּלָה ("Enlightenment") took on new strength.

Alexander's "generosity" was finally seen as a trick to lure Jews into the Gentile world and destroy their Jewish identity; later rulers were more direct. The government organized "spontaneous" attacks against the Jewish community which became known by the Russian word for "destruction"—POGROM. Anti-Jewish laws were passed, the worst being the "May Laws" which forbade Jews from living in rural areas of the Pale. These edicts put 65,000 Jews out of their village homes, caused terrible overcrowding in those cities where Jews were still permitted to live, and threw the economy of the area into chaos. The effects on the Jewish population were well thought out. In the words of a czarist official, "One-third of the Jews will emigrate, one-third will be baptized, and one-third will starve."

Two million Jews did leave, most for the United States, but the 5½ million who stayed neither starved nor converted. Despite all they suffered, they found ways to survive and to keep Jewish scholarship going. The Polish area of the Pale remained a world leader in Talmudic studies until Hitler. Furthermore, Jews became active in such movements as Zionism and socialism, which were dedicated to improving the lives of our people and of the world in general.

The Soviet state

The fall of the czars in 1917 brought a sudden end to anti-Jewish legislation, but the Communist revolution brought a new wave of Russian oppression. The Communist rulers, as part of their campaign against religion, closed most of the Russian synagogues, made religious education illegal, and placed great pressure on Jews to abandon their traditional ways. A great many did become nonreligious and might well have lost all Jewish identity, but this was not allowed. The Jewish people were said to be members of a separate nationality—even today Soviet passports call them Jews rather than Russians—and were forced to live under new restrictions. They were not allowed to leave the country, since the numbers eager to do so would have embarrassed Soviet authorities.

Until the 1950's, Russian Jewry was hidden from the rest of the world. It was widely feared that Soviet Jews would forget Judaism, much as the rest of the world had forgotten them. In the 1960's, how-

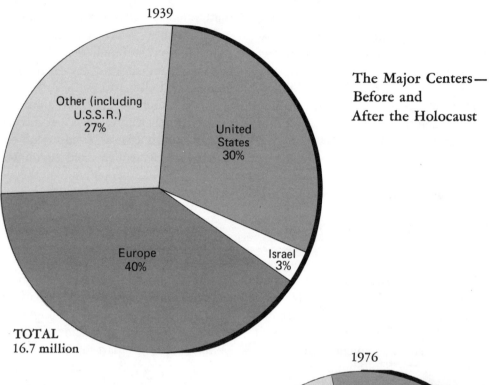

1939

Other (including
U.S.S.R.)
27%

United
States
30%

Europe
40%

Israel
3%

TOTAL
16.7 million

The Major Centers—
Before and
After the Holocaust

The two circle graphs
show the dramatic
effect of the Holocaust
on world Jewish
population. Not only
is the number of Jews
today less than the
prewar figure, but
Western Europe has
been wiped out as a
major center of Jewish
settlement. (Of course,
Jews still live there,
but far fewer than in
1939.) You can see by
comparing the two
circles where most of
the European
survivors went.

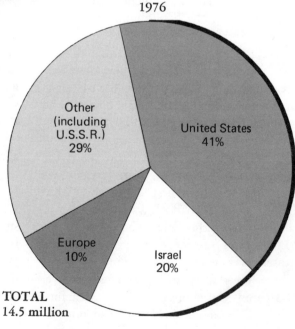

1976

Other
(including
U.S.S.R.)
29%

United States
41%

Europe
10%

Israel
20%

TOTAL
14.5 million

ever, international attention was turned on their situation and they began to demand their rights, including the right to leave Russia. In the 1970's the Soviet government did allow some tens of thousands to leave.

The rescue of the Jews who wish to escape from the U.S.S.R. and the resettlement of those who do reach non-Communist countries are major tasks facing the Jewish world today.

America—land of opportunity

The story of Jewish life in America is totally different. Very few anti-Jewish laws were passed in the colonial period, and those that did exist were done away with shortly after the American Revolution. In 1791 the First Amendment to the U.S. Constitution made freedom of religion the law of the land.

The Jewish community which enjoyed this liberty was very small. Even by 1825, the whole United States had only 6000 Jews and nine functioning congregations. In the 1840's, however, following the crushing of liberal movements in Central Europe, this picture changed rapidly. A large number of German Jews came to the New World, and by 1871 the American Jewish population numbered 250,000. The newcomers joined in every area of American life, building cities and towns, joining the California gold rush, and leading the development of large retail stores.

The German migration was dwarfed by the flood of immigrants who poured into America from Russia after the start of the pogroms and the passage of the May Laws. More than 2 million people jammed

The first Jewish settlers to reach New Amsterdam (now called New York) were twenty-three refugees from Brazil. This photo shows a model of their ship and the city they saw when they arrived in 1654.

into American ports, particularly New York. The Lower East Side of Manhattan Island became a bustling Yiddish-speaking city within the city, complete with its own schools and synagogues and a rich cultural life.

After World War I, the U.S. passed laws which all but ended immigration in general, and Jewish immigration in particular. Even during the Holocaust, only a trickle of Jewish refugees was permitted to settle here. Unhappy as this phase of American history was, it does not change the fact that never in history have so many Jews been allowed to live freely in one country or enjoy such success. Never has a Jewish community produced so many leaders in government, in the arts, in science, and many other fields. The United States has provided our people with freedom and opportunity, and we have been able to make valuable contributions to every part of American life.

The problem of identity

It is in the United States, however, that the problem of Jewish identity has become especially important. How are we to be Americans and Jews at the same time? How are we to mix in American society without losing our cultural and religious identities?

These questions have hardly been solved, but they are being faced very positively. While the generation born in America after the wave of Russian immigration

---

Jewish Identity

A modern menorah.

It seems that religion plays less of a role in many people's lives today than it did only a century or two ago. This is especially true in Communist countries, where the governments have tried very hard to stamp out all religious practices. But even in countries like the United States, where freedom of worship is protected, religious beliefs and institutions are no longer as important as they once were.

This is a problem for all religions, but a special problem for the Jews. For thousands of years, the Jews have survived as a people because they held fast to the idea that being Jewish matters. Often this was not easy. The temptation to become "one of the crowd" was strong—it always is. But Jews were proud of their heritage, and proud to be different.

Today you can carve out your own Jewish identity in many ways: by rediscovering Jewish traditions; by helping Israel and Soviet Jews; by studying the history and writings of our people; by thinking seriously about what it means to be a Jew in the modern world. Of course, being Jewish you will have to be different. But you will never be alone.

wanted to free itself from Old World religion, many today are eager to be involved in traditional Jewish life. Since World War II, synagogues have been built in record numbers. College students have demanded and received courses in Jewish studies. Concern for the State of Israel has caused many to re-identify with the Jewish people. Thus, not only because we have been given freedom in this country, but also because we are using that freedom to appreciate the value of our Jewish heritage, the future of the Jews in America is extremely promising.

A Jewish homeland

The State of Israel is, of course, the youngest of today's three great centers, yet it plays a central role in the thinking of all world Jewry.

Our people have lived in the Promised Land continuously since the time of Joshua (though at times in very small numbers), but the first modern Jewish settlers did not arrive until 1882. They were sixteen members of a group whose name, BILU (בִּיל"וּ), came from the initials of the Hebrew words for

בֵּית יַעֲקֹב לְכוּ וְנֵלְכָה

House of Jacob, come let us go up.
(Isaiah 2:5)

Their goal was to bring Jews back to the soil. Few Jews had been involved in farming since the Middle Ages, when our people had been forced from their farms by Christian laws, yet Jewish farmers were needed if there was ever to be a Jewish homeland able to feed itself. The members of Bilu worked for fifteen years, and in

that time built no fewer than eighteen farming colonies.

Their enormous effort, completed before Herzl convened the First Zionist Congress in 1897, set the stage for the immigration started by the founding of the international Zionist movement. By 1914 there were 90,000 Jews living in Palestine.

Palestine under the British

On November 2, 1917, hopes for a Jewish homeland were raised by a declaration of the British Foreign Secretary, Lord Balfour, that "His Majesty's Government view with favour the establishment in Palestine of a national home for the Jewish people." World War I was already being fought, and the Turks, who ruled Palestine, were allied with the Germans against England, America, and France. British troops, including three battalions of Jewish volunteers, set out to free the Holy Land. On the first day of Ḥanukkah, 1917, they captured the city of Jerusalem.

Great Britain soon conquered all of Palestine. After the war, the League of Nations gave the British control of the Holy Land until the area might be ready for self-government. There followed a short period in which there was a real chance for lasting peace in the Middle East. Local Arabs and Jewish settlers had often been able to work together. Moreover, Arab leaders understood that they had no historical claim to the land of Israel. The area had never been home to an independent Arab state, and even when it had been part of the Arab Empire it had been an unimportant district. Since 1517 the land had been ruled by the non-Arab Turks.

As late as 1936, a British royal commis-

In the Modern Era

The Jews came out of ghetto isolation ready to take part in Western society. From high-level diplomacy involving the State of Israel to supermarket freezers stuffed with frozen blintzes, everything in modern life has felt the impact of the Jewish people.

The modern world has changed us as well. Many forces have threatened Jewish values and weakened traditional Jewish institutions; but at the same time, new ideas and new forms have arisen. Perhaps no change has been more dramatic than the new rights of women. Educational opportunities have been opened in all Jewish groups, and among Reform Jews there are now female rabbis and cantors. In the State of Israel, women are drafted for military service.

One of the many changes in Judaism has been the emergence of the six-pointed star as an emblem for the Jewish people. The star was used for decoration from Biblical times, but it had no special Jewish meaning before the Middle Ages. Its first official use by Jews did not come until 1354, when the Jewish community in Prague was granted its own flag. The banner, in time known as "King David's Flag," featured a six-pointed star which took on the name MAGEN DAVID, מָגֵן דָּוִד ("Shield of David").

Not until the nineteenth century, however, did Jews begin to look for a symbol that would represent Judaism in the way that the cross represents Christianity. At this point the "Star of David" became widely accepted as the sign of the Jewish people. The badges which Hitler forced our people to wear were usually yellow six-pointed stars (the Jewish badges of the Middle Ages were simply circles).

But the "Jewish Star" has many happier memories. It was the symbol of the Zionist movement and was placed at the center of the Zionist flag. This, in turn, was adopted as the national banner of the State of Israel. And so, today, the Magen David represents both the Jews and the Jewish State to all the nations of the world.

Through bad times and good, the Magen David has become a symbol of our people. Opposite page: a Jewish child's view of a hanging during the Holocaust; the badge the Nazis made our people wear; a ship bound for Palestine, but forced by the British to return to Nazi Germany; the Israeli flag raised in triumph during the Yom Kippur War.

The Balfour Declaration, issued by the British government in 1917, was a turning point in Jewish history. At right, the declaration itself; above left, the man who signed it, Lord Arthur James Balfour, the British cabinet minister in charge of foreign affairs. The man who helped convince the British to issue the declaration was Chaim Weizmann; he is shown at upper right, attending the United Nations sessions that would finally result in the partition of Palestine and the creation of the State of Israel.

Foreign Office,
November 2nd, 1917

Dear Lord Rothschild,

I have much pleasure in conveying to you, on behalf of His Majesty's Government, the following declaration of sympathy with Jewish Zionist aspirations which has been submitted to, and approved by, the Cabinet.

His Majesty's Government view with favour the establishment in Palestine of a national home for the Jewish people, and will use their best endeavours to facilitate the achievement of this object, it being clearly understood that nothing shall be done which may prejudice the civil and religious rights of existing non-Jewish communities in Palestine, or the rights and political status enjoyed by Jews in any other country."

I should be grateful if you would bring this declaration to the knowledge of the Zionist Federation.

sion stated that if the Arabs were given independence in areas which they had traditionally ruled, they were willing to give "little Palestine" to the Jews. Unfortunately, the British government ignored the wisdom of its own commissioners as well as the commitment already made in the Balfour Declaration. It decided to establish an Arab-dominated state in which Jewish immigration and land ownership were to be limited. Arabs, now promised total victory, and Jews, facing total disaster, lost all ground for compromise, and the land became a battleground between the two forces. In the end, the British, unable to deal with the violent situation they had created, turned the matter over to the United Nations, which voted to divide the area into two states: one Arab, one Jewish.

Israel fights for survival

On May 14, 1948, David Ben-Gurion, a lifelong Zionist and the first prime minister of Israel, stood beneath a portrait of Herzl to proclaim to a crowded room, and to the world, the rebirth of the Jewish state. For the first time in 2000 years, the Jews had a home of their own; but it was theirs only as long as they could defend it. On the day the British left, Arab armies attacked the infant country. This began what Israelis call their War of Independence.

The miraculous victory of the Jewish troops against the mammoth Arab forces set the stage for several years of uneasy truce, during which Israel was in a state of siege. In 1956, after many signs that the Arabs were still bitterly opposed to Israel, the Israeli army (in coordination with attacks by the British and French) burst through the Egyptian lines and quickly conquered the Sinai Peninsula. The government returned the captured land in exchange for international guarantees which brought about the most fruitful, war-free decade in Israeli history. The state grew in population, economic strength, and international standing.

In 1967 the Arabs again took drastic action. Egypt expelled the United Nations Emergency Force, which had been maintaining the peace in Sinai and Gaza, and blockaded shipping to Israel, as it had in 1956. In a rapid campaign, called the Six-Day War, the Israeli army smashed Egyptian forces and reconquered the Sinai. Syria and Jordan joined the battle, but they too were defeated. Israeli troops captured the important Golan Heights and the fertile west bank of the Jordan River.

Most important, they freed the portion of Jerusalem which had been captured by the Arabs in the war of 1948. For nineteen years the Holy City had existed in two halves: the ancient half controlled by Jordan, the modern district ruled by Israel. At last Jerusalem was reunited as the capital of modern Israel.

Again victory bought a few years of peace, and again the Arabs attacked—this time on Yom Kippur, 1973. Thanks to the suddenness and surprise of their invasion, and to international agreements which prevented Israel from completing its counterattack, the Arabs, for the first time in any war, regained territory from Israel.

These gains gave the Arabs a new sense of power, and furthered their efforts to use oil as an economic weapon. The Arab governments also used their newfound wealth to support terrorist activities against Jews. Sometimes the Jewish state was again forced to take action—notably in July 1976, when Israeli commandos freed 103 hostages whose jet had been hijacked to Entebbe Airport in Uganda.

Young state, eternal values

But the State of Israel is far more than a country in a state of siege—or, rather, it has refused to let the state of siege keep it from building a life for its citizens. It has irrigated deserts and drained swamps, making the country once again "a land flowing with milk and honey." It has taken in 1½ million immigrants, giving them homes, education, and opportunity. It has built museums and developed cultural programs worthy of a country many times its size.

Perhaps most wonderful of all, it has developed an active and energetic democracy, the only one in the Middle East. Rising from a world in which the Jewish people have suffered unspeakable oppression, the State of Israel has promised freedom of religion to all. Standing on territory where Crusaders burned synagogues, the Jewish state has protected the holy places of all faiths. Living under constant threat from the Arab states, the government in Jerusalem has given its Arab citizens political equality.

Nothing else in the country's brief, magnificent history shows more vividly the eternal value of the ideals of Judaism, and the unshakable belief of our people in the right of every individual to life and freedom.

SUMMARY *Since World War II, the three great centers of Jewry have been the Soviet Union, the United States, and the State of Israel. The Soviet Union is the oldest of the three, and has oppressed the Jewish people for almost its entire history. A major problem of today's world is rescuing those Jews who wish to escape from Communist persecution. The United States, in contrast, has permitted the building of the most successful Jewish community in history, and it has profited from the contributions of Jews in government, culture, science, and other fields. The State of Israel, proclaimed in 1948, represents the fulfillment of the ancient dream of return. Despite constant threat from its Arab neighbors, Israel has maintained a remarkable cultural life and, even more amazingly, the only democracy in the Middle East.*

PART SEVEN

Past, Present, Future

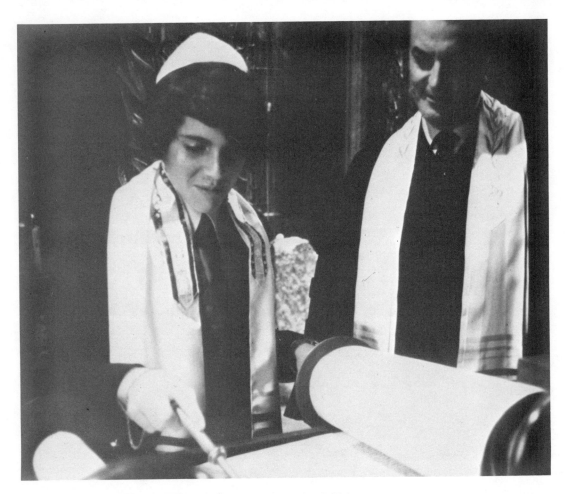

Bar Mitzvah—a link in the chain of Jewish tradition.

26

The Jewish
Role in History

The pagan religions of ancient times were concerned with survival. The purpose of worship was to win protection—to keep the sun god from burning the crops, to convince the rain god to water the fields—and so to make life as safe as possible. There was no thought of improving the world or putting an end to war.

Judaism split totally with these ideas. The Jews were not humble prisoners of the forces of nature, but partners with the one, all-powerful God. We had been chosen to teach His Law to the people of the earth, and thus to help humanity on its strange, halting, and unsure path to a future of goodness and peace.

We did not claim to have earned this special relationship with God. We knew we had not been especially righteous, and certainly did not claim racial superiority. Yet, for reasons we did not know, we had been called to bring the concepts of justice and righteousness to civilization. The Lord selected us. We became His "chosen people."

This idea raises many difficult questions. What kind of God has chosen us? How were we picked, and why? These questions cannot be answered here; but as students of history we must decide if the Jews, over the centuries, really *have* performed a special task. If not, if there is no special meaning to the Jewish experience, then all we have done and all we have suffered is, in a real sense, meaningless. So it is important for us to ask:

Does history show that we Jews have played a unique role in the life of humanity?

A unique history

Jewish history is unique in many ways. One striking thing about it is its great length. While empires have come and gone, the story of the Jewish people continues. This fact, striking in itself, is made all the more remarkable by the fact that we have so often been ruled by those who sought to destroy us.

Second, and in some ways even more startling, is how we have held to our principles. While the Pharaohs of Egypt would understand nothing of the religion of modern Arabs, and the ancient Chinese would have little in common with the Chinese Communists, the early Hebrews had the same basic ideas as we Jews do today. This is not to say that no changes have occurred in Jewish thinking over the centuries. The ability of Judaism to change over the ages has been a key fact of Jewish survival. Nevertheless, if Moses were to return to earth, he would recognize much of the Torah, the Hebrew language, and many of the traditional teachings of our people.

A third thing which sets Jewish history apart is the constantly high quality of Jewish intellectual and spiritual life. Of course, there have been Jews who were fools, scoundrels, and criminals, but an extraordinarily high number of Jews have worked as community leaders, scholars, scientists, physicians, lawyers, and artists. Furthermore, Jewish communities have kept their high ethical standards, even when thrown into horrible conditions. The rich have cared for the needy, and their record of charitable help to both Jewish and non-Jewish causes is unequaled.

Fourth is the Jewish commitment to the Promised Land. Nothing in human history is like the faith of our people, preserved over centuries of exile, in the Biblical promise that the land of our fathers would again be our home. Nor is any tale more miraculous than that of how this promise, against overwhelming odds, gave birth to the modern State of Israel.

Seeds of belief

But, granting that the Jews have had a very unusual history, have we performed the unique task for which we say we were chosen?

When the ancient Egyptians built the pyramids, every nation on earth believed in hundreds or thousands of gods representing each aspect of nature. Today, because of the Jewish experience, more than 1½ billion people have given up this idea for monotheism. Jews, Christians, and Muslims—about one-third of the world's population—trace their spiritual history back to the moment when the first Jew realized that one supreme force ruled the universe.

The belief in one God led to the belief in one humanity, in which all men and women are equal before the Lord. Significantly, the most dramatic event in early Jewish history was the Exodus, when God was seen to have favored slaves against the world's mightiest king. Now the days when all rulers claimed to be gods are gone forever—and the original sources of this change are the people of Israel.

Even this gives only part of the picture of the role of Jewish ideas and ideals. In ancient times, the major activity of kings was war. One of the most powerful nations of the ancient world, Assyria, dedicated its society to battle. The prophets of Israel were the ones who taught that conquest was not the proper goal of national life and gave us a vision of peace and brotherhood—beliefs which all nations now claim to share.

Building a better life

We must say "claim to share" rather than "share," for even the simplest glance at a newspaper shows how imperfectly the world has learned the principles of Judaism. There is good reason for doubt about the future of civilization.

But Judaism has not only changed world history: it has also taught us to look at it in a positive way. Other ancient civilizations pictured man as the plaything of fate, a helpless pawn in a meaningless universe. Eastern religions teach that life is endless suffering. Traditional Christian doctrine is rooted in the belief that man is a deeply sinful being.

Judaism, on the other hand, has taught that the world is fundamentally good:

וַיַּרְא אֱלֹהִים אֶת כָּל אֲשֶׁר
עָשָׂה וְהִנֵּה טוֹב מְאֹד. . .

God saw everything that He had made, and, behold, it was very good.
(Genesis 1:31)

Our religion insists on seeing the world as good, believing that God has a plan for the universe, a plan in which each of us plays a part. No individual is hopelessly evil. Every person can choose to do good, and in that way help perfect the quality of life on earth.

Most Jews throughout history have believed that there is some sort of life after death, but the main concern of our people has been to build a better world for the living. Perhaps no other idea with its roots in Judaism has been more widely accepted. Today, members of organizations as different as the Red Cross and the Communist Party share our basic interest in improving the conditions of humanity.

A test for all nations

Finally, we Jews have also provided a standard by which any government may be tested. No dictator has been able to tolerate the independent, inquiring, democratic Hebrew spirit. Thus, regardless of claims by national leaders of their belief in decency, justice, and equality, their true feelings have been shown by the way in which they treat their Jewish citizens. No other test so clearly shows the dictatorial nature of the Soviet government, for example, than its fear of permitting Jews to live and worship freely.

Similarly, the State of Israel presents a test to the nations of the world. They claim to believe in independence for *all* people. Do they believe in it enough to support independence for the *Jewish* people? Thus far, many countries have been prepared to say "No," or "Not if it would raise the price of oil." Still, the State of Israel survives, perhaps to play a leading role in creating a more democratic order in the Middle East and in the world.

The triumph of Judaism

Having looked at this evidence, can we say history shows that we Jews have a unique role in the destiny of the world? Our answer is a ringing and positive "Yes." Our special experience sets us apart from any other people. During our history we have changed the life and thought of humanity, bringing to the world ideals of equality, decency, and morality which, however imperfectly carried out, are the driving forces of today's civilization.

Whether this development has been slow or rapid is a matter of opinion. If one remembers that the dinosaurs ruled the earth for more than 100 million *years*, and that human civilization has been recorded for barely 2 million *days*, then the speed of these changes is breathtakingly fast. If one uses the scale of a human life, the change has been painfully slow. Yet, by any standard, the remaking of human thought has been remarkable—and it has been brought about through the Hebrew people.

The tasks ahead

Clearly our task is far from over. The world is horribly imperfect, and the safety and welfare of many people, especially our own, is threatened. What will the future hold? Can we peer into the unknown and predict the situation that will exist in the years ahead? That is really the job of prophecy, not of history; but still, using our insights into Jewish history, we can confidently make a few predictions.

First, the Jewish people will survive. There is no scientific way to prove this. A purely "objective" person may wish to say simply that since the Jews have survived in the past, we will probably continue to do so. A religious person may state that the Jews will survive to complete the task for which God has chosen us. We may accept either view, or both, but the prediction remains the same: Jewish history, though very old, has a long future ahead.

This is not, however, a cause for feeling satisfied and doing nothing. Our second prediction must be that Jewish survival will be bought at the cost of great dedication and sacrifice. Hopefully this will not mean facing more wars, pogroms, and massacres, but it will require acts of courage and determination by many people.

Some of these will be dramatic, but most will seem very small. Your decision to finish studying this book, for example, means that you now have more knowledge of your Jewish heritage and can be a stronger link in the chain of Jewish tradition. If you continue your Jewish education, take part in Jewish activities, contribute your talents and effort to Jewish causes, and lead a Jewish life, you will be one of the millions who, for forty centuries, have used their daily acts to strengthen and preserve the Jewish people.

In the footsteps of the prophets

Third, we predict that Jewish survival will matter. This is not just because Jewish individuals will dedicate themselves to learning, to beauty, to the healing arts, and to bettering the lives of others—though they will do that—but because the teachings of Judaism will continue to be among the highest goals of humanity.

And, because of this, we make one final prediction. Or rather, we will offer a prediction made by the prophet Isaiah some 2700 years ago:

And it shall come to pass in the end of days,
That the mountain of the Lord's house shall be established as the top of the mountains, . . .
And He shall judge between the nations, . . .
And they shall beat their swords into plowshares,
And their spears into pruninghooks;
Nation shall not lift up sword against nation,
Neither shall they learn war any more.
(Isaiah 2:2–4)

Glossary

AGGADAH "narration"; the stories, legends, and sayings that make up about one-third of the TALMUD and the greater part of the MIDRASHIM.

ANTI-SEMITISM hatred of or prejudice against the Jewish people.

ASHKENAZIM Jews who lived in the Christian lands of Germany and Eastern Europe during the Middle Ages, and their descendants.

AUTO-DA-FÉ "act of faith"; the public execution of MARRANOS and others in Spain or Portugal by the INQUISITION.

B.C.E. Before the Common Era. Because B.C. means "Before Christ" and refers to Jesus, Jews use the abbreviation B.C.E., which means before the year 1 in the Western calendar.

BLOOD LIBEL the lie, invented during the Middle Ages, that Jews murdered Christians in order to use their blood in Passover matzah.

C.E. Common Era. Because A.D. means *Anno Domini* ("In the year of the Lord") and refers to Jesus, Jews use the abbreviation C.E. to mean after the year 1 in the Western calendar.

COURT JEW a Jew who held a privileged position as financial advisor to a Christian noble in Central or Eastern Europe during the 17th and 18th centuries.

DEAD SEA SCROLLS documents written in Roman times and discovered at Qumran in 1947; they may have been the sacred texts of the ESSENES.

DIASPORA "scattering"; Jewish settlements outside the Holy Land.

ESSENES Jewish religious sect in Roman times; they withdrew from society in order to live a life of strict piety.

ETHICS teachings which help us to know right from wrong.

GAON (*pl.* GEONIM) "Excellency"; title held by the leaders of Babylonian Jewry from about 600 to 1000 C.E.; later applied in Europe to a man of outstanding piety and learning (for example, the Vilna Gaon).

GEMARA "Completion"; commentaries on the MISHNAH; part of the TALMUD.

GHETTO "cannon factory." At first this was the name for the Jewish district of Venice, which was located next to a cannon factory. Later the name was used for any walled section (of a city) where Jews were required to live.

HALACHAH "the rule by which to go"; the legal materials which make up about two-thirds of the TALMUD, later codified in the MISHNEH TORAH, SHULCHAN ARUCH, and other works.

HASID (*pl.* HASIDIM) "pious one"; a follower of HASIDISM.

HASIDISM "religion of the pious"; Jewish religious sect based on the teachings of the Baal Shem Tov (1700–1760 C.E.) and stressing joy and devotion rather than study.

INQUISITION organized effort by the Roman Catholic Church to stamp out heresy; especially in Spain and Portugal, a campaign to eliminate the practice of Judaism.

KABBALAH "Tradition"; Jewish mystical beliefs and practices; see ZOHAR.

KARAITES Jewish religious sect dating from the eighth century C.E.; the Karaites followed the TORAH literally, rejecting rabbinic tradition.

KIDDUSH HA-SHEM "sanctification of God's

name"; in the Middle Ages, the decision by some Jews to die rather than abandon their religion.

LADINO mixture of 15th-century Spanish with Hebrew, and written in Hebrew characters; still used by Jews whose ancestors lived in Spain before the expulsion of our people in 1492.

MARRANOS "swine"; term applied by Spanish Catholics to the New Christians—Jews who had converted to Christianity but who often continued to practice Judaism in secret.

MASORETIC TEXT from *masora*, "tradition"; standard version of the Hebrew Bible, completed during the 8th century C.E.

MESSIAH from *maschiach*, "anointed one"; a descendant of King David who will reestablish the Kingdom of Israel.

MESSIANISM belief in the coming of a MESSIAH.

MIDRASH (*pl.* MIDRASHIM) "interpretation"; commentary on the Bible, often through maxims or brief sayings and stories.

MISHNAH "Study"; sacred book of Jewish law compiled at Yavneh about 200 C.E.; part of the TALMUD.

MISHNEH TORAH "Repetition of the Torah"; legal and ethical code written by Maimonides in the 12th century C.E.

MONOTHEISM belief in one God; the opposite is polytheism, or belief in two or more gods.

MYSTICISM the belief that a person can have special and direct contact with God.

ORAL TORAH Jewish beliefs and traditions passed down verbally from generation to generation, until recorded by the sages of the TALMUD.

PHARISEES Jewish religious-political party during the Roman period; while faithful to the spirit of the TORAH, the Pharisees were flexible in interpreting its laws.

POGROM massacre of Jews, especially in Russia and other countries of Eastern Europe.

RABBI "my master"; title given to the religious leaders of the Jewish community since the time of the Roman Empire.

RABBIS Jewish leaders during the Age of the Rabbis, from about 100 to 500 C.E.

SADDUCEES Jewish religious-political party during the Roman period; the party of the priests

and the upper classes, the Sadducees were rigidly conservative in matters of Jewish law.

SEPHARDIM Jews who lived in Muslim lands (especially Spain) during the Middle Ages, and their descendants.

SEPTUAGINT "The Seventy"; translation of the Bible into Greek, completed in the 3rd century B.C.E.

SHOFTIM "judges"; chieftains and heroes of the Hebrew tribes between the time of Joshua and the anointment of Saul.

SHULCHAN ARUCH "Prepared Table"; code of Jewish practice compiled by Joseph Karo in the 16th century C.E.

TALMUD "Learning"; second only to the TORAH as a sacred book of Jewish law. The Talmud consists of the MISHNAH and the GEMARA. The Palestinian Talmud includes the Gemara compiled in Israel between 200 and 400 C.E.; the more influential Babylonian Talmud includes the Gemara produced in the Babylonian academies between 200 and 500 C.E.

TORAH the Five Books of Moses (Genesis, Exodus, Leviticus, Numbers, Deuteronomy), the most sacred text of Judaism; also, more generally, the whole of Jewish learning.

TOSAFOT "additions"; commentaries written on the Babylonian TALMUD by the followers of Rashi.

TZEDAKAH "righteousness"; because aiding the poor is an act of righteousness, this word is also used to mean "charity."

WESTERN WALL the only part of the Jerusalem Temple to survive the Roman attack in 70 C.E.; it was returned to Jewish control in 1967.

YIDDISH language of the ASHKENAZIM; an old German dialect mixed with many Slavic and Hebrew words, written in Hebrew characters.

ZADDIK (*pl.* ZADDIKIM) "Holy Man"; the leader of a Hasidic sect (see HASIDISM).

ZEALOTS Jewish religious-political party during the Roman period; the Zealots used terrorist methods to fight both their Jewish rivals and the Romans.

ZIONISM in modern times, the movement to reestablish an independent Jewish state in the Holy Land.

ZOHAR "Brilliance"; a key text of the KABBALAH, apparently written during the 13th century C.E.

Index *

* Entries in italics refer to photographs or illustrations. To save space, the following abbreviations have been used: B.C.E., Before the Common Era; c., circa, about; C.E., Common Era; cent., century; d., died; r., reigned. All dates above 100 are C.E. unless otherwise noted.

The editor and publisher gratefully acknowledge the cooperation of the following sources of photographs for this book:

A.I.C.F., 210; American Friends of the Hebrew University, 68; Australian Government Tourist Office, 202; Bibliothèque Nationale de Paris, 135, 139, 175; British Library, London, 85, 122, 158; CDJC, 229; CEDOK, 157 (all photos); Geoffrey Clements, 142; Curaçao Tourist Board, 204.

Also: Czechoslovak Ministry of Culture, 156; Frank J. Darmstaedter, 112, 162, 179; Harry S. Dash, 169; Eastfoto, 203; Editions Artaud, 12; T. Gidal, 28; Giraudon, 4; Globe Photos, 199 (Roy Pinney), 200; David Harris, 42, 86; HUC Museum, 214.

Also: Israel Consulate General, New York, 212, 229; Israel Ministry of Tourism, 69; Israel Museum, Jerusalem, 11, 86, 121, 158; Italian Government Tourist Office (E.N.I.T), 39; Jewish Museum, New York City, 64, 79, 120, 137, 155, 196, 209, 226; Jewish Theological Seminary, 108, 116, 146.

Also: Kulturinstitut, Worms, 150; Magnum, 167 (Cornell Capa), 200 (Charles Harbutt), 202 (Leonard Freed), 203 (Erich Hartmann), 234 (Sepp Seitz); Metropolitan Museum of Art, New York City, 6 (both photos), 85 (Rogers Fund, 1913); Museo del Prado, Madrid, 119; National Gallery of Art, Washington, D.C., 120.

Also: New York Public Library, 181; Novosti from Sovfoto (two photos), 203; Oriental Institute, University of Chicago, 22; Popperfoto, 204; Rapho/Photo Researchers, 15 (George Holton), 48 (Dr. Eugene A. Eisner), 206 (Jan Lukas); Religious News Service, 225.

Also: Gail Rubin, 3; Shostal Associates, 205; South African Government, 205; Spanish National Tourist Office, 97; Union of American Hebrew Congregations, Art and Architecture Library, 40, 42, 83, 122, 204, 206; Roman Vishniac, 167; Wide World, 91, 210; YIVO, 167, 194, 220, 229; Zionist Archives, 230.

On the cover: Babylonian lion, Metropolitan Museum of Art; Spanish synagogue, UAHC Art and Architecture Library; Cardiff rabbi, Magnum (Erich Hartmann); Horb synagogue, Israel Museum, Jerusalem; archaeological dig, Martin S. Rozenberg; Egyptian painting, Metropolitan Museum; Rosh Hashanah plate, Jewish Museum; Arabic medical manuscript, Metropolitan Museum (Rogers Fund, 1913); schoolboys playing soccer, Australian Government Tourist Office; Torah crown, CEDOK.